Principles of Macro-Monetary Theory

■

Fourth Edition

Kishore G. Kulkarni

Professor of Economics
Metropolitan State College of Denver
Denver, Colorado

Adjunct Professor
University of Colorado-Boulder
Colorado School of Mines
Graduate School of International Studies
University of Denver

KENDALL/HUNT PUBLISHING COMPANY
4050 Westmark Drive   Dubuque, Iowa 52004

Copyright © 1986, 1992, 1997, 2003 by Kendall/Hunt Publishing Company

ISBN 0-7872-9972-3

Library of Congress Control Number: 2003100360

Printed in the United States of America
10 9 8 7 6 5 4 3 2

*To the three beautiful
girls in my life:
Jayu, Lina, Aditi*

Contents

List of Illustrations

Preface to the Fourth Edition

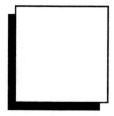

More than 22 years of teaching economics principles has allowed me to meet thousands of students in different educational institutions I have taught for. In fact it is their unending curiosity and conscientious studentship that prompts me to work for this fourth edition of "Principles of Macro-Monetary Theory." To all those curiously sharp minds I owe a big debt. I am particularly happy that in this edition we have moved from single space to double space printing which will be easier on the eyes. I know readers and students will like the simplicity and straight-forward analysis in this edition as in earlier editions.

Several individuals have helped me in rewriting this edition. My colleagues Drs. John Cochran and Arthur Fleisher make the work-place worth coming back to with lively discussions on a daily basis. Dr. Robert McNown played an inspirational and supportive role for my activities. The magnificent staff of Kendall/Hunt Publishing Company helped in their usual cheerful ways. Besides being on a permanent faculty at the Metropolitan State College of Denver, I have taught on a visiting (or Adjunct) basis at the Colorado School of Mines, University of Colorado-Boulder and the Graduate School of International Studies in University of Denver. I want to express my gratitude to all individuals I am interacting with in these institutions.

I am also thankful to all my family members for being there for me.

Kishore Kulkarni
Denver, Colorado

Introduction and a Few Definitions

1.1

To start any book on economics, it is a good idea to define a few concepts. Many students have noticed that some of the economic concepts are so special that they do need a complete clarification. There is also an unanswered question of "Is economics an art or a science?" This is important because several schools in the U.S. classify the economics department in the college of arts while others put it in the college of business.

Another point that has given many individuals a lot of material for thought is the one of attempting to define "economics." Some have called it a science of supply and demand, some have referred to it as the art of trade-off, and others have even termed it as the science of managing money! In fact, Jacob Viner of Harvard University has defined economics as "a thing that the economists do." This is a sign of frustration rather than an escape from the question of defining economics correctly. John Maynard Keynes, one of the greatest economists of the 20th century, has elaborately described economics as, "an easy subject in which few excel." In essence, Keynes has also attempted to describe at great length the economics profession in general in 1924, a description that holds true even now. He writes, "the study of economics does not seem to require any specialized gifts of an unusual order. Is it not, intellectually regarded, a very easy subject compared with the higher branches of philosophy and pure science? Yet good or even competent economists are rarest of birds. An easy subject, at which few excel! The paradox finds its explanation, perhaps, in that the master economist must possess a rare combination of gifts. He must be a mathematician, historian, statesman, philosopher—in some degree. He must understand symbols and speak in words. He must contemplate the particular in terms of the general, and touch abstract and concrete in the same flight of thought. He must study the present in the light of the past for the purposes of the future." Perhaps, when Viner defined economics as what economists do, he had this broader definition of economist in his mind.

Nonetheless, the most acceptable definition of economics that comes close to defining economics correctly and completely is given by Lionel Robbins of Cambridge University. His definition is as follows: Economics is a science that studies human behavior as a relationship between ends and scarce means that have alternate uses. Of course several questions come to mind: What are ends to satisfy? What are the means to satisfy these ends? Peoples' ends are called wants and there are two types of wants; 1) individual wants and 2) collective wants.

Individual wants are those that have to be satisfied by every individual and depending upon the circumstances, examples of individual wants are such things as water, shelter, clothes, food, etc. These are therefore wants that have to be satisfied individually. Collective or social wants are those that have to be satisfied collectively. Several examples of collective wants can be pointed out as education, health, public parks, transportation, defense, etc. The means to satisfy wants are the resources owned by the people. For individual wants, these resources can be such things as income of the person. For many people this resource is scarce. Even millionaires complain about not having enough resources to satisfy all their wants. Moreover, this resource has "several" (what Robbins called "alternate") uses. One can use the income to buy groceries, medicine, automobiles, or any number of other things. Now according to Robbins' definition, when means are scarce, and when there is an abundance of wants to satisfy, how people behave is studied by a science called "economics." Hence it is resolved that economics is a science and it studies the human behavior under special conditions.

There are two major branches of general economics: *micro-economics* and *macroeconomics*. *Micro*, the Latin term, means something small, tiny or little. Hence, economics of small things like the behavior of only one firm rather than the whole economy is studied under microeconomics. In fact, theory of the firm forms a big segment in microeconomics. Similarly, decisions of only the consumer about what to consume is studied under microeconomics which is popularly called consumer theory. On the other hand, *macro*, another Latin term, means something big, large or huge. Hence, economics of large things, like decisions of the whole economy about how much to produce (GDP calculation), behavior of all prices taken together (inflation) is studied under Macroeconomics.

Another important definition that is frequently used in economics is the one of factors of production. Factors of production are those basic things needed for any productive activity to take place. In pure economic theory we recognize four factors of production: *land*, *labor*, *capital* and *enterprise*. Land needs no explanation, as it can be the basic piece of land either located in a field or on the high floor of a high-rise building. Labor involves availability of manual labor or a skilled labor input that is endowed in heavy human capital. Human capital is a concept that is used extensively in economic development theory that means the sanitational, cultural, educational, or health conditions of a labor force. Clearly, there are differences in labor quality according to the human capital involved in it, but one can easily see that labor is a basic factor of production. Capital requires a special explanation since it can be of two types: financial capital and physical or real capital. Financial capital includes such things as liquidity (or cash), equity capital, bonds, stocks (or shares). Physical capital involves such things as machinery, tools, equipment, and natural resources, etc. Obviously for a real productive activity one needs physical rather than financial capital. In short, a knowledge of technology means the enterprise. Clearly, without it no production can be possible. In fact, many times the technology known to a producer may not be as valuable, but that is when he/she receives losses from such productive activity!

Quite related to the factors of production, another important definition is that of returns (or rewards) to the individual factors of production. For allowing the use of land one must receive rent, hence, rent received is considered as a reward for land.

Similarly, for labor the reward is the wage rate, for capital the return is the interest rate (one can borrow financial capital and use it to buy real capital) and for the use of enterprise one receives profits. Thus, there are specific rewards for specific factors of production.

Opportunity cost is another concept that is used quite often in economic literature. What do we mean by an opportunity cost? In short, it is the value of the second best use of a resource. It is the benefit one has to forgo to use a resource for a specific reason. Since this is a broadly defined term, for every decision there is an opportunity cost. Suppose, for example, time is a resource and taking an economics class at a certain time is your decision to use that time resource. Then what can you think as the opportunity cost of that decision? Of course, how you could have used this resource otherwise determines the answer to this question. Suppose you would have eaten at the cafeteria, or watched a TV show, earned a few wages, or done nothing at all at this time. Then values of all these opportunities define the second best alternatives that are foregone by taking this economics class at this specific time. Now economists always worry about opportunity cost calculation to make any decision. As against opportunity costs there is an accounting cost, or the direct cost of the decision being considered. Clearly the tuition you paid for the class, textbook bought, or parking expenses paid are a part of accounting costs.

The concept of opportunity cost is quite useful in explaining the famous economic saying that, "there is no such thing as a free lunch." Even if a friend of yours asks you to go eat lunch with him/her and she is buying, many times you ignore that invitation because of the opportunity costs involved. One may ask, "what can be an opportunity cost of a free lunch?" Of course, the second best use of that time will determine it, or how about the fact that you have to listen to her boring life stories at the time of that lunch? No wonder then that free lunch invitations are turned down all the time. (It is quite obvious that you will accept a free lunch invitation if the opportunity cost is less than the benefit you will receive from the free lunch.)

In a similar fashion, by using the concept of opportunity cost, one can also explain the frequently observed fact that in a boring ball-game, a higher proportion (or percentage) of empty seats are seen in a high priced section. If we assume that high priced tickets are bought by rich people (with high opportunity cost) and low priced tickets are purchased by poor people (with relatively low opportunity cost), then it is quite clear that high priced seats people will leave the boring ball-game much earlier than low priced seats fans.

Economic system is another concept used quite often in economic literature. Economic system is technically defined as a "set of arrangements used by an economy to mobilize its resources to answer three fundamental questions: what to produce, how to produce, and for whom to produce?" Answers to these basic questions determine production, technology and income distribution in an economy. Clearly, the answer to the question of what to produce decides production combinations that will take place in an economy. Similarly, the answer to the question of how to produce determines technology to be used to produce these production combinations. Third, when the economy answers the question of for whom to produce, the income distribution in an economy is determined by deciding recipients of the produced goods and services.

There are basically two types of arrangements any economy can make to answer these questions. One type of arrangement is to let the government sector possess all resources in the economy and government policy makers are responsible for answering these three basic questions. That type of arrangement is popularly called socialism or communism. Private property has little meaning in socialism. Another arrangement is to allow private individuals to keep the resources and private individuals make decisions of how to answer the above three basic questions. This arrangement is called "pure capitalism." In this economic system there is little meaning to the government sector and private property is closely guarded.

Without government, the most dominant sectors of pure capitalism, consumer sector and producer sector, have a constant flow of exchanges going on between them. This flow of exchanges is popularly called the *circular flow*. There are basically two *types* of circular flows to be recognized: *real flow* and *money flow*. In real flow we do not consider the role played by money. In real terms therefore, the consumer sector gives to the producer sector the factors of production and in return gets from the producer sector goods and services. As shown in Figure 1.1, the real flow therefore recognizes this basic exchange between consumer and producer sectors.

However, if we consider the role played by money then we can turn real flow into money flow. Consider that in money terms, for giving up factors of production the consumer sector receives returns to the factors of production from the producer sector. Similarly, in money terms the producer sector receives consumer expenditure for the goods and services given to the consumer sector.

Figure 1.1
Circular Flow: Real and Money Flows

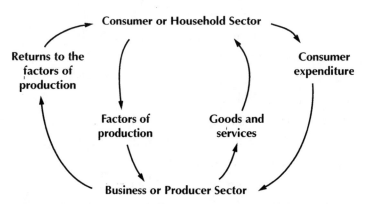

Besides looking at economics in terms of *micro* and *macro*, there is another way in which one can divide economics into *normative economics* and *positive economics*. Positive economics considers all those issues that have only information, data, historical events, etc., included in them without any value judgment about them. These can include such things as the economic history of a country or information about institutions such as the Federal Reserve System or governmental behavior in a war, etc. It also includes such things as surveys, data gathering and other things that do not have any value judgments. In short, there is not much to disagree about in positive economics.

However, in normative economic issues, such things are included as the policy options for the government, or forecasting of future economic growth or effects of certain policy action on other economic variables. Clearly in this area there is a lot to disagree with because each economist can come up with different answers depending upon his/her value judgment. Hence when economists disagree with one another, which they do all the time, then they are basically discussing the normative economic issues.

1.2   A Technique of Drawing Graphs

If you think that your background in geometry is strong enough that you do not need information on the technique of drawing graphs, then you can conveniently skip this section without a loss of continuity. However, many times students in principles classes come up with little background in geometry, and hence find this information useful to revise the concepts in geometry which will help them to read and draw graphs that are used quite extensively in economic literature.

Technically the word "graph" only means a pictorial representation of a relationship between two variables. Then a question naturally arises, what do we mean by variables? Of course, as you may have heard in your first mathematics class, variable means any concept that can be measured in numbers. For example, age of students in a class is a variable since it can be measured by changing numbers. Similarly, height or weight of students in a class are other examples of variables. Thus, any concept that can be measured by changing values can be referred to as a variable. It is quite possible that if we conveniently pick some variables, then their values can depend on each other's values. When this happens we say that two variables have a relationship. Consider, for instance, two variables: 1) income of a person and 2) the amount of saving she makes in a bank. As the values of income go up we shall expect that she will save more in a bank. Hence, values of saving depends upon values of income made by that person. Clearly then these two variables have a relationship.

There are basically two types of variables we can recognize: 1) a dependent variable and 2) an independent variable. A dependent variable is the one whose values depend upon the values of other variables. In the above example then, saving of a person is the dependent variable. On the other hand, an independent variable is the one whose values dictate the values of other variables. In our example, income of the person is the independent variable.

Similarly there are two types of relationships variables can have with one another. The first type is called an inverse or negative relationship and the other type is called a direct or positive relationship. When the values of the independent variable go up and they make the values of the dependent variable to go up too, we say that the two variables have a direct relationship. For example, the above relationship (income and saving) is clearly a direct relationship, but we can think of several others as well. How about the relationship between interest rate (independent) and saving (dependent)? Or the one between height (independent) and weight (dependent) of a person?

When the values of the independent variable go up and make the values of the dependent variable go down we say that the two variables have an inverse or negative relationship. A classic example of an inverse relationship is the one between mortgage interest rate and the number of houses bought in a town. As the interest rate charged by banks for mortgages goes up, the number of houses bought in a town will go down. Similarly, the relationship between wage rate demanded by workers and the number of workers employed by businesses will be of an inverse kind. In the following table we shall discover a sample of a positive relationship discussed above between saving and income of a person.

Table 1	
Income in dollars	**Savings in dollars**
1000	200
2000	400
4000	800
6000	1200
8000	1600

Now, a graph only represents in a pictorial form the above relationship between two variables. But there are some systematic ways in which we do the process of plotting points on a graph. First, recognize that for any graph there are four parts as shown in Figure 1.2 below, popularly called quadrants. They are first (I), second (II), third (III), and fourth (IV) quadrants and the most used quadrant is the first one. The two sides of the first quadrant are called "axes," more specifically, the horizontal axis is called the X axis and the vertical axis is called the Y axis. In order to show the relationship in Table 1 on a graph, traditionally we measure the values of the independent variable on the X axis and values of the dependent variable on the Y axis. Nonetheless, many times this tradition is broken, but no harm is done until we define the slope of that relationship, which we shall discuss later. While drawing the graph, here we shall go along with the tradition and plot the independent variable on the X axis. Hence we measure the values of income of the person on the X axis while values of saving are measured on the Y axis. Our next job is to plot a point, like point K, that has the coordinates of the first combination of values shown in Table 1. Coordinates of a point are the values of variables to which that point corresponds. In fact, with the coordinates we can say point K has X axis value of 1,000 and the Y axis value of 200. In mathematical terms, 1,000 is called point K's X coordinate and 200 is called point K'sY coordinate. Similar to plotting point K we can also plot points J, F, S, T, etc. When we join these points by a straight line we call this line a *saving line*. The shape of the *saving line* plotted in Figure 1.3 is many times referred to as "upward sloping from left to right." Just as a rule of thumb, we can remember that all positive or direct relationships are shown by lines that are upward sloping from left to right. Similarly, if we had plotted an inverse relationship, then the line showing that relationship would have been downward sloping from left to right because all negative relationships, by definition, are shown by a downward sloping line from left to right.

Figure 1.2
Four Quadrants of a Graph

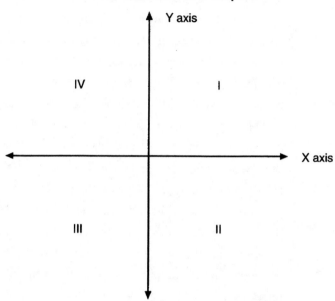

Figure 1.3
Graphing Variables from Table 1

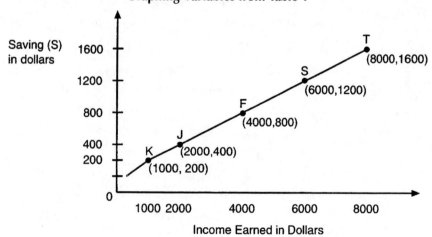

Our next job is to define the slope of a line. Generally speaking, the slope is a concept that tells us what will be the change in a dependent variable when there is a change in independent variable values. For example, how much will be a change in the saving of a person when there is a change in income? In other words, by observing the above relationship, can we tell how much will be an increase in saving if income increases by say, 100?

The slope usually gives us that answer. However, we can have a relationship whose slope is different at different points. That type of relationship is called a non-linear relationship and it is shown by a non-linear curve on the graph. The relationships that are shown by a straight line are called linear relationships and they have a constant slope at all points on that straight line.

To define the slope of a linear relationship, consider once again the *saving line* plotted in Figure 1.3 that shows the positive relationship between income and saving of a person. The same relationship is reproduced in Figure 1.4 below. In general, the slope is defined by the ratio of rise and run when we consider a movement on that line from one point to another. Hence consider two points on that line such as, say points F and S, and define their coordinates.

Figure 1.4
Slope of a Linear Relationship

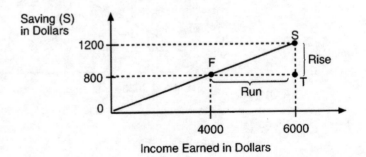

When a movement from point F to point S is considered, the rise is by the amount of change in Saving that has occurred. It is measured by the distance ST and it is equal to 400. The run is measured by the distance FT and is equal to 2,000. Hence the slope of this relationship is equal to 400/2,000 = .2.

Since the slope of a linear relationship is constant it does not matter which two points we select to calculate the rise over run ratio. However, in the case of a non-linear relationship, we have to change the process of defining the slope. Consider a classic economic non-linear relationship between total product of a company and the number of employees employed in it. As the number of employees goes up, the total product will increase but eventually the company will be a crowded place and the total product will start declining. This is shown in Figure 1.5.

To calculate the slope of this relationship we must ask a question: is the slope of this curve the same at all points? The answer is obviously *no*. Hence, we first need to determine at what point the slope of this curve is to be calculated. Suppose therefore, that we want to define the slope at point L on this total product curve. The procedure to do that is to initially draw a tangent to this curve at point L. A tangent is a straight line that touches the curve at only one point. Once the tangent is drawn, the slope of the tangent is the slope of that curve at that point. Hence, at point L the slope of the non-linear total product curve is defined by the ratio LM/MN.

Figure 1.5
Slope of a Non-Linear Relationship

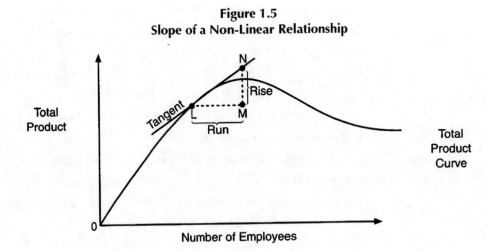

Total Product

Total Product Curve

Number of Employees

Economic hypothesis is a statement that hypothesizes human behavior. For example, an increase in income of the consumer will make an increase in his/her consumption. A bunch of related economic hypotheses is used to construct the *economic model*. Hence, an economic model is developed to show the behavior of humans or an economy. We shall discuss such models in the future. Testing such models is what economists do very efficiently.

This should complete our review of the technique of drawing graphs. In economic analysis we use several relationships. To show these relationships economists make an extensive use of graphs. One such relationship we discuss in the next chapter.

Suggested Additional Reading for Chapter 1

1   Arnold, Roger. *Macroeconomics*, 3rd ed. West Publishing Company, 1996. Chapter 1.

2   Baunol, William, and Allan Blinder. *Economics*, 6th ed. Prentice Hall Publications, 1995. Chapters 1 and 2.

3   Byrns, Ralph, and Jerald Stone Jr. *Economics*, 6th ed.Harper/Collins Publishers, 1994. Chapters 1 and 2.

4   Case, Karl E., and Ray C. Fair. *Principles of Economics*, 4th ed. Prentice Hall Inc., 1996. Chapters 1, 2, and 3.

5   Samuelson, Paul, and William Mordhaus. *Economics*,13th ed. McGraw Hill Publishing Company, 1994. Chapters 1, 2, and 3.

6   Sharp, Ansel M., Charles A. Register, and Paul W. Grimes. *Economics of Social Issues*, 12th ed. Irwin Publishers, 1996. Chapter 2.

7   Stiglitz, Joseph. *Economics*, 2nd ed. W.W. Norton and Company, 1996. Chapter 2.

8   Tregarthen, Timothy. *Microeconomics*. Worth Publishers, 1996. Chapter 2.

Laws of Demand and Supply

2

2.1

One of the most important relationships that economists have long recognized is the one between the price of a product and the quantity demanded (or quantity supplied). The relationship was originally discussed even in the writing of Adam Smith who is considered as the father of economics. In his famous book of 1776 entitled *Wealth of Nations*, he formulated the role of the price of a product. In his opinion, in the market system, the price of a commodity serves as a signal for producers to produce higher or lower quantity of a certain product. Mr. Smith was aware of the fact that when consumers need and are able to buy a certain commodity, then they cast their "price votes" for that commodity and as a consequence the market price goes up. Producers whose self-interest is to maximize profits take this price increase as a signal for producing a higher quantity of that product. In order to reap new and increased profits in the production of that commodity they increase the production and supply higher quantities of that commodity. In this special way the market system automatically satisfies the wishes of consumers. Smith refers to this mechanism as the "invisible hand of nature."

Other economists expounded on this original idea of Adam Smith to clarify what is popularly called the *market mechanism*. Strictly, "market" is a conceptual idea rather than a "place" or "region" as its name tries to indicate. In fact, some markets are not even "located" anywhere. It is therefore a concept where producers (or suppliers) and consumers (demanders) meet to make their wishes known to each other. When the actual transactions take place there is a certain payment made by consumers (for what they get) that we call "price." Changes in price can dictate the changes in quantity the consumers are willing and able to buy. The willingness and ability of consumers signifies the demands for the products.

One has to recognize the difference between needs and demands. Only the needs that are backed up by purchasing power of a consumer can become demands. Clearly, a lot of times consumers or individuals need several things but when they do not have purchasing power to buy those things, then these individuals do not form a part of demand for those commodities. For example, in order to come to my office I "need" a very expensive and roomy car, but do I make a part of demand for an expensive car? Then the answer is, of course, *no*, because my need is not backed by purchasing power for an expensive car.

2.2   Law of Demand

Once we recognize the demands as separate from needs, then we can also see an inverse relationship between the price of a product and the quantity demanded of that product by an individual or a market. Strictly, the relationship can be seen in both directions. When the price is seen as the dependent variable, then an increase in quantity demanded can raise the price and a decline in quantity demanded can lower the price. Hence, the relationship between quantity demanded and price is positive, but mind well that is not what is depicted by the law of demand. In fact, in the statement of the law of demand, the quantity demanded is treated as a dependent variable and the price of a product is taken as an independent variable. In essence, the law of demand is stated as follows: When the price of a product goes up, then by "keeping all other things constant" and in a given time, the quantity demanded for that product will go down. Thus, the relationship between price and quantity demanded is inverse, if price goes up then quantity demanded goes down, by keeping all other things constant.

Now instead of saying "keeping all other things constant" one can also use the two Latin words "ceteris paribus" which have the same meaning. We shall see later what these other things are that have to be kept constant for the law of demand to hold. Currently we need to notice a difference between a demand schedule and a demand curve.

The demand schedule is a table of values of price and quantity demanded that shows the inverse relationship between price and the quantity demanded like Table 2.1. When this demand schedule is plotted on the graph it shows the demand curve like in Figure 2.1.

Table 2.1
Demand Schedule

Price of a product in dollars	Quantity demanded of the product in units
5	10,000
10	8,000
15	6,000
20	4,000
25	2,000
30	0

Figure 2.1
Demand Curve and Inverse Relationship

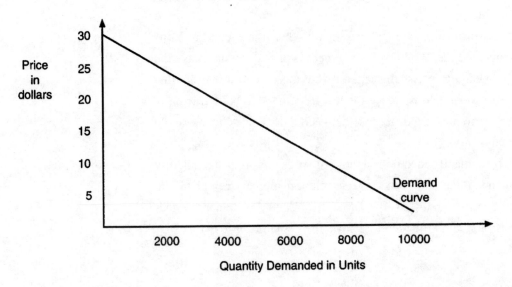

As shown above, the inverse relationship between the price of a product and the quantity demanded is shown by the demand curve that has a downward sloping shape from left to right. The main question is, "How can we justify the law of demand?" According to Alfred Marshall of Cambridge University who is considered as the father of the demand curve, there are two reasons why an increase in price will lower the quantity demanded and they are referred to as the substitution effect and the income effect. When the price of a product goes up and the consumer has the same money income, his/her real income goes down and he/she feels poorer than before. This leads him/her to reduce the quantity demanded for all products, including that of the product whose price has increased. This effect of decline in real income on the quantity demanded is called the income effect.

The second, substitution effect, on the consumption side is also explained in a similar manner. When the price of a product goes up, consumers will substitute its consumption by the consumption of other similar products. For example, if the price of coffee goes up, then people will start drinking more cups of tea. This is called the substitution effect on the consumption side. Thus, due to both the income and substitution effects, the law of demand is justified.

Our next task is to explain the other things that have to be held constant for the law of demand to be valid. These other things are as follows: 1) income of the consumer(s), 2) tastes of the consumers for the product, 3) prices of related products, 4) number of consumers in the market, 5) expectations of consumers, 6) income and population distribution of the consumers, 7) wealth of the consumers, and 8) government's policy of such things as income taxes. The important thing to remember is that if these things are allowed to change then the relationship between price and quantity demanded will change and the demand curve will shift from one location to another.

We can examine these things one by one as follows: 1) Income of the consumers. As the income of consumers changes there will be more or less quantity demanded at the same price. Hence, at the price of say $5, by looking at Figure 2.2, we can say that initially consumers demand 50 units of a product, then with the increase in income of consumers, at the same price they will start demanding more than 50, say 70, units of the product and the point K of the original demand curve will move to the right to, say, point F. In this similar fashion, all points of the original demand curve will move to the right and a new demand curve will be drawn to the right of the original one. Thus, with an increase in income there will be a right-ward shift of the demand curve as shown in Figure 2.2.

However, you can imagine that not all products will be demanded with higher quantity when there is an increase in income of the consumer. Consider, for example, a product that is a poor person's food like, say hamburger. Suppose further that if a consumer consumes five hamburgers in a week, then with an increase in her income, she will start eating less than five hamburgers and switch to an occasional big meal of steak instead.

Thus, with an increase in income of the consumer in this case, the quantity demanded of hamburgers will go down. All these types of products whose quantity demanded declines with the increase in income of the consumers are popularly called inferior goods. The goods that are consumed more after an increase in income are called normal goods, and clearly for normal goods, with an increase in income of the consumers, the demand curve will shift to the right. Recognize that with an increase in income of the consumers for inferior goods there is a shift of the demand curve to the left. This is because with an increase in income, at the same price, consumers buy lower quantities of the inferior good. For example, all the generic goods compared to brand names are inferior goods: people demand lower quantities of generic goods when their income goes up.

The second factor that has to be held constant for the demand curve to be stable is the tastes of consumers for that product. Clearly, tastes can change in favor of the product or they can change so that it will make consumers go away from the consumption of that product.

Figure 2.2
Shifts of the Demand Curve

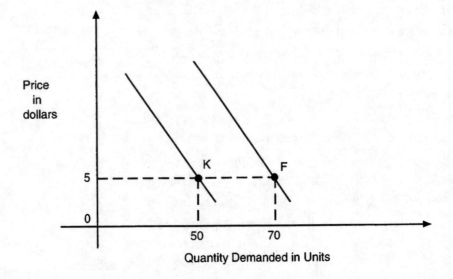

Quantity Demanded in Units

Consider, for example, a product like coffee. Suppose further that a new study makes its finding known that coffee consumption causes cancer. Then there will be a change in tastes of consumers in disfavor of coffee consumption and at the same price consumers will start buying a lower quantity of the coffee. This can make the demand curve of coffee to shift to the left.

The third factor that has to be held constant in the above list is the price of related products. For any commodity there are two types of related products: substitutes and complementaries. Two goods are said to be substitutes of each other if they can be consumed for one another. Examples of substitutes are goods such as coffee and tea, or Pepsi and Coke, or automobiles and buses, or scooters and bicycles.

Now, if we are looking at the demand curve of coffee and the price of tea goes up, then for the same price of coffee people will start drinking more cups of coffee and the points of coffee's demand curve will shift to the right. Thus, an increase in price of a substitute product makes a rightward shift in the demand curve of the product under consideration.

Complementary goods are those that have to be consumed together. Such combinations as cement and brick, or tires and a car, or toothpaste and a toothbrush, or sanitizer and a cleaning cloth are complementary to each other. If two goods are complementary and the price of one good increases, then the demand curve of the other good will shift inward to the left as well. This is because if the price of cement goes up, then the quantity demanded of cement will go down and even if the price of bricks is unchanged, people demand lower quantities of bricks. Hence, the demand curve of brick will shift if the price of cement is changed.

The next thing to be held constant in our list is the number of consumers. Clearly an increase in the number of consumers will shift the demand curve to the right, and a reduction in the number of consumers will shift the demand curve to the left. The expectations of consumers for the future price of the product are also important. If the consumers expect the price of the product to increase in the future, then even if the price currently remains unchanged, they will start demanding a higher quantity of the product. Thus, expectations of an increase in price in the future can shift the demand curve to the right.

Income and demographic distribution of population (sixth on our list) can also have an effect on the position of the demand curve of a certain product. This is because as income distribution changes in favor of the rich population, different products like perfumes, fancy cars, expensive motorboats, and luxurious housing will be demanded more. Hence the demand curves of all these goods will shift to the right. Similarly, as the poor people become fewer in number, the demand for such products as hamburgers, tacos, budget store items, and generic foods will go down. Hence, the demand curve of these products will shift to the left.

Demographic distribution of the population depends upon ages of the population. One can easily imagine that as the baby boom moves over the period of time and as baby boomers reach retired age, they will demand some specific products a whole lot more than some others.

Clearly with greater numbers of aged consumers in the population, products like pain killers, pillows, and dentures will be demanded more and the demand curve of these products will shift to the right. The demand curve of such products as tours and travel, motorbikes, and fancy clothes will shift to the left.

Wealth of the consumers (7) can also have some special consumption patterns. An increase in wealth makes the demand curve of all products that wealthy individuals use to shift to the right. Income tax structure (8) can also change the location of demand curves of inferior and normal goods in a predictable way. An increase in income taxes will make people demand a lower quantity of all normal goods and a higher quantity of inferior goods. Hence, for the normal goods, the demand curves will shift to the left and for inferior goods the demand curves will shift to the right. All in all, we have found several reasons why the demand curve can shift from one position to another. Of course, for the demand curve to be stable, all these things have to be held constant.

We can now make a clear distinction between the change in quantity demanded and the change in demand. When there is a change in price of the good whose demand curve we are considering, there is a "change in quantity demanded," and the change in quantity demanded is explained by a movement along the demand curve (no need to shift the demand curve when this happens). On the other hand, when there is a change in one of the other things that have to be held constant, there is a "change in demand" for the product. Only the change in demand is explained by the shift of the demand curve. Thus, clearly we should never talk about a change in demand when the price of the product under consideration is changing. Similarly, a change in quantity demanded never happens when there is a "change in one of the other things." Economists are particular about this terminology, hence, it is a good idea that we master it once and for all and not make a mistake in using it.

The next important definition that can be useful is the one of consumer surplus. Consider in Figure 2.3 the demand curve for a certain good, say good X, and observe that the maximum price someone in the market is ready to pay for the first unit of good X is OJ. Suppose further that the market price of good X is OK and the quantity demanded of good X is 0Q. Now, due to the fact that the market price is OK, there are at least some consumers who are getting satisfaction that the price is less than what they would have paid for the first unit of it. A measure of this satisfaction is called, "consumer surplus." On the graph, consumer surplus is defined by the area of the triangle under the demand curve from the market price to the maximum price someone would have paid for that product. In terms of Figure 2.3, the area of triangle KJL

Figure 2.3
Consumer Surplus: Area Under the Demand Curve

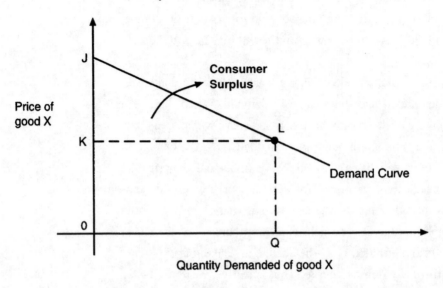

defines consumer surplus. An increase in consumer surplus represents a gain for the consumer class in the economy and a reduction in consumer surplus means a loss to the consumer class.

2.3   Law of Supply

Just like there is a special relationship between the price of a product and the quantity demanded, there is also another relationship between the price of the product and the quantity supplied by the producers of that product. That relationship is explained by the law of supply. In short, the law of supply is expressed as, "when the price of a product increases, then the quantity supplied (by producers or suppliers) of that product increases by keeping all other things constant." Thus, there is a positive (or direct) relationship between price and quantity supplied. Let us keep in mind, however, that in this relationship, price is seen as the independent variable and quantity supplied is the dependent variable. (Of course, one can come up with an

inverse relationship when quantity supplied is seen as the independent variable and price as the dependent variable, but that is
not what the law of supply is describing!)

The main question is, how can we justify the validity of the
law of supply? Clearly there are two basic reasons. They are
referred to as the profitability effect and the substitution effect on
the production side. As the price of a product goes up, suppliers
(or producers) expect higher profits in the production of that
product. Maximizing profits is a self-interest of producers so they
increase the quantity supplied of that product to the market. This
increase in quantity supplied is due to the profitability effect.

Moreover, as the price of a product increases, producers will
substitute production of other products by the production of the
commodity whose price has gone up. Hence there is a substitution effect on the production side. Thus, if a producer can produce
two goods, say X and Y, and if the price of good X increases,
then the producer will switch production from good Y to good X.
Thus, due to the substitution effect on the production side, the law
of supply is justified. A direct relationship between price and
quantity supplied is shown in Table 2.2. The table of values that
shows a positive relationship between price and quantity supplied
is called the "supply schedule." When the supply schedule is plotted on the graph it shows the supply curve.

Table 2.2
Supply Curve

Price	Quantity Supplied
3	50
6	80
9	110
12	140
15	170
18	200

Figure 2.4
Supply Curve: Price and Quantity Supplied

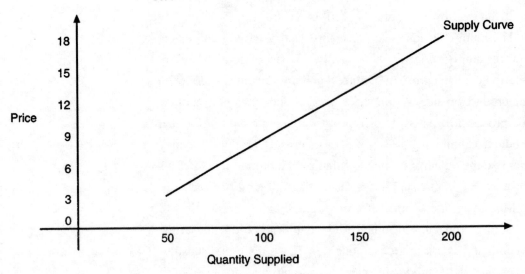

Just like in the case of the demand curve, we should pay attention to the other things that have to be held constant for the supply curve to stay at the same location. Because if any one of these things change then there will be a shift of the supply curve.

The things that are important for the supply curve are: 1) number of suppliers of that product, 2) prices of related commodities on the production side, 3) technology of production, 4) resource cost or the cost of production, 5) expectations of the producers for future prices, and 6) business taxes.

The number of suppliers will obviously have effect on the quantity supplied even if price stays the same. An increase in the number of suppliers will make a higher quantity supplied at the same price and the points on the supply curve will shift to the right (or down). Hence, an increase in the number of suppliers will make the whole supply curve shift to the right.

On the production side, products can be related to each other if they have to be produced jointly or if they have to be produced one after the other. Examples of joint products are easy to find, such as: automobiles and tires, grapes and wine, oranges and orange juice, etc. Clearly, if products X and Y are jointly pro-duced and the price of good Y increases then the quantity sup-plied of good X will increase even if there is no change in the price of good X. Thus, all points on the supply curve of good X will shift to the right when the price of good Y increases. Tech-nology of production can also change the quantity supplied of any product. Consider such production as mining, done by sending individuals to dig inside a mine. Suppose further that miners find a new machine that drills the mine faster and more effectively so that there is an improvement in technology of mining production. Due to this improvement in technology, at the same price the quantity supplied of the product will increase and the supply curve will shift to the right.

Cost of production or resource cost can also influence the loca-tion of the supply curve. An increase in the cost of production will make it harder to supply the same quantity at the same price. Hence, an increase in resource cost will force producers to lower the quantity supplied of the product, creating a leftward shift in the supply curve. Consider the supply curve of a product such as a shirt and suppose further that the price of cotton increases. Clearly, at the same price of shirts, the producers will produce a lower quantity of shirts and the supply curve of shirts will shift to the left due to the increase in price of cotton. Last, but not least, business taxes can also dictate the position of the supply curve. An increase in business taxes will make it harder for producers to supply the same quantity of a product at the same price. Hence an increase in business taxes will shift the supply curve to the left. In the reverse case, a subsidy from the government can shift the sup-ply curve to the right, showing an increase in quantity supplied at the same price of the product.

There is an important difference between a change in quantity supplied and a change in supply. When the price of a product increases there is an increase in quantity supplied as shown by the law of supply. This is shown by a movement from one point to

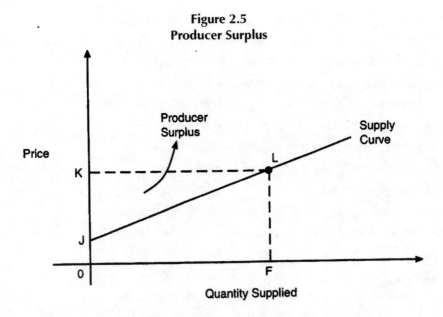

Figure 2.5
Producer Surplus

another on the supply curve and is called a "change in quantity supplied." However, when there is a change in one of the other factors that have to be held constant, there is a "change in supply" and it is shown by a shift of the supply curve. Hence one should not talk about shifting the supply curve when the price of the product changes. There is also no change in supply in this case, only a change in quantity supplied. When the technology changes, one should shift the supply curve and should talk about a change in supply. It is important that we use this terminology in the right way.

Producer surplus is also a concept that shows the satisfaction on the part of producers by having a market price greater than the minimum price the first producer would have accepted for that product. Consider the minimum price of good X in Figure 2.5 as OJ. At this price (OJ) some producers in the market would have produced the first quantity of good X. Suppose that the market price is OK and the quantity produced at that price is OF.

Clearly, all the producers who would have produced at least some quantity of good X at prices below OK are satisfied that the market price is at OK. The measure of this satisfaction is called producer surplus and it is defined by the area above the supply curve up to the market price. Thus, in Figure 2.5, triangle KJL defines the producer surplus. An increase in producer surplus makes gains for the producer class and a reduction in it makes losses for the producer class.

2.4 Derivation of Market Demand Curve from Individual Demand Curves

By using the information of individual demand (supply) curves one can easily get the market demand (supply) curves. Consider a small market that has only three consumers Mr. A, Mr. B and Mrs. C. Suppose further that this is a market of some commonly used commodity such as a wristwatch. The individual demand curves for watches is shown in the following figures. At a $10.00 price for each wristwatch, the quantity demanded by Mr. A in a span of say one year is 5, by Mr. B is 10, and by Mrs. C it is 15. Then the quantity demanded by the whole market at the price of $10.00 is total of individual quantities demanded, which is 30. Hence, in the following graph of market demand curve point J can be plotted at co-ordinates of $10.00 price and 30 units of quantity demanded.

By a similar exercise we can find out the quantity demanded at other prices of wristwatches by the market of these three individuals and then we can derive the market demand curve. The procedure that we used here is called the horizontal summation of individual demand curves. Thus the market demand curve is derived by a horizontal summation of individual demand curves. The market demand curve derived in this fashion is shown in the following Figure 2.6.

Just like deriving the market demand curve, market supply curve can also be derived by the horizontal summation of individual supply curves. Therefore to get points on the market supply curve, one can consider the quantity supplied by producers in the wristwatch market at different prices. Suppose further that the

Figure 2.6
Market Demand Curve from Individual Demand Curves

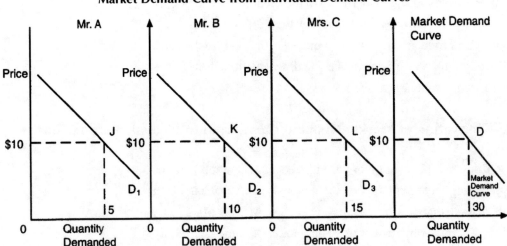

market of wristwatches is made up of say, four suppliers. Then at a given price one can find out the individual supplier's quantity supplied. By adding those quantities one can find the points on the market supply curve.

When taken together with the market demand curve, the market supply curve can provide equilibrium condition of market for the wristwatches. Consider therefore Figure 2.7 in which the market demand curve is sloping downwards from left to right and the market supply curve is sloping upward from left to right. The point at which they intersect one another is called the equilibrium point. At the equilibrium point the quantity demanded by consumers is just equal to the quantity supplied by the producers. Indeed at the equilibrium point both consumers and producers have the same plans hence both are relatively happy to have arrived at the price resolution.

Price that equates the quantity demanded and quantity supplied (such as price P1 in Figure 2.7) is called equilibrium price. Economists are champions in arguing that if there is no out side force on this market of wristwatches then the "market mechanism" will always make price of wristwatches to gravitate towards the equilibrium price. It is relatively simple to prove that at any price above equilibrium price there is a higher quantity supplied than the quantity demanded. Consider therefore any price above equilibrium price, say price P2. At P2 price, the quantity demanded by the market (in Figure 2.7) is Q1 and the quantity supplied is Q2. Hence, there is a surplus of Q1Q2 at P2 price. Now if there is a surplus of any good, its price will start going down. Hence the surplus will be responsible for pushing price down from P2 toward the equilibrium.

In the similar fashion at any price below equilibrium there is higher quantity demanded than supplied making a shortage of the product. Consider therefore a price below equilibrium—say at P3. The quantity demanded by consumers at price P3 (in Figure 2.7) is Q3, and quantity supplied is Q4. This creates a shortage of wristwatches by Q3Q4. If there is shortage of any product then its price starts going up. Hence, from P3 there will be force on price to move upward toward equilibrium.

Figure 2.7
Market Equilibrium Stage

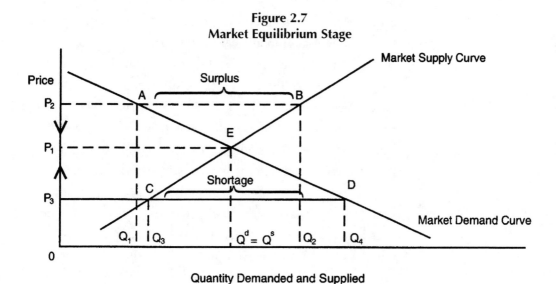

Quantity Demanded and Supplied

Thus the above described market mechanism guarantees the establishment of equilibrium in any market when there is no outside force on it. This mechanism is also referred to as *paradox of flexibility*. It is a paradoxical to observe that if price is left to itself, (or when it is flexible) it tries to reach to a "constant" or inflexible level of equilibrium level. Clearly market clearing process or market mechanism works the best when it is left to itself or if there is no outside force on this market. Alas, reality is full of cases when the market of a product is far from being left to itself.

2.5   Outside Forces on Market Mechanism

On the theoretical level we can recognize at least two types of outside interventions on the market mechanism: 1) three groups of individuals: middlemen, arbitrators and speculators and 2) government policy of price control.

Middlemen are those individuals who buy from a producer and sell the product to a consumer. Clearly all the departmental stores, store outlets in malls are classic examples of the middlemen. While their activities reduce the transaction costs of exchanges the middlemen benefit from information cost incurred by consumers and middlemen receive reward for helping consumers get information about the product. Obviously the price consumers pay for these products is different than the price producers receive for these products. Individuals who buy a product in one regional market and sell it in another regional market are called arbitragers. Thus arbitragers carry out arbitrage activities. An important word in the above definition is the "regional."

Therefore, there are arbitrage activities in all types of products. Some famous arbitrage activities are in the foreign exchange market or in the gold market. If price of a product is higher in New York than in Los Angeles then the arbitrager will buy the product in Los Angeles and sell it in New York. Obviously a large number of arbitragers will reduce the price differences in two regional markets. This is because as arbitragers buy in Los Angeles, price will increase and as they sell the product in New York price will go down.

People who buy and sell products according to expected future prices of the products are referred to as *speculators*. Speculators try to buy when the price is low and sell when the price is high. Obviously whether price will go up (or go down) in the future depends upon one's expectations. Hence, when speculators expect the price to go down in the future, they sell the product and when they expect the price to increase in the future they buy that product. If there are large number of speculators in the market one can show that the price fluctuations are sometimes lower. Thus speculations can be stabilizing or destabilizing for the price fluctuations.

Many times, hoping to help either producers (or consumers), governments get into market mechanism and start dictating the prices. These policies of the government are called *policies of price control*. There are numerous examples of price controls all over the world, but primarily in developing countries. Economists rarely are in support of price control of any kind because they perceive that price control is neither necessary nor beneficial to the party it is supposed to help. A simple model of demand and supply can help one show the effects of price control policy.

Strictly speaking price control has two ways to be enforced. When government intends to help the consumers it fixes a maximum price producers can charge for that product and puts a ceiling on the price. This price ceiling policy has several bad side effects to it. Consider Figure 2.8. The ceiling is expected to help consumers, the sealed price has to be selected that is below equilibrium price of P_1. This selection of Pc price to be the maximum price is obvious because market forces will take the price to equilibrium due the *paradox of flexibility* explained earlier. Hence, no amount of government intervention (or price fixing) is needed to keep price at the equilibrium. If the government selects price to be greater than equilibrium then of course the consumers are hurt

Figure 2.8
Price Control Policy To Help Consumers: Price Ceiling

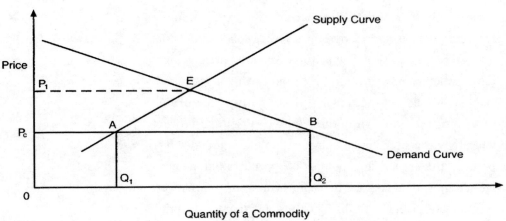

Quantity of a Commodity

rather than helped by the government. Therefore if helping the consumers is government's objective then the selected price better be below equilibrium price.

Notice however that at price Pc that is below equilibrium, there is higher quantity demanded than quantity supplied. Thus government's policy of putting a maximum allowable price in the market creates an arbitrary shortage of the product. At Pc price consumers demand the commodity more than producers are willing to supply to the market. This shortage of the product makes the future price (when the ceiling is lifted) zoom up to equilibrium level and instead of consumers being helped, they are hurt. There are several other consequences of price ceiling if it is not lifted soon enough. Producers obviously start substituting production of this commodity by the production of other goods and services. Consumers, who are willing and able to pay a higher price than the sealed price, carry out their purchases illegally leading to an "illegal/black market." Thus there is also an administrative cost of keeping the price at the sealed level.

The hardship in keeping a maximum price for the product is also duplicated when the government tries to keep the minimum price of the product by adopting the price floor policy. As against price ceiling, price floor is adopted to help the producers, hence a minimum price is guaranteed to the producers to produce a certain product such as wheat or rice. But again as Figure 2.9 shows, the price floor policy creates an arbitrary surplus of the product and instead of helping the suppliers it hurts them by creating a surplus and forcing the future price to go down, once the price floor is lifted.

In Figure 2.9 the selection of price Pf to have the floor, that is above equilibrium, has the same logic as in case of price ceiling. If suppliers have to be helped then the price better be above equilibrium, since the market forces will naturally take the price to equilibrium level. Clearly if one selects price floor to be at price below equilibrium then no help is given to the suppliers. A classic example of a price floor is the laws such as minimum wage law.

But as shown in Figure 2.9 the government only ends up creating surplus of the product and suppliers are not benefitted. In conclusion one can easily argue that governmental policies of price control do not lead to consequences that are beneficial to the

Figure 2.9
Price Control Policy to Help Suppliers: Price Floor

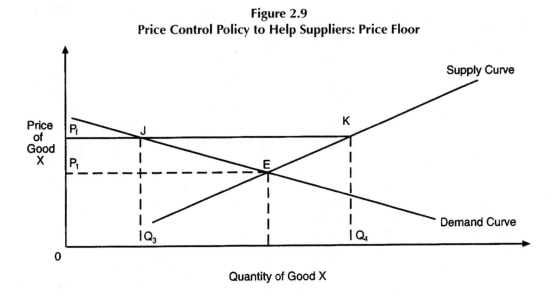

parties they are designed to benefit. Hence it is much better that government does not interfere with market mechanism and the prices determined by market are socially much more efficient than the ones dictated by outside entity such as the government.

In this chapter we have accomplished several tasks. We have stated, proved and derived the law of demand and the demand curve. Similarly we stated, proved and derived the law of supply. We also derived the market demand and supply curves, and with their help we have shown the market mechanism that reinforces the price determination without outside influence. With the help of Paradox of Flexibility we have shown the process in which price is kept at equilibrium when it is flexible. Last, but not least, we have also evaluated the role played by three groups of individuals, and we have seen the inefficiency inherent in governmental policy of price control. In the next chapter we discuss role played by money in an economy by defining money and by considering its evolution and functions.

Suggested Additional Reading for Chapter 2

1. Arnold, Roger. *Macroeconomics,* 3rd ed. West Publishing Company, 1996. Chapters 2 and 3.

2. Baumol, William and Blinder, Allen. *Economics,* 6th ed. Prentice Hall Publications, 1995. Chapters 3 and 4.

3. Byrns, Ralph and Stone, Jerald Jr. *Economics,* 6th ed. Harper/Collins Publishers, 1996. Chapters 3 and 4.

4. Samuelson, Paul and Nordhaus, William. *Economics,* 14th ed. Prentice Hall Publications, 1995. Chapter 4.

5. Sharp, Ansel M., Register, Charles and Grimes, Paul. *Economics of Social Issues,* 12th ed. Irwin Publishers, 1996. Chapter 3 and 4.

6. Stiglitz Joseph. *Economics,* 2nd ed., WW Norton and Company, 1996. Chapter 4.

7. Tregarthen, Timothy. *Microeconomics.* Worth Publisher, 1996. Chapters 3 and 4.

Definition, Evolution and Functions of Money

3

Our problems start popping up as soon as we try to understand the meaning of the word *money*. This happens partly because there is no one acceptable definition of money which can yield everything derived from the word "money." Money is often defined on the conceptual basis as something generally accepted as a medium of exchange. This definition can be labelled as a "behavioral" or "functional" definition of money because it emphasizes the unique function of money: "medium of exchange." This brings us to the question of how to define medium of exchange itself. We may get some help from P. Wickstead[1] who writes ". . . the special characteristic of a medium of exchange is that it is acceptable by a man who does not want it, or does not want it as much as what he gives for it, in order that he may exchange it for something he wants more." However, the functional definition does not pin-point the exact amount of money supply which we see in day-to-day transactions. Hence, out we go in search of another definition of money to find out what the money supply is constituted of. Another (probably better or more acceptable) definition of money defines money as a total debt on the part of government and commercial banks. Debt on the part of governments everywhere is in terms of coins and notes, bills, or in general, "currency." Also, debt on the part of commercial banks is in terms of deposits held by the public.

---

[1] Wickstead. *The Common Sense of Political Economy*, Vol. 1. London: Routledge and Kegan Paul, 1933. Page 136

Hence, money defined in this way should include the coins, currency, and deposits of the banks. Therefore, money = coins + currency + deposits. This definition of money can be termed as a "physical definition." In contrast to the behavioral definition, it does pinpoint what exactly money is. However, our problems are not over until we decide whether all deposits of all banks are included in the money supply or not. Obviously, banks everywhere in the world have (a) demand deposits (called checking accounts in the U.S., and current accounts in the U.K., and India); (b) time deposits (called savings accounts in the U.S., the U.K., and India); and (c) certificates of deposits or fixed deposits, etc. In most countries, this problem is resolved by defining money in several ways like M1, M2, and M3, depending upon what type of deposits are included in that component of the money supply. The part of the money supply which is legally made acceptable as a medium of exchange is called legal tender. Obviously, bank deposits are not a legal tender because anyone can refuse to accept one's check, and that is perfectly legal. (One cannot do anything but offer cash as a payment.)

The financial assets which are not included in the definition of money, but which can readily be converted into a medium of exchange, are called near monies. These assets are things like bonds, stocks, commercial paper, shares and equities, etc. The big question is, should we or should we not include these assets when we are considering money? It is useful to point out the consequences of the existence of near monies. First, due to their existence, the definition of money supply still remains very arbitrary. Because it is still not possible for us to decide what exactly is the money supply, and any attempt to do so is likely to fail over any period of time. Second, the existence of near monies changes the consumption habits of people. If there are substantial amounts of near monies in existence, then people are likely to consume more. The effect of these financial assets on consumption is known as the real balance effect.[1] Third, the existence of near monies is likely to widen the fluctuation of business cycles. In an inflationary stage of a business cycle, if people have stock of near monies, then they are likely to convert them into the medium of exchange to consume more. This obviously increases the demand for goods and services and makes inflation even worse. In the case of a recession (or deflation) people tend to convert their money into near monies and consume less, which reduces demand for goods and services and brings down the price level even further. Thus, due to near monies, business cycle fluctuations are made wider. Lastly, the existence of near monies makes the job of monetary policy—the policy which makes changes in the money supply— much harder. This is because it is much more difficult to pinpoint the target level for a money supply that, due to near monies, fluctuates over a period of time.

Today, we are left with several definitions of money supply depending upon which near money component of money we include or exclude. Availability of several definitions of money is one of the reasons for the confusion between words like money, wealth, income, and property. Once and for all, let us erase these confusions one by one. There is a basic conceptual difference between money and income. Money is a stock concept, and income is a flow concept. A stock concept is something we have to measure "at a point in time." Hence, it is meaningful to say that the money supply is so and so, in so and so currency unit on a certain date. We do not have to measure it per week or per month. Income, on the other hand, is a flow concept and has to be measured over a period of time, such as per week, per month, or per year. Hence, if someone mentions to you that he or she is making a lot of money, what someone really means is that he or she is earning a high income. Money, as a stock, can be changed (or made) only by banking authorities on a central or commercial

---

[1] Several studies of the real balance effect have been done. See Kulkarni (1979). Studies conclude that the real balance effect does appear in several economies.

level. A difference between money and wealth should also be understood. Both money and wealth are stock concepts, however, wealth consists of several physical things and has a meaning only in real terms. Money, on the other hand, has no meaning in physical terms (it is just a piece of paper), but has meaning only in monetary terms. Wealth, like property, consists of things like buildings, machinery, resources, etc.

Despite the above distinctions, money as a commodity is desired by every man and woman on earth. There is glamour associated with its control and severe economic consequences are attached to its increase or decrease. Why is it, then, that money is so important? What are the origins of its modern form? These questions are answered in the following sections.

3.1   Evolution of Money

In traditional society, the metal or any other commodity which served as a monetary unit had an unchanged value for both monetary and non-monetary uses. Since it was possible to use the metal for both purposes, the stability of its value was almost guaranteed. This also increased its general acceptability as a means of payments. In older times, cattle, tobacco, tea, and liquor have served as a medium of exchange, but, in a short time, metal became more popular than any other media because of its several properties. First, metals were scarce in availability and were stable in supply. Both these characteristics guaranteed a constancy of their value, (assuming no drastic changes in its demand) hence, rapid and shocking inflations were impossible. Second, metals are more durable than any form of monetary unit mentioned above. According to Lloyd Thomas, Jr., "This property enabled metallic coins to serve the store-of-value function effectively and thereby to permit the separation of purchases and sales over time."[1] This was obviously not possible for tobacco or cattle.

---

[1] Lloyd Thomas, Jr. (1980, p. 13)

Third, using metals as a monetary unit was much easier because metal coins could be conveniently minted and transferred from one place to another. All these properties gave metals a distinct advantage over any other form of money. Among metals, iron, silver, copper, and gold had served as money in one time period or another. Iron and copper eventually encountered the problem of abundance of supply. Hence, in order to keep the value of metal the same for monetary, as well as non-monetary purposes the coins had to be bulky and heavy. Gold was too scarce to be used as money. Hence, silver became popular for a long time. The monetary system in which the metal serving as money has the same value for monetary and non-monetary purposes is called full-bodied commodity money. In the later period, governments realized that it is also sufficient to introduce a monetary unit whose value is backed up by a stock of precious metal. This gave rise to a representative commodity money. In this system, even if value of the monetary unit was higher for a monetary purpose than for a non-monetary purpose, it could always be exchanged with the government's stock of the precious metal. When representative commodity money was introduced, it ultimately replaced all the metal coins over a period of time. This case is an application of Gresham's law.[1] The law can be stated as, "when good and bad money circulated at the like value, people would prefer to hoard the good and pass away the bad; so that the former would disappear from, and the latter remain in circulation." The law, originally written in 1552, still holds quite true.

Depending upon how many metals are used in making coins for circulation, there were three distinct monetary standards in the past: Monometallism, bimetallism and symmetallism. As the name suggests, monometallism used only one metal to redeem

---

[1] Alexander Del Mar (1968, p.68). Gresham's law is named after Sir Thomas Gresham. He was an English textile merchant who served King Edward VI, Queen Maryland Queen Elizabeth I as financial representative in Antwerp. Though he was certainly not the first to explain it, the law is always credited to him.

the coins, bimetallism used two metals to make two separate coins and symmetalism used two metals to make the same coin. The gold standard was the classic case of a monometallic system and its operation will be discussed in detail in the next chapter.

In modern times, governments have realized that as long as people accept a currency as a medium of exchange, there is absolutely no reason why it has to be backed up by any amount of a precious metal. The very fact that an unbacked currency can work for all of the purposes that it is supposed to serve, has led to the new monetary system known as a fiduciary money system. Money whose value in the physical terms is less than its value in monetary terms and is not backed up by any precious metal which can be exchanged with it, is known as fiat or credit, or fiduciary money.[1] In Lloyd Thomas' words, "In a real sense, the backing of our money today consists of an implicit faith and confidence that our government will keep the supply of money in reasonable control so that the buying power of a dollar (monetary unit) does not deteriorate appreciably in a given week of a month. Given the existence of this faith, money can serve its functions effectively without any commodity backing." After this survey of possible monetary systems, it is now time to look at the different functions that money performs.

3.2   Functions of Money

The first important function money performs is known as a medium of exchange. The importance of this function of money is best understood by imagining an economy without money, namely, a barter economy. In a barter economy, all exchanges are made in physical terms which means that good X has to be exchanged directly for good Y. Moreover, in order for an exchange to take place, a barter economy requires what is known

---

[1] Following Thomas (1979, p. 19) even if we use these three words synonymously, technically credit and fiduciary monies are broader than fiat money.

as "double coincidence of wants." A possessor of good X must have information about the existence of a seller who would offer to him the good he desires and is ready to accept good X in exchange. In other words, both individuals should have enough information to answer the following questions:

Who offers the goods desired to be purchased? In what quantity is the offer made? Is the ratio of exchanges acceptable to both parties? To collect the needed information is a costly, time consuming and inefficient process. Therefore, the requirement of a double coincidence of wants in a barter economy make exchange particularly difficult.

It is obvious that in a money economy, a person can transfer goods and services for money and then exchange money for any other desired commodity. There is not as great a need for information in a money economy as there is in a barter economy. Since acquiring information is a costly endeavor, exchanges in a money economy are less costly and therefore much easier. Moreover, this reduction in transaction costs for exchange leads to more exchanges which is better for the economy. A higher number of exchanges enhances the specialization process in the economy, and specialization is beneficial because, given enough competition everywhere, one can use one's resources in the most efficient way. Without money, exchanges are so costly and rare that growth and prosperity are out of the question. Service of the monetary unit as a medium of exchange is, therefore, the most important and desirable function that money performs.

The second important function of money is that it also serves as a measure of value. All goods and services can be expressed in terms of money.[1] When the values of goods and services are expressed in terms of money, they become prices. Money serves as a standard or as a numeraire in measuring the value of goods and services in exchange. Due to this function of money,

---

[1] Sometimes this function is also referred to as the function of "unit of account."

economic life is much more simple in a money economy than in a barter economy. In a barter economy, all goods would have to be measured, and their value expressed, in terms of all the other remaining goods. Hence, if there are 'n' goods, each good would have to be expressed in terms of those remaining (n−1). The number of exchange rates needed in such an economy would be given by a formula:

$$J = \frac{n \quad (n-1)}{2}$$

where: J = total number of exchange rates needed in the barter economy; n = number of goods in the barter economy.

To use a simple example, a barter economy with only 100 goods would need 4,950 exchange rate (or price) expressions! In the case of a money economy, this can be done with only 100 prices. In reality, we have tens of thousands of goods. Hence, one might imagine how cumbersome it would be to deal with a very large number of prices. A money economy is more efficient than a barter economy because the former has a standard of value.

The third function which money performs is called a store of value. Because people are aware of the fact that money can always function as a medium of exchange, they can store their wealth in terms of money. Thus, this function is related to the first function performed by money. However, in a modern society since the income is received periodically, there is a need for saving purchasing power for a time. Given a wide spectrum of other financial assets in which purchasing power can be stored, there is a special reason why people prefer money to several other assets. This is called the "liquidity" property of money. By liquidity, we refer to the ease with which we can convert a financial asset into a medium of exchange. Liquidity is greatest for money as an asset because money itself is a medium of exchange. Compare this with any other financial asset like bonds or stocks. It takes some time period to convert these assets into something that can be exchanged for goods. Obviously, there are some people who do not have a very high "liquidity preference" who store their wealth in terms of other nonliquid assets. The decision about choice of the financial assets according to liquidity risk and returns is called a portfolio decision. However, we can be confident that when using money as a medium of exchange is necessary, money also performs the useful function of a store of value.

Lastly, money serves the function of a measure of deferred payment. Often people engage in exchanges that involve payments over some period of time. There will be some inconvenience inherent in the receipt of payments at a later date because people prefer liquidity in a shorter time over liquidity in a longer time. To measure this inconvenience and to pay for this waiting time, money is useful. We refer to this "additional reward for waiting" as the interest rate. The contracts which involve such waiting time and interest rates are known as debt contracts.

It is important to get acquainted with some other concepts related to money. One such concept is the value of money which is measured by the amount of goods and services one unit of money can buy. In other words, the value of money is nothing but the purchasing power of money. It is inversely dependent upon the supply of money. If the supply of money becomes scarce, then the value of money increases. But more about this will be considered in other chapters. Another important concept is called "postponement of payments." This is done by the use of credit cards. Strictly speaking, the use of credit cards solves only the problem of carrying cash in the pocket. Even though credit cards sometimes are used indirectly as a medium of exchange, they are not considered a part of the money supply.

To summarize, in this chapter, the word "money" has been defined. Also discussed were the usual misconceptions of the word money, and the differences between money and wealth and money and income. The consequences of the existence of near monies were also noted. Further, the evolution of money was reviewed. In it, a brief survey of historical monetary systems was presented. The later section described the functions of money, namely, medium of exchange, unit of account, store of value, and standard of deferred payments. By evaluating the important functions that money performs, this chapter also emphasized the inconvenience of a barter economy. It is seen that money holds a crucial position by the virtue of its functions. In the next chapter, the working of the gold standard system is analyzed.

Suggested Additional Reading for Chapter 3

1. Armen, Alchian. "Why Money*?" Journal of Money, Credit and Banking*, February 1977.

2. Brunner, K. and A. Meltzer. "The Uses of Money: Money in the Theory of an Exchange Economy." *American Economic Review*, Vol. 61, No. 5, December 1971.

3. Chetty, V.K, "On Measuring the Nearness of the NearMonies." *American Economic Review*, June 1969.

4. Fisher, Douglas. *Monetary Theory and the Demand for Money*. New York: John Wiley and Sons, 1978. (Chapter 1 features a very good theoretical treatment of the definition of money.)

5. Goldfeld, L. V. and S. M. Chandler. *The Economics of Money and Banking*, 7th ed. New York: Harper and Row Publishers, 1979. Chapter 1.

6. Johnson, I. C. and W W Roberts. *Money and Banking: A Market-Oriented Approach*. New York: The DrydenPress, 1982. Chapters 1 and 2.

7. Kulkarni, Kishore G. "Comparison of the Existence of Real Balance Effect in Six Countries." *Economic Affairs*, Vol. 24, No. 8-9, August-September 1979:193-203.

8. Thomas, Lloyd. *Money, Banking and Economic Activity*. New Jersey: Prentice Hall Publications, 1979. Chapters 1 and 2.

9. Thorn, Richard S. *Introduction to Money and Banking*. New York: Harper and Row Publishers,1976. Chapters 1 and 2.

10. Tullock, G. "Competing Monies." *Journal of Money, Credit, and Banking*. November 1975.

Gold Standard Mechanism and Empirical Evidence

4

4.1   What is the Gold Standard?

The gold standard is a monetary system which existed in several forms throughout history. The classical gold standard existed in the United States and in several other countries in the years between 1880 and 1917, although aspects of it persisted in various forms until the 1971 breakdown of the Bretton Woods system. In the classical gold standard monetary system, each country was committed to keep the value of their monetary unit constant in terms of gold. Before 1821, most countries were on a bimetallic standard based on silver and gold. After the Napoleonic War inflation episode, Great Britain returned to a gold standard. Throughout the period 1821-80, the gold standard steadily expanded as more and more countries turned to it. By 1880, the majority of countries in the world were on a gold standard. According to Bordo, "The period from 1880 to 1914 known as the 'heyday' of the gold standard, was a remarkable period in world economic history, characterized by rapid economic growth, the free flow of labor and capital, virtually free trade, and in general, world peace. These external conditions coupled with the elaborate financial network centered in London are believed by many observers to be the *sine quanon* of the effective operation of the gold standard."[1]

---

[1] See Bordo in the Suggested Reading List.

After 1914, the gold standard temporarily broke down because of World War I but was reestablished from 1925 to 1931, as the gold exchange standard. However, due to large outflows of gold stock from the U.K. and U.S. economies, the gold exchange standard broke down in 1934. Another reason for this breakdown was the unwillingness of most of the countries to let the gold outflow happen. The Bretton Woods System (which existed from 1944 to 1971) is the most recent attempt to adopt some kind of gold standard mechanism. Bordo has summarized the reasons for the breakdown of this system by saying, "In the post World War II period, persistent U.S. deficits helped finance the recovery of world trade from the aftermath of depression and war. However, the steady growth in the use of U.S. dollars as international reserves and persistent U.S. deficits in balance of payments steadily reduced U.S. gold reserves and the gold reserve ratio— which in turn reduced confidence in the ultimate ability of the U.S. to redeem its currency in gold. This so called confidence problem, coupled with the aversion of many countries to paying seigniorage to the United States as well as paying an "inflation tax" to the United States in the post-1965 period, ultimately led to the breakdown of the Bretton Woods System in 1971. Thus, even if the gold standard does not exist now, it has been the most influential monetary system of the past. it, therefore, deserves a careful examination in this chapter.

4.2   The Working of Pure Gold Standard: Rules of the Game

In the gold standard, governments of each member country had to adhere to at least three strict rules. First, each government had to keep the price of gold constant in terms of the currency circulating as money. This fixed price was called the "mint price." For example, in the U.S. the mint price was established as 35 dollars per ounce of gold. At the mint price, the government must be ready to buy or sell any amount of gold offered to it by the general public. The readiness of the government to do these activities guaranteed the equality of actual market price of gold and the announced mint price. This is because, if the actual price of gold happened to be lower than the mint price of gold, then the public would tend to sell gold to the government. Consequently, the supply of gold in the market would go down and the actual price of gold would move upwards[1]. in the reverse case, if the actual price of gold is greater than the mint price, then the public would buy gold from the government. In turn, the supply of gold in the market would go up, lowering its market price. Thus, due to this second rule, the mint price was no different than the market price. Third, the governments under the gold standard also had to legalize the melting of gold. Due to this rule, the price of gold for monetary and non-monetary use was made equal, and this rule supported the equality of the mint and the actual prices of gold.

With the help of these rules and Figure 4.1, let us now determine the exact value of the money supply under the gold standard. Notice that in Figure 4.1 the horizontal axis denotes the quantity of the total gold supply in the economy and demand for gold for non-monetary purposes such as making rings, necklaces or just for hoarding. On the vertical axis, we plot the price of gold per ounce. The inverse relationship between the price and the quantity demanded of gold for non-monetary purposes is shown by the downward sloping demand curve from left to right. As the price of gold increases, people would tend to demand less of it because of the income and substitution effects. The supply curve of gold for the economy would be upward sloping from left to right. This is so because a higher price of gold makes the producers of the gold, who supply the quantity, work harder and supply more.

---

[1] As the principles of economics may have taught you, due to an increase in the price of a good, the real income of the consumer goes down, making him demand less of all goods. Second, an increase in the price also causes the consumer to substitute for the consumption of gold by the consumption of related commodities such as silver, In ordinary terms, an increase in the price of gold would make people wear more silver and less gold.

Figure 4.1
Quantity Supplied of Gold and Quantity Demanded of Gold for Non-Monetary Purposes

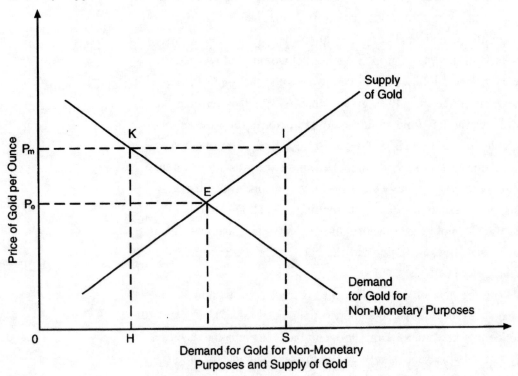

At the point where these two curves intersect, the equilibrium price, Pe, is determined. Interpreted carefully, this means that at price Pe, all of the supply of gold in the economy is being demanded for non-monetary purposes such as making rings. Obviously that means there is no excess supply of gold left to make the coins from. Hence, a rational government would fix the mint price above Pe (certainly not equal to or below Pe because in those cases there would be no gold left to support the money supply of the economy). Let us assume that the government in question fixes the mint price at the level Pm. At Pm, the quantity supplied of gold in the economy is OS, (Pm) given by the supply curve, and quantity demanded of gold for non-monetary purposes is PmK (or 0H) given by the demand curve. This results in an excess of gold supply of HS (or K1) to be used as the money supply. In a pure gold standard, the quantity HS is available for making coins. Now, if we define the value of the money supply as the product of the price of gold and the quantity of gold used as money, then the value of the money supply, in terms of Figure 4.1, is 0Pm (price) x HS. The product of 0Pm and HS defines the area of the rectangle KISH. Thus, the value of the money supply under the gold standard can be expressed as the area of KISH.

Does this mean that it is only the locations of the demand and supply curves in Figure 4.1 which determine the amount of the money supply under the gold standard? Or to ask the question differently, does this mean that the money supply (under the gold standard) is likely to change if there are shifts in these curves? The answers to both questions are, importantly, *yes*. Hence, the sources of changes in the money supply under the gold standard derive from the factors that shift the demand for gold and supply of gold curves. Our preliminary understanding of principles of economics tells us that the demand curve for gold shifts if there is an increase in income of the consumers. Since the demand for gold we are considering is the demand by the whole economy, it is the income of the nation or economy (national income) which would be influential in this case. A higher income tends to make consumers demand more gold at a given price.[1] Hence, an increase in income would indicate a shift of the demand curve to the right. It would reduce the area of KISH which means the value of the money supply would go down. Second, the price of related commodities, silver in this case, can also influence the location of the demand curve. If the price of silver goes up, people would demand more gold (less of silver) and the demand curve for gold would shift to the right. This reduces the value of the money supply under the gold standard. Similarly, the tastes of the consumers, prices of complementary goods, and expectations of the consumers also

---

[1] Following the effects of income changes, an interested reader may want to analyze the effects of these changes on the money supply under the gold standard.

Figure 4.2
Demand for Gold for Non-Monetary Purposes and Supply of Gold

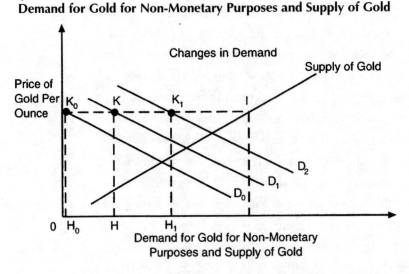

Demand for Gold for Non-Monetary
Purposes and Supply of Gold

have an effect on the location of the demand curve. Refer to Figure 4.2 for shifts in the demand curve due to changes in demand.

In general, when the demand curve shifts right to D_2 from D_1 the value of the money supply goes down from KISH to K_1ISH_1 and when the demand curve shifts downwards from D_1 to D_0, the money supply increases from KISH to $K_0 ISH_0$.

The supply curve of gold may shift because of the changes in any of the factors which affect the quantity supplied except for the price of gold.[1] These factors include changes in the cost of production, new discoveries of gold mines, expectations of producers, and changes in technology of the production. To clarify, for example, an increased cost of production would reduce the gold supply, causing the supply curve to shift to the left. This reduces the area of rectangle KISH making the value of the money supply under the gold standard lower. Similarly, the new discovery of a gold mine, optimistic expectations of producers, and improved technology of gold production, may shift the

---

[1] In theory, one may argue that by announcing a different mint price of gold, the government can exercise some control on the money supply. However, in practice, each member country had agreed to keep the mint price unchanged for an indefinite period.

supply curve to the right, increasing the area of rectangle KISH, and increasing the value of the money supply.

In terms of Figure 4.3, a rightward shift of the supply curve from S_1 to S_2 increases the value of the money supply from KISH to KI_0S_0H. A leftward shift of the supply curve from S_1 to S_0 is responsible for decreases in the money supply from KISH to KI_1SH_1. Notice carefully the consequences of the above shifts in terms of making changes in the money supply. Since the money supply determination was left for a free-play of demand and supply curve location, it was obvious that the government had no control of it. However, it is interesting to know that the system in which governments could not change the money supply at will, functioned efficiently for a long time. There were some apparent benefits of the gold standard.

First, since governments could not increase money supply excessively, the gold standard was an era of price stability. It provides evidence for the belief that excessive increases in the money supply are the only reason for inflation, always and everywhere. It can also be deduced that if governments cannot control

Figure 4.3
Supply for Gold and Demand for Gold for Non-Monetary Purposes

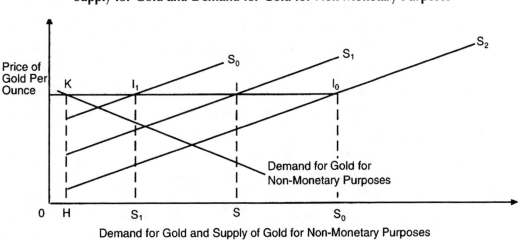

Demand for Gold and Supply of Gold for Non-Monetary Purposes

the money supply, then any business fluctuations whose basic cause is the governmental actions, were absent under the gold standard. That gives us one less reason for having business cycles in the economy. Evidently, governmental actions are not the only cause of business cycles, therefore, even in the era of the gold standard there were business cycles.

Second, even if there happens to be inflation (defined as an increase in the general price level of goods and services), there is an automatic cure for it under the gold standard system. For example, in case of inflation, producers would tend to divert their resources from the production of gold to the production of goods and services. In the long run, this would lead to an increase in the supply of goods and services and also to decreases in the gold supply. Both of these consequences lead to a decrease in the general price level of goods and services because a higher supply of goods would bring their prices down and because a lower gold supply leads to a lower money supply in the economy which also makes the inflation less vulnerable. Thus, some economists believe that in the gold standard system, inflation should be no problem in the first instance, and even if it happens to become a problem, it would be cured automatically.

Third, the gold standard system is also beneficial for price equalization on an international basis. (This is sometimes referred to as "the law of one price.") The price equalization happens in the following manner. Suppose there are two economies, A and B, and the price level in country A, say P_A, initially happens to be greater than the price level in country B, say P_B. In this situation, assuming free trade, country A will import more from country B. As she does so, she will have to pay money for the goods and services she is importing. Hence, the money supply in country A will go down and the supply of goods and services will go up. Both forces would reduce prices in country A. As far as country B is concerned, she would lose goods and services and obtain additional money supply. Hence, the tendency of the general price level would be to go up in country B. Theoretically, the process would continue until the price levels in both economies are equal. Hence, on an international level, the countries could achieve the same price level for their goods and services. It appears that this was probably the most significant benefit of the gold standard, for even in modern times (as late as 1980) several economists have argued for returning back to the gold standard to solve the problem of worldwide inflation. Now the questions are, if there are so many benefits of the gold standard, in theory, then why did it break down in the first place? Are there any economic causes for this break down or were they all purely political? Questions like these can be answered by looking at the costs that were incurred in the adoption of the gold standard.

First, under the gold standard, the government authorities were trapped in a strange situation. They had to follow the stringent rules mentioned before, and in return, they had no control of the money supply. This gave rise to contempt on the part of the government and an unwillingness to obey the rules. In the longer run they realized even more fiercely that an active government has to influence the money supply to carry out an increase in activities. Thus, more and more governments became reluctant to obey the rules of the gold standard and that endangered its existence.

Second, the government, which is able to defect from the system, can be seen as a beneficiary from its actions. To make this point clear, let us continue with the same example of country A and country B as before. Let us assume that country A, who is importing goods and services from country B decides to move away from the gold standard and to not abide by its rules. Then it is possible for country A to continue importing from B and make the payment for the increased imports by printing more currency. Country A would keep on obtaining more goods and services from country B by giving up a lower cost commodity—its money. It is thus possible for a defector (country A) to be at an advantage by failing to observe the rules of the gold standard. Several economists feel that this was the basic reason why many countries were suspicious of other members under the gold standard, and it was the major reason why the gold standard broke down.

The third reason for the breakdown of the gold standard can be identified as the greater awareness on the part of the governments about the necessity of providing for a greater supply of the medium of exchange in order to achieve economic growth. The reasoning behind this is as follows. A higher number of transactions in the economy are needed for a greater level of gross national product because only more exchanges can best do the job of producing higher by encouraging specialization. Exchanges are facilitated only by more—not by constant or declining—money supply. Hence, it appears that by not having more money, there is a guarantee of economic stagnation. It is, therefore, the strict mandate on governments not to be able to increase the money supply according to their own liking, which constituted a serious drawback in the gold standard system. No wonder it failed in the past, and no wonder in the modern time, when governments are so active in the process of economic advancement, very few economists support readopting the gold standard. Having reviewed this, let us now consider some of the major developments in the present monetary system in the world economy.

4.3 Empirical Evidence on the Gold Standard Mechanism: A Critical Appraisal

Having discussed the theoretical foundation underlying the gold standard mechanism, now we will critically review the performance of the gold standard era and put it in historical perspective.

The Classical Gold Standard (1879-1914)

The use of precious metals as a medium of exchange can be dated back several centuries. However, gold was particularly popular due to its scarcity, durability and the relative ease with which it could be minted into coins of uniform value. As economies grew over the years and the volume of transactions expanded rapidly, slowly the currency or paper money replaced gold as a medium of exchange. This was because paper money was safer and lighter to transport, while each unit could still be converted into gold on demand. Thus, the so-called gold standard, in which currency fully backed by gold served as the medium of exchange, emerged simultaneously in many countries as a viable monetary arrangement.

The international gold standard was not consciously established through international treaties. Instead it evolved over time, partly due to the series of unforeseen events leading to gold discoveries and partly due to the economic problems inherent in maintaining a bimetallic standard. Under a bimetallic standard, a nation's currency would consist of a specified amount of one metal (gold) or another (usually silver). For example, the United States (U.S. from now on) Coinage Act of 1792 stipulated that a dollar should consist of 24.75 grains of gold or 371.25 grains of silver. This, in turn, fixed the mint ratio of silver to gold at 15:1 (371.25/24.75 is approximately 15), i.e., 15 ounces of silver for one ounce of gold. Thus, whenever the market price of gold (in terms of silver) differed from the mint price of gold, profitable arbitrage opportunities existed. The market price, in turn, depended on the relative supplies of gold and silver which were tied to the unforeseen circumstances concerning the timing of gold and silver discoveries. For example, in the U.S., the market price of a unit of gold fluctuated between 15.6 and 15.8 units of silver after the 1820s. This prompted the traders to buy gold cheap at the U.S. mint for 15 ounces of silver and sell it high in the market. As the U.S. mint lost gold and acquired silver, the new coins had to be struck in silver; despite the government's official commitment to a bimetallic standard. The situation reversed itself when the Coinage Act of 1834 changed the mint price of gold to 16 ounces of silver, in response to a shortage of gold coins in circulation. Since gold was now overvalued (relative to the market price) at the mint, it drove the silver coins out of circulation.[1]

Britain was one of the first countries to tie the pound sterling more closely to gold than to silver as early as the 17th century. Towards the latter half of the 18th century, Germany, Japan and other major countries followed suit, attracted by Britain's economic dominance and hoping to achieve similar economic success by imitating British institutions. The United States officially joined the gold standard in 1879 when it restored full convertibility of paper dollars into gold which was temporarily suspended to finance the Civil War. With Britain, the United States and major European nations on domestic gold standard, the international monetary system evolved toward the gold standard in 1879 and lasted until the outbreak of World War I.

As discussed in section 4.2, under the gold standard, the monetary authority in each country defined the value of its domestic currency in terms of gold, commonly referred to as the "par value." For example, the U.S. dollar value of an ounce of gold was defined as $20.67 compared to £4.24 per ounce in Britain. The monetary authorities stood ready to buy or sell gold at the stipulated price to keep the par value of domestic currency fixed. Such practices, in essence, fixed the mint exchange rate between any pair of currencies through their ties to the gold. For instance, the mint exchange rate between dollars and pounds was $4.87 per pound sterling. The arbitrage activities ensured that market exchange rates between currencies did not deviate from the official

---

[1] Such a situation illustrates Gresham's law; that bad money (i.e., the money that is overvalued at the mint) drive out the good money (i.e., the money that is undervalued at the mint.)
$20.67 = 1 ounce gold =£4.24 or $4.87 = £1

mint exchange rates more than the amount of transportation costs incurred in shipping gold across national boundaries. Thus, the gold standard came to represent a special type of fixed exchange rate system amongst nations' currencies.

The viability of gold standard also required that the monetary authority issue no more currency than it could back by gold. Besides, the way the classical gold standard system was designed, as discussed in the theory section, money supply was allowed to change passively in the face of balance of payment difficulties. This, in turn, meant that nations could not actively use monetary policy to achieve domestic full employment with price stability. However, this did not undermine the confidence of the classical economists in the gold standard, who held that in the long run, there is an automatic tendency for a market oriented system to achieve full employment without inflation.

In retrospect, how well did the Classical Gold Standard work? The economists, by and large, agree that the gold standard was successful in maintaining a stable exchange rate between major currencies. During 1879-1913, there were no changes in the mint exchange rates between the U.S. dollar, British pound, French Franc and the German mark.

The U.S. also experienced rapid economic growth accompanied by a low inflation rate whereas nations unable to maintain gold convertibility (e.g., Latin America) suffered from frequent devaluations of their currency. Such empirical evidence has prompted some economists to conclude that the gold standard also contributed to price stability. However, a closer examination of behavior of prices during the 18th and 19th century reveals that price stability was not attained, either in the short run or in the long run. According to Richard Cooper, "Price stability in the sense of a return to earlier levels of prices was obtained over longer periods only by judicious choice of the years for comparison. If one chooses 1822, 1856, 1877, late 1915, and 1931, for instance, the U.S. wholesale price level indeed appears unchanged. But between these dates there were great swells and troughs" (See Cooper, 1982, p. 7). In retrospect, this is not surprising, since the growth of the gold stock itself has been historically erratic due to unforeseen circumstances relating to gold discoveries or new extraction technologies. So even if the monetary authorities had followed the rules of the gold standard closely in creating no more money than they could back by gold, the growth in the money stock and the associated price movement were expected to be quite volatile. To make matters worse, the monetary authorities frequently circumvented the rules by changing the laws to require less gold backing for each unit of currency, when it was in their national interest to do so.

To summarize, it appears that during the tranquil period of pre World War I, the nations on the gold standard indeed enjoyed economic prosperity and low inflation rates. But the question remains as to whether the gold standard was responsible for such economic prosperity, or was it the prosperity of these nations that allowed them to remain faithful to the gold standard? It is worth noting that the gold standard era coincided with a period of rapid technological evolution designed to improve the living standard of the masses. Besides, the world economy was still not subjected to severe shocks such as the World War I and II, the Great Depression of the 1930s or the OPEC oil price shock of the 1970s which would have profound influence in shaping the international monetary system of later years.

The classical gold standard era came to an abrupt end with the outbreak of World War I. Financing the war became the prime focus of the belligerent nations. Most of the nations accomplished it by issuing paper currency. In the absence of new gold to back the paper currency, the nations were forced to suspend the convertibility of their currency into gold. However, the U.S. returned to gold immediately after World War I in 1919. Attracted by the comparative financial stability of the gold standard era, other European nations followed suit. Austria and Sweden restored convertibility in 1923, followed by Germany in 1924. Fearing isolation and a loss of its dominance as the world's leading financial center, Britain restored the convertibility of the pound to gold in 1925 at the prewar price of gold. With return of all the major nations to gold, the international monetary system was back on the gold standard once again.

In retrospect, England's return to gold at the prewar parity level proved fatal. Although prices had been generally falling since the war, in 1925 it was still much higher than it was in the prewar days of the gold standard. As had been correctly predicted by John Maynard Keynes, at the prewar parity level, the British pound was seriously overvalued. This adversely affected Britain's international competitiveness and in turn, caused slow economic growth and high unemployment rates. An overvalued pound also led to higher imports and lower exports resulting in current account deficits and consequent gold outflow. Given that Britain's gold reserves were limited, the persistent outflow of gold undermined confidence of other nations in Britain's ability to honor its commitment to exchange pounds for gold at the prewar parity level. Thus, the panic-stricken foreign holders of pounds began converting their pounds to gold and Britain was eventually forced off gold in 1931.

At around the same time, the world economy was plagued by the Great Depression (1929-1933) which had an enormous impact on the international monetary system. International monetary cooperation took a back seat as country after country suspended the convertibility of their currencies to gold. To "protect" domestic jobs from foreign competition, countries erected trade barriers, instituted quotas, and more important, resorted to predatory devaluations to increase their own international competitiveness at the expense of foreign countries. Such currency devaluation often provoked foreign retaliation and left all countries worse off in the end. For example, it is often argued that U.S. devaluation of 1933 when the dollar price of gold was raised from $20.67 per ounce to

$35 per ounce (nearly 60% devaluation of the dollar in terms of gold) was undertaken in response to the pound's devaluation of 1931. The turbulence in the world markets continued until the outbreak of World War II in 1939 and the period was characterized by great instability stemming from flexible exchange rates. According to many economists, such interwar experience prompted the Allies at the close of World War II to establish an international monetary system with some degree of exchange rate flexibility but with primary emphasis on some sort of exchange rate stability that was prevalent during the classical gold standard era.

The Interwar Years

Unlike the gold standard, the Bretton Woods System was a deliberate creation. In 1944, representatives of 44 nations including the United States and Britain (led by Harry White of the U.S. Treasury and Keynes respectively) met in Bretton Woods, New Hampshire in the U.S. in an effort to lay out the rules of a stable and open international trade and monetary system that would preserve the fixed exchange rate aspects of the gold standard within a framework allowing for moderate exchange rate changes. The International Monetary Fund (IMF) was created to serve as a forum through which countries could meet to solve their exchange rate and balance of payment problems.

Under the rules of the agreement, the U.S. dollar had to be pegged to gold within 1% of its par value of $35 per ounce of gold. This required that the Federal Reserve of the U.S. stand ready to buy or sell gold in unlimited amounts to maintain the fixed price of gold. On the contrary, other nations participating in the IMF had the choice of tying their currencies either to the dollar or to gold. In practice, other nations chose to peg their rate of exchange to the dollar and thus, were indirectly tied to gold. It was the responsibility of these nations to keep the dollar values of their respective currencies unchanged at the agreed upon pegged rates through buying and selling of dollars. In essence, the Bretton Woods System was a gold exchange standard rather than a pure gold standard in which the dollar played a central role as the reserve currency.

The Bretton Woods agreement, in theory, incorporated the desirable features of a flexible exchange system into a gold exchange standard. Following World War II, some nations were growing rapidly, while other nations were struggling to recover from the devastations of war. The agreement recognized the need for some sort of flexibility in the international monetary system to periodically realign currencies of nations in widely divergent circumstances. Nations could change the exchange rate between the dollar and their own currency by less than 10% of par value through intervention in the foreign exchange market. A larger change in the exchange rate stemming from a fundamental disequilibrium[1] in balance of payments required IMF consent. Thus, the Bretton Woods agreement was referred to as an "adjustable peg," exchange rates were to be pegged but adjustable.

In retrospect, how did the Bretton Woods system work? Despite the flexibility, most of the nations suffering from current account deficits were reluctant to devalue their currencies because of national pride. Instead, the deficit nations would wait until such a devaluation was long overdue. By then, the individuals fearing an imminent devaluation would sell the nation's currency and exacerbate the deficit. On the other hand, the nations enjoying current account surpluses were equally reluctant to revaluate their currencies fearing that such a move will adversely affect their international competitiveness. This, in effect, robbed the Bretton Woods system of the flexible adjustment mechanism which was designed to correct the balance of payment disequilibria. The adjustable peg regime of Bretton Woods turned into a de facto fixed rate regime.

---

[1] The term "fundamental equilibrium" was nowhere clearly defined in the agreement; however, it was broadly defined as large and persistent balance of payment deficits and surpluses.

The Bretton Woods System (1944-1971)

The Bretton Woods system also meant contradictory responsibilities for the U.S. On one hand, the central banks of other nations needed large stocks of dollars to carry out large scale intervention in the foreign exchange market in order to keep the dollar price of their currencies fixed. But the accumulation of large sums of dollars in the hands of foreign central banks, if not backed by adequate gold reserves, would undermine confidence in the convertibility of the U.S. dollar to gold. During the 1960s, the U.S. began experiencing huge balance of payment deficits, partly resulting from overly expansionary monetary policies pursued to ease the impact of the Vietnam War. Fearing that the U.S. would be unable to maintain the dollar price of gold, the foreign central banks were reluctant to accumulate dollars at the rate at which they were being created. Since the U.S. did not have the option under the Bretton Woods agreement to devalue the dollar, it tried to persuade the surplus nations (particularly Germany and Japan) to revalue their currencies, but without success. Eventually, on August 15, 1971, President Nixon was forced to suspend the convertibility of dollars into gold. Recognizing the end of the Bretton Woods system, many nations let their currencies float against the dollar and the era of flexible exchange rates had begun.

4.4   Future of International Monetary Regime

The sharp exchange rate fluctuations of the 1980s have rekindled interest in the pegged rate systems of earlier years. Despite its limitations, the Bretton Woods system, in retrospect, appears to have coincided with a period of exchange rate stability and rapid economic growth. Inflation was moderate and the national income in the G7 countries rose more rapidly than in any comparable period before or since. According to Bordo and Eichengreen (1993), "it is tempting to assume, as many have done, that the key to this admirable performance lay in the international monetary agreement concluded in 1944 (Bordo and Eichengreen, 1993, preface). The European Monetary System (EMS) was the first serious attempt at another adjustable peg system since the demise of Bretton Woods in 1971. The EMS was established in March of 1979 under the auspices of the European Economic Community (EEC)[1] to create a "zone of monetary stability" among its members. Many of the member nations have established fixed par values among their currencies and agreed to maintain market exchange rates within a band around these par values. Their currencies float jointly against the dollar and together they comprise a composite currency (the so called European Currency Unit, or ECU) representing a very large economic area.

After numerous initial doubts, the EMS is now widely viewed as a resounding success. It seems to have evolved into a full Economic and Monetary Union (EMU) with a single currency. If successful, the EMU is likely to induce a substantial portfolio adjustment away from the dollar into the Euro—the common currency. The resulting appreciation of European currencies against the dollar will distort the pattern of trade, invoke protectionist sentiments and destabilize global arrangements. According to many economists (e.g., see Bergsten, 1993) the U.S. and Japan should engage Europe in negotiations on the global monetary system while the latter has worked out its regional arrangements.

In that spirit, Bergsten (1993) and Williamson (1987) at the Institute for International Economics (U.S.) have advanced a "target zone" proposal. They suggest that a limited number of major countries (e.g., the U.S., Germany and Japan to begin with) negotiate a set of mutually consistent targets for their real exchange rates. The participating countries would be expected to conduct their macroeconomic policies with a view to limiting exchange rate fluctuations within 10% (approximately) around the target

---

[1] Includes U.S., Germany, Japan, France, United Kingdom, Canada and Italy.

rates. As Williamson puts it, "there is no point in pretending that the world economy can perform satisfactorily . . . to achieve sensibly aligned and reasonably stable exchange rates without the official sector explicitly asking itself what those rates are and being willing to adjust monetary policy to achieve them" (Williamson, 1987, p. 204).

McKinnon (1988) has advocated a new monetary regime centered on fixed exchange rates between major currencies—"a gold standard without gold," as he calls it. He believes that the great variation in exchange rates among the industrial nations in recent years can be attributed to the fact that the investors continually shift their preferences among yen, mark, dollar, and sterling assets according to their expectations as to how each exchange rate will move in the future. According to McKinnon, the appropriate solution to this portfolio instability would be for the U.S. Federal Reserve System, the Bank of Japan, and the Bundesbank to adhere to a common monetary standard by announcing fixed nominal targets between yen/dollar and mark/ dollar exchange rates (within narrow bands). The three central banks would adjust their domestic money supplies from time to time to maintain the nominal exchange parities and concomitantly, maintain roughly the same rates of domestic inflation as under the classical gold standard.[1]

To conclude, the international monetary regime is evolving over time. The newly liberalized economies of Eastern Europe or Commonwealth of Independent States are presenting challenges never experienced before. Whatever the shape of the future monetary regime, the lessons learned from the fixed exchange rate system of the classical gold standard or the Bretton Woods is certainly going to play a crucial role for many years to come.

---

[1] The aim would be to set targets such that the nations' current accounts will be in balance and at the same time, fastest domestic economic growth will be achieved without igniting new inflation.

4.5 Modern Time Money Supply: Credit Money

The commodity money, or a representative paper money, at one time, was backed up by a 100% stock of a precious metal like gold or silver. In modern society, governments have realized that no such backing is necessary for money to perform any of its functions effectively, Governments have legally made some currency like coins and notes a medium of exchange. This part of the money supply, as we mentioned in Chapter 3, is called legal tender or fiat money. If we include in fiat money other types of financial assets which also serve as a medium of exchange like checking accounts with commercial banks, then we get credit money or fiduciary money. For changes in the supply of credit money, one does not need an increase in the stock of any precious metal to be held by the government. The credit money functions as money because people have full confidence in the system. Governments can change the money supply, hence, economic growth is easily achievable. If governments had no control on money, it may be argued that business cycles caused by the governmental actions would have been absent. However, one has to notice that in some cases, the government's stabilization policies do help rather than hurt in reducing the fluctuations of business cycles. Also, the Great Depression of 1929 to 1933 has shown that without an active government, the lengths of various stages of business cycles can be increased.

Suggested Additional Reading for Chapter 4

1.   Aghevli, Bijan B. "The Balance of Payments and Money Supply Under the Gold Standard Regime: U.S. 1879-1914." *American Economic Review,* March *1975: 40-58.*

2.   Barro, Robert J. "Money and the Price Level Under the Gold Standard." *Economic Journal,* March 1979: 13-33.

3.   Bergsten, C. F. "The Collapse of Bretton Woods: Implications for International Monetary Reform," in Bordo, M.D. and B. Eichengreen, eds. *A Retrospective on the Bretton Woods System: Lessons for International Monetary Reform.* Chicago: University of Chicago Press, 1993. 587-593.

4.   Bordo, Michael D. "The Classical Gold Standard: Lessons From the Past." *The International Monetary System: Choices for the Future*, ed. Michael Connolly. Praeger Special Studies. Praeger Publishers, 1982. 229-265.

5.   Bordo, M. D. Preface. *A Retrospective on the Bretton Woods System: Lessons for International Monetary Reform.* Chicago: University of Chicago Press, 1993.

6.   Cooper, R. N. "The Gold Standard: Historical Facts and Future Prospects." Brookings Papers on Economic Activity 1982: 1-56.

7.   Enders, W and H. E. Lapan. *International Economics: Theory and Policy.* Prentice-Hall, Inc., 1987.

8.   Ford, A. G. *The Gold Standard 1880 to 1914, Britain Argentina.* Oxford: Claredon Press, 1960.

9.   Kemmerer, E. W. *Gold and the Gold Standard.* New York: McGraw-Hill, 1994.

10. Krugman, P. R. and M. Obstfeld. *International Economics: Theory and Policy,* 3rd ed. Harper Collins College Publishers, 1994.

11. Lindert, P. H. *International Economics*, 9th ed. Richard D. Irwin, Inc., 1991.

12. McCloskey, D. N. and J. K. Kecher. "How the Gold Standard Worked." *The Monetary Approach to the Balance of Payments*, eds. J. Frenkel and H. G. Johnson. Toronto: University of Toronto Press, 1978.

13. McKinnon, R. I. "Monetary and Exchange Rate Policies for International Financial Stability: A Proposal." *Journal of Economic Perspectives* 1(1988): 83-103.

14. Salvatore, D. *International Economics*, 4th ed. Macmillan Publishing Company, 1993.

15. Tew, Brian. *The Evolution of the International Monetary System: 1947-1977.* London: Hutchison Press, 1977.

16. Thomas, Lloyd. *Money, Banking and Economic Activity.* Prentice-Hall Publications, 1979. Chapter 2.

17. Williamson, J. "Exchange Rate Management: The Role of Target Zones." *American Economic Review Papers and Proceedings*. 2(1987): 200-204.

Determination of and Differences in Interest Rates

5

5.1 Introduction

After analyzing the definitions, functions, and evolution of money, and upon an understanding of the history of the gold standard, we can now examine the theories of the determination of the price paid to borrow money, called the "interest rate." The interest rate is defined in several ways: (a) it is the reward for postponing the current consumption, (b) it is the opportunity cost of holding money, (c) it is the price paid to borrow a loan from a bank, and (d) it is the reciprocal (or inverse) of the price of bonds. Even if in reality we observe that all these concepts do not give us the same rate, in theoretical economic literature, there is generally only one interest rate considered. The interest rate is the crucial link between the monetary sector of the economy and the real sector of the economy. To put briefly, a change in the interest rate not only affects the demand for and supply of bonds, but also makes producers borrow differently and review their real investment decisions. Hence, it is important that we closely examine the determination of the interest rate. The most well-known of theories of the interest rate determination is the Loanable Funds Theory. In this chapter we will evaluate that theory first.[1]

Second, the causes for the differences in interest rates will be considered, because in reality, instead of observing one interest

---

[1] The main theories are the Classical, Keynesian and the Loanable Funds Theory. For excellent review of these theories refer to Hansen (1953) in the suggestion list. Here we will concentrate only on the Loanable Funds Theory.

rate, we see several levels of interest rates. Some of the reasons for the existence of differences in the interest rate are marketability, default risk and expectations about future bond prices. We examine these causes in detail in the present chapter

5.2   The Loanable Funds Theory

The classical theory of the interest rate pointed to the interaction of saving and investment schedules as the basic determinants of the interest rate, bringing up the following problem. However, in classical theory it may be that no solution is possible, because the position of the saving schedule will vary with the level of national income. As income rises, the saving curve will shift to the right. Hence, one will not be able to determine saving unless one knows income, and one cannot know income unless one knows the interest rate (and investment). Thus, classical theory could not explain how the interest rate could finitely be determined.

The *loanable funds theory*, on the other hand, hypothesizes that the interest rate is decided by the intersection of demand for and supply of loanable funds. The loanable funds approach emphasized the availability of total credit in the economy. A producer who sells bonds to borrow money creates the demand for loanable funds and the supply of bonds. One who invests money in buying bonds creates the demand for bonds and the supply of loanable funds. Thus, the demand and supply forces in the loanable funds market operate in opposite directions to the demand and supply forces in the bond market. Next, we should note that the supply of loanable funds can come from a surplus in the budget of any entity in the economy. If we consider the economy to be composed of two major sectors, the private sector and the public sector, then the supply of loanable funds can be augmented if the private sector saves more than it invests. In the public sector, the supply of loanable funds can be augmented in two ways. First, because of the surplus in the budget of the government (that happens when government tax revenue is more than the amount of government expenditure), and second, because of the excess supply of money created by the monetary policy. Thus, saving, surplus in the government budget, and an excess supply of money, are the primary sources of the supply of loanable funds.

On the opposite side of the market, the demand for loanable funds is created by the private sector if it invests more than it saves, and by the public sector, if the government runs a deficit in its budget and/or if there is excess demand for money. With an increase in the interest rate at a given time, there will be a reduction in the quantity demanded of loanable funds and an increase in the quantity supplied of loanable funds. Hence, as shown in Figure 5.1, the supply of the loanable funds (LF) schedule will slope upwards from left to right, and demand for LF will slope downwards from left to right.[1] The intersection point of these two schedules determines the equilibrium interest rate. According to Dennis Robertson and other loanable fund theorists, at the end of a transitory period (or adjustment period) r_E is the only rate that would persist. This is obvious because at any interest rate above r_E (like at r) the supply of loanable funds given by $r_E I$ (or OS_0); and demand for LF will be given by $r_0 K$ (or OD_0), creating an excess supply of LF; that would lead to the reduction in the interest rate. On the other hand, if the interest rate happens to be below r_E, say $r_1 J_1$, (or OD_1) there will be pressure on the interest rate to move up. In the long-run, r_E is the only interest rate that would exist. Thus, according to the loanable funds theory, the interest rate can be determined by looking at the supply and demand forces in the loanable funds market. However, as Hansen points out, the loanable funds theory does not escape from the criticism levelled against the *classical theory*. If there is a change in national income, Hansen points out that the saving part of the total supply of LF does not remain constant and the supply

---

[1] Strictly, any direct relationship between two variables is shown by an upward sloping curve, and any inverse relationship is shown by a downward sloping curve from left to right.

Figure 5.1
Supply and Demand for Loanable Funds

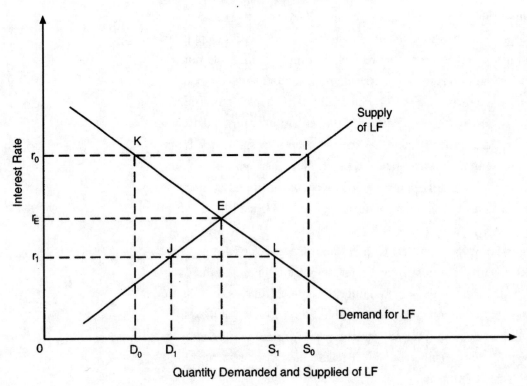

schedule shifts. Hence, one cannot determine saving (hence, supply of LF), unless one knows income, and as mentioned before, the interest rate has to be predetermined to decide the level of investment, and therefore, income.

Secondly, according to Irving Fisher (1930), the expectation of inflation can make it necessary to modify the conclusion of the loanable funds theory. If people expect that the inflation rate is going to be higher in the future, then both the demand for and the supply of loanable funds can be affected. The quantity demanded of loanable funds, in general, will increase and the quantity supplied will go down. Hence, the demand curve for LP will shift rightward and the supply curve of LF will move leftward. As shown in Figure 5.2, this would give a higher interest rate than r

which we should—really speaking—observe. Hence, according
to Fisher, we should differentiate between the nominal interest
rate (which we do observe) and the real interest rate (which we
should observe, but we do not, because of the expected inflation
rate). Therefore, the following relationship is established:

Real Interest Rate = Nominal Interest Rate − Expected Inflation Rate.

In modern days it is believed that it is the real interest rate
which is crucial in making decisions about the real investment
and bond market.

Figure 5.2
Demand for and Supply of Loanable Funds

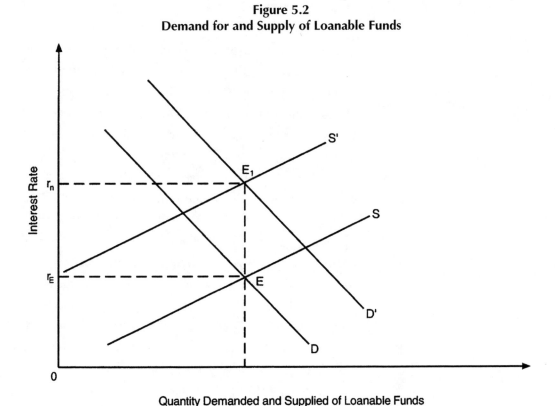

Quantity Demanded and Supplied of Loanable Funds

5.3   Terms Structure of Interest Rates

When we look at the reality, we obviously do not observe only one interest rate. There are different interest rates on bonds, saving accounts, and other time deposits. Our next aim is to find out the reasons for these differences in interest rates.

(a)   Default Risk: A supplier of each bond carries with it a certain risk of default. Default is a breach of one or more contractual agreements between a supplier and a buyer of the financial asset. It is obvious that a small company which has not established itself (when it goes into the financial market to sell its stocks) would have a harder time than a company that is well established. The obvious reason is that the former company implies a larger default risk. Hence, the stock of a company with a higher default risk would need to be offered at a higher yield (lower price) to remain marketable. The difference in interest rates that occurs due to the risk of default is called the default premium. If a company is more stable and secure, then it can afford a smaller risk premium. On the other hand, the bond of a stable firm can easily be marketable and hence, will carry with it a very low-risk premium.

(b)   Differences in the marketability of financial assets is another reason why there are different interest rates. The marketability of a financial asset depends upon three important characteristics of its secondary market. First, the depth of a market is measured by the number of orders ready for the asset at the same price. The greater the depth is, the greater will be the marketability for that asset. Second, the breadth of a market is decided by the number of orders for that asset at different (lower or higher) prices. Again, a higher breadth generates higher marketability for the financial asset. Lastly, the resiliency of a market measures the responsiveness (or elasticity) of demand for that financial asset. Each financial asset has a different market-ability depending upon the depth, breadth and resiliency of the secondary market. If a financial asset is widely market-able, then the yield rate (or interest rate) on it will be lower, and its price will be higher.

(c)   The third reason for the differences in the interest rate is given by tax considerations. In several economies, the yields on bonds are taxed differently. Of course, a higher tax rate will have to be compensated by the higher yield on that financial asset. Hence, tax considerations cause different bonds to carry different interest rates.

(d)   Lastly, but most importantly, interest rates also differ according to the time period required for the maturity of the financial asset. It is conceivable that a bond which has a short maturity period yields a lower interest rate than the bond which matures after a long time. In reality, there is no guarantee that this will always happen; the relationship between the yield on a short-run bond and a long-run bond can be direct, inverse or nonexistent. In terms of Figure 5.3, in which the vertical axis measures the yield rate and the horizontal axis measures the time of maturity, the possible relationships can be shown by either upward sloping line 3, or by downward sloping line 1, or by a horizontal line 2. To explain which of these three lines would be more commonly observed in reality, there are three theories we must consider.

i)   *Liquidity preference theory*: This theory originated in the magnificent work of Lord Keynes in 1936. He and his followers claim that a person would always prefer cash to no cash. If liquidity is defined as the ease with which a financial asset can be transformed into a medium of exchange, then higher liquidity is preferred to lower liquidity. If we believe in it, then a long-run bond which is less liquid, is less preferable to a short-run bond which is more liquid. Hence, in order to sell a long-run bond, one must offer a higher interest rate (or a lower price). According to this theory, since people have a liquidity preference, the short-run bond would show a lower yield rate than a long-run bond, therefore, line 3 on Figure 5.3 would appear feasible. However, there may be incidences in reality when we may observe higher interest rates for short-run bonds than for long-run bonds. The liquidity preference theory cannot explain those incidences.

(ii) *Expectation theory*: This theory holds that interest rates behave according to the expectations of wealth holders. Also, there is a greater chance of gain from financial assets that have a longer maturity when it

Figure 5.3
Term Structure of Interest Rates

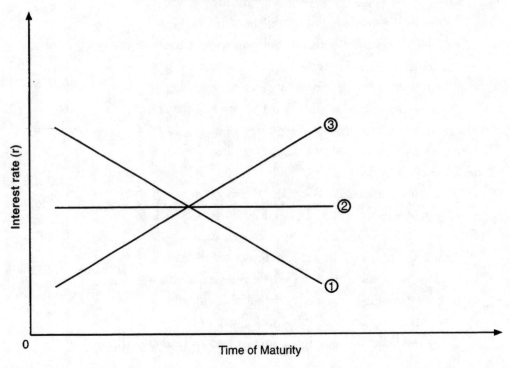

becomes necessary to sell them for cash. And if wealth holders are risk averters, then they would need a higher interest rate to buy the long-run financial asset. In other words, only a higher interest rate on the long-run bond can attract the buyers. Hence, the relationship shown by line 3 in Figure 5.3 is possible when the expectations of the wealth holders are as described above. But there is no reason why wealth holders (or financial investors) should expect that yields on both short-run bonds are about equal.

It may very well happen that wealth holders expect interest rates to either fall or rise in the future. If they expect the interest rate to rise in the future (i.e., price of a bond of a long-run nature to be lower than the price of a bond of a short-run nature) then they may decide to hold more short-run bonds which would create higher demand for those bonds and interest rates on them may become higher than interest rates on long-run bonds. This would create a term structure as shown by line 1 in Figure 5.3. In the reverse case, when they expect interest rates to fall in the future, they would demand more long-run bonds which would make a lower interest rate for long-run bonds. The term structure shown by line 3 (even steeper than before) is plausible in this case. Thus, according to the expectations theory, the correct term structure is guided by the expectations spectrum of the wealth holders.

(iii) *Hedging theory of market segmentation theory*: The most satisfactory explanation of the term structure of the interest rate is presented by the market segmentation theory. It claims that the market of financial assets is segmented because the demand and supply forces which decide the interest rate on short-run bonds are totally different than the demand and supply forces which decide the interest rate on long-run bonds. This bifurcation results from the observation of the fact that suppliers of short-run bonds are such entities as (a) small firms which have a short production lag and need money only for a short-run (b) local government (c) retailers (d) middlemen, etc., and the demanders of short-run bonds include people from middle income group or small banks and other financial institutions. These demanders have a high liquidity preference and hence, they cannot afford to tie up their cash in the long-run bonds. On the other hand, the demanders of long-run bonds are individuals who are ready to part with their money for a long duration, who have a low liquidity preference, and therefore, those who are wealthy. The suppliers of long-run bonds include (a) the big and stable firms which have a long production lag and need money on a long-run basis (b) federal and state governments which have huge projects to be completed only after a long time (c) wholesalers, etc. Depending upon the demand and supply forces in each of these two separate markets, there could be two different interest rates. And since there is minimal interaction between markets of short-run bonds and those of long-run bonds, the interest rates decided by these markets should not have any specific relationship. In other words, it is unlikely that a correct judgement can be made "a priori" regarding the shape of the curve in Figure 5.3. It is possible that the interest rates for short-run bonds and for long-run bonds may have relationships shown by line 1, or by line 2, or by line 3, or by none of them. Thus, the market segmentation theory suggests that the true relationship between two interest rates cannot be found out unless we look at the two separate markets for these bonds.

In summation, we conclude that expectations and liquidity preference theories can explain a part of those differences in interest rates, while the market segmentation theory offers a more systematic explanation. Nonetheless, we must note that all interest rates generally change in a similar manner. An increase in one interest rate, let us say on bonds, causes an increase in another interest rate, perhaps on equities or stocks, and therefore, all of them move together. The reason for such similar movement is obvious. All financial assets act as substitutes for each other. Hence, when the price of one asset goes up, so does that of the others.

In this chapter we attempted to explain the procedure in which the interest rate is determined. We also tried to give several reasons for the existence of differences in the interest rates as observed in the real world. In the next chapter we will enter into theoretical principles regarding the effects of money supply changes on other economic variables.

Suggested Additional Reading for Chapter 5

1.   Fisher, Irving. *The Theory of Interest Rates*. New York: MacMillan, 1930.

2.   Hansen, Alvin. *A Guide to Keynes*. New York: McGraw Hill Paperbacks, 1953. Chapter 7.

3.   Homer, Sydney. *A History of Interest Rates*. New Brunswick, New Jersey: Rutgers University Press, 1963.

4.   Robertson, Dennis H. *Money*. Chicago: Harcourt, Brace Publishers, 1964.

5.   Thomas, Lloyd. *Money, Banking and Economic Activity*. New Jersey: Prentice-Hall Publishers, 1979. Chapter 4.

6.   Thorn, Richard S. *Introduction to Money and Banking*. New York: Harper and Row Publishers, 1976. Chapter 16.

Old Quantity Theory of Money and Classical Economics

6.1   Some Important Definitions of Economic Variables

In this chapter we present the theoretical elements of the quantity theory of money—the theory that was prevalent before its revision by Professor Friedman. However, in order to discuss the development of the quantity theory we must become acquainted with several economic variables. Hence, in this chapter we start with some important definitions.

(a)   Gross National Product (GNP) or Gross Domestic Product (GDP): GNP is a measure of development of an economy. Just like any businessman would analyze the total productivity of his business, economists examine the total product of the whole economy. GNP is defined as the total market value of all final goods and services produced in an economy over a period of time. Two key concepts in the above definition are (i) market value and (ii) final goods. *Market value* is calculated as the product of the price of a commodity times the quantity produced of that commodity in the given period of time. A total market value of all final goods will constitute the GNP of that economy. *Final goods* are those goods which are consumed directly by the consumers (or those goods which directly satisfy wants). Many times they are also referred to as consumer goods. This obviously means that intermediate goods which are not directly consumed but are used in the production of other goods are excluded from the definition of GNP. An exclusion of these goods is necessary to avoid the danger of their double counting. Similarly, GNP calculation also excludes purely financial transactions like transfer payments, etc. Now, having defined GNP as the total market value, we may run into a problem that GNP's value is affected by mere changes in price level. For example, if only the price of a commodity increases, its market value goes up, and so does the GNP. Hence, GNP which is a measure of development will be affected by the increase in price level in spite of the constant quantity produced. In order to avoid this problem, economists construct a price index.

(b)   Price Index: A *price index* measures the general (or average) price level of goods and services in the economy. It is constructed by considering the price level of commodities in the current year (the year for which we are constructing the price index) and the average price level of the same commodities in the base year (the year which is used to compare the prices, and generally it is about 10-12 years before the current year). The price index is constructed by using the following formula:

$$\text{Price Index} = \frac{\text{Average Price Level in Current Year}}{\text{Average Price Level in Base Year}} \times 100$$

More technically, it can be written as,

$$\text{Price Index} = \frac{\Sigma p^c_i \times q_i}{\Sigma p^b_i \times q_i} \times 100$$

where p^c_i = Prices in current year,

p^b_i = Prices in base year,

q_i = Quantities of goods

Now the question is, what types of commodities do we include in defining the price index? If our answer to this question is to include only consumer goods and define price index in the above manner, then we will have a consumer price index (CPI) defined. If we answer the question to include only producer goods or primary goods or intermediate goods (all words are synonyms referring to the goods sold in the primary market) then we would have another type of price index called "Producer Price Index" (PPI). And lastly, if we include both primary as well as consumer goods, then we define the third type of price index as the GNP deflator. Hence, there are three types of price indexes; the consumer price index (CPI), the producer price index (PPI), and the GNP deflator. Depending upon the preference and emphasis on different sectors of the economy, a researcher may choose any one of these indexes to serve as a measure of the general price level. The most popular to measure the inflation rate, etc., is the CPI.

(c) Real GNP and Nominal GNP. Since the major purpose of defining the price index is to avoid the changes in prices which affect the value of nominal GNP (the total market value), we use the following formula to define real GNP.

$$\text{REAL GNP} = \frac{\text{NOMINAL GNP}}{\text{PRICE INDEX}}$$

If observed carefully, real GNP as defined above gives us a solution to the problem mentioned earlier. It remains unchanged by the mere changes in the price level. For example, if prices increase, nominal GNP increases, but so does the price index, so real GNP stays constant. However, one has to note that even if real GNP is called "real," it is measured in money value (such as in dollars or in any other monetary unit).

Using the key economic variables, described above, we can now survey the historical developments in monetary theory.

6.2   Historical Background of Monetary Theory

Now we are in a position to observe carefully the process by which the money supply affects other economic variables. The theory which explains this process is known as monetary theory. The oldest monetary theory that is popular with economists of modern times is the one developed by the classical economists such as Henry Thornton, Jeremy Bentham, David Hume and Irving Fisher. Other notable names are John Gray in England in the 1830s and 1840s, and Paul Douglas of the University of Chicago in the United States in the 1930s.

Jeremy Bentham's work can be traced back as early as the 1800s.[1] It was a time when England had undergone price inflation and Bentham attempted to explain it. In his writings, one can see some seedlings of the quantity theory of money. His statements such as "the sum of all prices given for all the salable articles sold within a year cannot be anything but the total of money given for them" or "the rapidity of circulation must also enter into account" give us the impression that Bentham had described the modern quantity theory which Irving Fisher eventually elaborated. The quantity theory proposes, directly or indirectly, that an increase in the price level of the economy is caused only by an excessive increase in money supply. Hence, for reasons which we will discuss later, quantity theorists believe that the effect of a change in the money supply is seen in terms of change it causes in the general price level. Bentham's earlier work was the first to recognize the equality of aggregate demand (the money side of his equation) and aggregate supply (the real side of his equation). Given this equality, Bentham argued, "we can look for the cause of the permanent increase in prices only in the increase of the effective force, i.e., the

---

[1] *The True Alarm.* Jeremy Bentham. London, 1801. P. 136.

quantity and the rapidity of circulation, of the mass of money."[1] This was his attempt to explain England's inflation of the early 1800s. Economists also see the origins of monetary theory in Henry Thornton's book: *Paper Credit* (1802).[2] In it, one can find statements like, "the effect produced by paper credit on the price of articles depends not merely on the price of paper in existence, but also on the rapidity of circulation." It is clear from this statement that Thornton was aware of the changes in the velocity of money. As argued by Harris (1981), there were several other economists of earlier years, like Wicksell and J. S. Mill who had attempted to describe the effect of the money supply on the price level.

6.3   The Quantity Theory of Money

The most elegant and elaborated analysis of the effect of the money supply on other variables was done by Irving Fisher of Yale University in 1903. He formulized his theory known as the quantity theory of money, in terms of an equation called the "equation of exchange." Since Fisher used this equation so extensively, it is also called, the Fisherian equation. And because this equation is used to analyze the quantity theory of money, it is also referred to as the "quantity theory equation." This equation is expressed in the following form:

$$MV = PY$$

Where   M   =   the amount of money expended in the economy during a given period of time.

V   =   the Velocity of Money, defined as the turnover rate of money. More technically, "Velocity of money completes the circular flow in the given time period." Hence, V is a certain number like 4 or 5 or 2.5, etc.

---

[1] Ibid., p. 136

[2] *Paper Credit*, Henry Thornton, London, 1802, p. 242.

P   =   General Price Index measured by one of the price indexes discussed earlier.

Y   =   real output or total transactions in the economy in a given time period.

Hence, if P_i is the price of the ith commodity and q_i is the quantity transacted (bought or sold) of that commodity, then $\Sigma P_i q_i$ is called the market value of all commodities, which is on the right hand side of the Fisherian Equation:

$$P_1 q_1 + P_2 q_2 + P_3 q_3 + \ldots P_n q_n = \Sigma P_i q_i = PY$$

By analyzing this relationship Fisher concluded that, "a normal effect of an increase in the quantity of money is an exactly proportional increase in the general level of prices." The first observation he thought we should make is that "velocity of circulation, as an institutionally determined factor influenced primarily by such things as the public's payment habits, the extent of the use of credit, the speed of transportation and communication as it influences the time required to make a payment, and other technical factors that bear no discoverable relation to the quantity of money in circulation." In simpler terms, this means that the velocity of money is independent of the stock of the money supply.[1] Similarly, Fisher viewed real income (Y) of the whole economy to be determined by such exogenous factors as the stock of natural resources in the economy or the labor productivity. In short, the real output (Y) can also be considered to be independent of changes in the money supply. Hence, under these conditions, with any change in an equal supply (M), the price level (P)

---

[1] A reader may remember that in a purely capitalistic economy where there are two sectors, namely, consumer (or household) sector and producer (or business) sector, there is a constant flow of exchanges going on called the circular flow, the business sector provides goods and services to the household sector and in return gets the factors of production from it. The velocity of money is the number of times an average monetary unit must change hands to complete transactions by the given money supply.

would have to change in an equal and direct proportion to warrant the equality specified by the Fisherian equation.[1] A doubling of money supply will be responsible for the doubling of the price level. This obviously means that the expansionary monetary policy of any government is responsible for the price increases an economy experiences. The effect of any consistent expansionary monetary policy will be to create inflation in the economy. A conclusion of this sort gives a message to the monetary authorities to be as inactive as possible because any action of increasing the money supply, on its part, would be ineffective in influencing the level of real output of the economy.

Nonetheless, anxious economists attempted to search for inconsistencies in Fisher's arguments. To summarize the criticisms of the quantity theory of money, we note the following points. First, in the equation of exchange, some may observe that the left hand side (money supply times the velocity of money) represents the value of total income generated (price level times total real output). In 'ex post,' since this indicates an identity (tuotology, truism or an equation which is true by definition), total expenditure for the economy, as a whole, is always equal to total income generated in it. Hence, the quantity theory equation cannot be used to derive policy consequences. For instance, one should not (and cannot) argue that an increase in the money supply causes the price level to go up. As an identity, any increase on the left hand side of the equation must be compensated by an equivalent increase in the right hand side. In other words, an identity cannot be used to assert a cause and effect relationship. The matter of the quantity theory equation being an identity did not escape Fisher's mind, and he had an answer for it in the following manner; "One of the objectors to the quantity theory attempts to dispose of the equation of exchange . . . by calling it a mere truism. While the equation equivalence, in all purchases, of the

---

[1] See Fisher—Suggested Additional Reading

money or check expended, on the one hand, and what they buy on the other, . . . this equation is a means of demonstrating the fact that normally, the P's (price levels) vary directly as M, this is, demonstrating the quantity theory. 'Truisms' should never be neglected. The greatest generalizations of physical science, such as that forces are proportional to mass and acceleration, are truisms, but when duly supplemented by specific data, these truisms are the most fruitful sources of useful mechanical knowledge."

The second criticism of the quantity theory's conclusion comes from a group of economists from Cambridge University in Cambridge, England. Notable economists in this group were A. C. Pigou, Alfred Marshall and R. G. D. Allen; who on their behalf, created a modified version of the quantity theory equation known as the Cambridge equation. The main thrust of the formulation of the Cambridge equation was its emphasis on the store of value function of money. In doing so, they formulated an equation which can be stated as follows:

$$M = K * P * Y$$

Where K is defined as the proportion of national income kept in money terms. The above equation is also a definitional identity. According to Pigou and others, people have several reasons to keep money in terms of cash. To put in his words, ". . . everybody is anxious to hold enough of his resources in the form of titles to legal tender (money) both to enable him to affect the ordinary transactions of life without trouble, and to secure him against unexpected demands due to a sudden need, a rise in the price of something he cannot easily dispense with." If the money supply goes up, the value of K is expected to increase, because with more liquidity available, people would tend to use more money as a store of value.

By comparing the Cambridge equation (M = KPY) and the Fisherian equation (MV = PY) we can deduce easily the value of

K as being equal to the inverse of the velocity of money. Hence, $K = 1/V$; and as money supply (M) increases, the value of K will go up (as discussed before) which obviously would mean that the velocity of money would fall.

Hence, the Fisherian contention[1] that the velocity of money is independent of changes in the money supply is questionable. The observations that money also serves as a store of value, and that a money supply increase would make people use money more and more as a store of value, are indeed a challenge for the quantity theory's conclusion. According to Havrilesky and Boorman; "This orientation led the Cambridge economist to formulate a first line of monetary inquiry from which emanate many of the modern developments in monetary economics. By emphasizing the individual's demand for money and the utility which money balances may yield, Cambridge economists were led to examine choices facing the individual."[2]

However, being a clever economist as he was, Fisher did not miss the point, that any increase in the money supply may "temporarily" affect the value of velocity of circulation. But he ignored any significant consequences of this because they occur only in the transitory periods. (In modern times, economists have picked up the idea of money serving as a depository asset and not merely as a medium of exchange. The velocity of money is believed to be dependent upon the extent to which money performs the store of value function.)

The third criticism of the conclusion of the quantity theory was put forward by John Maynard Keynes in his revolutionary book, *The General Theory of Employment, Interest and Money* (1936). The main thrust of his argument is that a capitalistic economy is characterized by underemployment equilibrium. In a typical economy we may see a lack of sufficient aggregate demand to warrant employment of all resources including, of course, that of

---

[1] Suggested Additional Reading—see Fisher.

[2] Suggested Additional Reading—see Havrilesky and Boorman.

labor. The type of unemployment caused by insufficient demand for business output is labelled as involuntary unemployment. An existence of involuntary unemployment guarantees us that the real output (Y) cannot stay constant when the money supply is increased. Moreover, Keynes proved in a rather systematic process how an increased money supply can be effective in raising the level of economic activity. He believes that the Fisherian conclusion does not hold because of the likelihood of an increase in real output (Y) on the right hand side of the equation.

In spite of these strong criticisms against its conclusion, the quantity theory is credited tremendously for its observation of dependence of the price level on the money supply. As Friedman pointed out later in 1956, whether we believe in absolute proportionality of Fisher's conclusion or not,[1] the fact still remains that the major cause of consistent increases in the general price level is an excessive growth in the money supply. As we will examine in the later chapters, the revised version of the quantity theory of money holds a crucial position in the modem monetary theory. One has to admire the efficiency and depth shown by Fisher in noticing the fact that the money supply may cause an increase in the price level, at least in the long-run. The long-run observation of several capitalistic economies have shown that increases in the price level were, in fact, associated with wide increases in money supplies. We may have to wait a while in this book to find out what other factors can cause inflation in the economy, but thanks to Fisher's work in the early 1900s, we have realized already that one of the important factors in that list is an excessive money supply.

---

[1] On page 161 of Fisher's *Purchasing Power of Money*, one can see the following statement, ". . . a sudden change in the quantity of money and deposits will temporarily affect their velocities of circulation and the volume of trade. . . ." Therefore, the quantity theory will not hold true strictly and absolutely during a transition period.

Suggested Additional Reading for Chapter 6

1. Bentham, Jeremy. *The True Alarm*. London: 1801.

2. Fisher, Irving. *The Purchasing Power of Money*. New York: Macmillan Publishers, 1911.

3. Friedman, Milton. "The Quantity Theory of Money," in *Money, the New Palgrave*, eds. John Eatwell, Murray Milgate and Peter Newman. New York: W.W. Norton, 1989.

4. Harris, Laurence. *Monetary Theory*. McGraw-Hill Book Company, 1981. Chapters 4, 5, and 6.

5. Havrilesky, T. M. and J. T. Boorman. *Money Supply, Money Demand and Macroeconomic Models*, 2nd ed. Harlan Davidson Publishers, Inc., 1982.

6. Keynes, J. M. *General Theory of Employment, Interest and Money*. London: Harcourt, Brace and World, 1936.

7. Mill, J. S. *Principles of Political Economy*. London: J. W. Parker Publishers, 1848.

8. Pigou, A. C. "The Value of Money." *The Quarterly Journal of Economics,* Vol. 32, November 1917: 41.

9. Tavlas, George. "Some Initial Formulations of the Monetary Growth Rate Rule." *History of Political Economy*, Vol. 9, Winter, 1977: 535-547.

10. Wicksell, J. G. K. *Interest and Prices*. Trans. by R. F. Kahn, Macmillan Publishers.

7
The Keynesian System: Commodity or Product Market

7.1 Introduction

The main aim of this chapter is to analyze the Keynesian system in the most crucial market of an economy: the product market. Monetary theory gained significantly from the Keynesian ideas of the multiplier, the marginal efficiency of capital (MEC), the marginal propensity to consume, and several others. Keynesian thoughts were quite different from his predecessors whom he refers to as Classicals. Strictly speaking, classicals were neither organized in their writing nor did they communicate with each other to come up with any identical philosophy. Nonetheless, some common ideas persist in the writings of John Stuart Mill (1806-73), David Ricardo (1772-1823), Alfred Marshall (1842-1924), Irving Fisher (1867-1947), and J. B. Say (1767-1832). Since it was the classical school of thought that Keynes disassociated himself so strongly with, and criticisms of whose writing led to special Keynesian feelings, it is imperative that in this chapter we initially review the main contentions of the classical economists.

If we assume that in an economy, three markets exist, namely the product (or commodity) market, the labor market and the capital market, then according to classical economists, in the long-run, the price, wage rate and interest rate flexibility assures the existence of equilibrium in each of these markets. In the product market, if the price level of commodities is assumed flexible, then the shortages (or surpluses) will be automatically cured. In case of a shortage (surplus) the price level is expected to go up (down) and in the long-run, the shortage (surplus) will disappear. By using Figure 7.1 this can be shown very easily.

The demand curve shows an inverse relationship between the quantity demanded of a product and its price while the supply curve shows the direct relationship between quantity supplied and the price level. Classical economists used to think that price levels other than P_0 are improbable to persist for a long time. At a price level above P_0 like at P_1, the quantity supplied will be Oq_2 and the quantity demanded will be Oq_1 creating a surplus in the market. Obviously, there will be pressure on the price level to move downwards. At any price level below P_0 the contrary is evident. At price level P_2 the quantity demanded is Oq_3 and quantity supplied is Oq_0. The shortage of q_0q_3 is responsible for an upward pressure on the price level. Hence, in the long-run, P_0 is the only price level that would exist. In other words, the price flexibility automatically clears the product market.

Considering that the capital market of an economy consists of saving and investment forces, the interest rate flexibility will guarantee that the capital market would be in equilibrium in the long-run. At interest rates higher than the equilibrium interest rate, there will be an excess saving, forcing the interest rate to come down, and at interest rates lower than the equilibrium interest rate, there will be higher investment than saving, causing that rate to go up. All in all, there will be only one interest rate that can persist for a long time. The same reasoning is applied to the labor market analysis, assuming wage rate flexibility. The demand for labor and supply of labor are the two forces that define the labor market. At a wage rate higher than the equilibrium wage rate, there will be a higher supply of labor than the demand for labor, and the wage rate will go down. In conclusion, it can be said that due to assumed price, wage rate and interest rate flexibilities, the classical economists were champions in showing the existence of general equilibrium in the economy.

Figure 7.1
Classical Model: Commodity Market

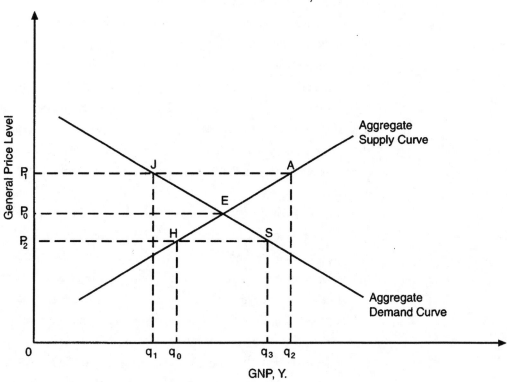

Together, with the above explanation, there was an important contribution made to the classical theory by the French economist, Jean-Baptiste Say (1767-1832). Say's law of the market is an observation that an activity which is intended to supply a commodity to exchange it with another commodity, creates demand of an equal value. "Supply creates its own demand" can be taken as a brief statement to summarize this law. In a barter economy, where money does not exist and goods are only exchanged with other goods, Say's law of the market states the obvious. This is so because the factors of production are paid in kind with the product they helped produce and the total payments made to households will equal the total output. In a barter economy there can never be over production. However, what seems obvious in a barter economy may not always be possible in a monetary economy because money not only serves as a medium of exchange, but also as a store of value.

Just as the classical economists were experts in showing an automatic mechanism of establishing general equilibrium in the economy, they were also staunch advocates of a *laissez faire*[1] policy. In other words, the most common thread that runs among all classical economists is their faith that the capitalistic economy possesses a built-in force that leads to automatic general equilibrium. Hence, no action on the part of the government is needed to cure the business fluctuations, since in the long-run, they will probably not persist.

Starting in late 1929, the major industrial economies of the world experienced what is rightly called the Great Depression. For four years unemployment was increasing—eventually reaching the highest number ever, output was declining, the price level was going down, industrial output, money supply and the number of banks were shrinking. The most striking fact about these events was that they persisted for a relatively long time, contrary to the expectations of the classical view. Even the United States' economy, which was supposed to be a land of the most plentiful resources in the entire world, experienced one of the worst moments in its history. Now the vital question was, what went wrong? Why did the prices, wages and interest rate not decline, and thereby influence aggregate demand to pick up and eliminate the glut? What had happened to the automatic mechanism? The classical economists had no answers to these crucial questions. With this background of events, in 1936, Keynes wrote the most pathbreaking book of modern times, *The General Theory of Employment, Interest and Money*. It was obviously a very difficult job to explain the paradox of poverty in the midst of potential plenty. On one hand, Keynes challenged the critical but crucial assumptions of classical theory, and on the other, he developed his

---

[1] The English meaning of these two french words is 'to leave something alone' or 'to not interfere.'

own ideas about the consumption, investment and saving behavior of people in a capitalistic economy. From Keynes' perspective, the most important factor in the economy was the aggregate demand.

Aggregate demand is the total expenditure in the economy. If we assume that a typical economy is composed of a consumer sector, a producer sector, a government sector, and a foreign trade sector, then each sector has an expenditure of its own, and the total expenditure in the economy consists of the following elements. The consumer sector expends on final goods and services and that expenditure is called consumption. The producer sector has its own expenditure on machinery, tools and equipment, which is known as investment. And the government sector's expenditure is known as government expenditure. In the foreign trade sector, expenditure takes place in two parts. When the residents of our economy expend on foreign goods, it becomes imports, and when foreigners expend on our goods, their expenditures are seen as our exports.

If all the above categories of total expenditure are taken into consideration, the aggregate demand in the economy is represented as Consumption (C) + Investment (I) + Government Expenditure (O) + Exports (Ex) − Imports (M). It is important to notice that imports are subtracted from the total expenditure stream because they represent expenditure on foreign products. Hence, foreign countries should include that production in their GNP. Having pointed out what constitutes aggregate demand, we can concentrate on each of its factors.

7.2 Consumption

As mentioned before, consumption constitutes expenditure done by the consumer class on such final goods as groceries, homes, cars, medicine, clothing, etc.[1] In the whole expenditure stream, consumption is by far the largest category and therefore, the most important one. The general behavior of consumption is stable and households tend to consume even when income earned is very little. Nonetheless, the most crucial explanatory variable for consumption is the total income. If income increases, then a typical household is likely to consume more in absolute terms. In other words, the relationship between income and consumption is seen to be a direct relationship. In the consumption theory of Keynes, what seems to be logical for household behavior is also assumed to be true for national behavior. Hence consumption, in general, of an economy depends upon the national income. The relationship is direct because as Y goes up, C is expected to increase and is assumed further to be linear. Denoting consumption by (C) and national income (or GNP) by (Y) we can write this relationship as:

$$C = a + bY \text{———— (1)}$$

The linear, direct relationship shown by equation (1) is known as the *consumption function*. This relationship, when plotted on the graph, is depicted by an upward sloping curve from left to right.

In equation (1), letters 'a' and 'b' deserve some more explanation. The letter 'a' is obviously the constant term in the equation. Geometrically, it is the intercept of the Y axis (or vertical axis) and, in common sense, it becomes equal to consumption (C=a) when income is zero. In other words, it is the bare minimum consumption an economy makes even when GNP is zero. In economic literature, 'a' is called *autonomous consumption*. Hence, autonomous consumption is the value of a constant in the consumption function.

---

[1] One does not find consensus among economists as to which level of income decides consumption. Relative income (Duesenberry), permanent income (Friedman), and current income (Keynes) are the three most popular answers to that question.

If one variable increases in value and influences the other to increase, we say the relationship between these two variables is direct, on the other hand, the relationship is said to be inverse if one variable increases in value and influences the other to go down.

The second letter, 'b,' in equation (1) algebraically is the coefficient of Y in the consumption function. In geometric terms, it is the slope of the consumption function. Just like any other slope, it is measured by considering a movement on that line from one point to another (like from point G to G' in Figure 7.2). In such movement, we consider the value of the rise (i.e., KG') and the run (GK) and define the slope as rise/run. In the case of Figure 7.2, the slope of the consumption function is KG'/GK. In some other notational form, KG' is denoted as AC since it is the 'change in consumption.' Also, GK is ΔY as it is the 'change in income.' Hence, the slope of the consumption function, (b), is equal to $\Delta C / \Delta Y$. In economic terms, it is known as the *marginal propensity to consume* (mpc). Thus, mpc is the slope of the consumption function and is the coefficient of the Y term in the equation. What is the 'propensity' to consume? As Heilbroner and

Figure 7.2
Consumption Function

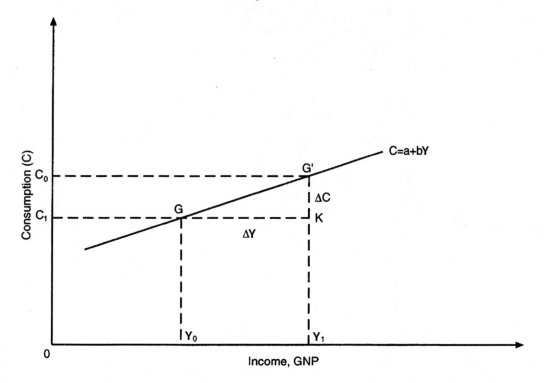

Thurow (1984)[1] put it, 'it means that the relationship between consumption behavior and income is sufficiently dependable so that we can actually predict how much consumption (or how much saving) will be associated with a given level of income.' The marginal propensity to consume when numerically found, gives us an idea of the exact increase (or decrease) in consumption when income increases (or decreases). However, one should not get the impression from the above discussion that income is the only determinant variable that affects the consumption, but before we examine these variables closely, we have to acquaint ourselves with another Keynesian invention—*average propensity to consume* (apc). While 'marginal' propensity to consume considers a movement from one point to another on the consumption schedule, the 'average' propensity to consume concentrates on only one point of that schedule. Hence, at any given income level, the level of consumption gives us apc. In notational form, apc is the ratio of the consumption (C) level at a given Y level. Hence apc = C/Y. The relationship between apc and mpc can be shown by the following simple derivation:

$$apc = C/Y$$

From the consumption function, putting the value of C = a + bY we get:

$$apc = \frac{a + bY}{Y} = a/Y + b = a/Y + mpc$$

Hence,

$$apc = a/Y + mpc \text{———— (2)}$$

---

[1] Suggested Reading list: Heilbroner and Thurow (1984), p. 192.

From equation (2) it is obvious that apc and mpc are different concepts. Nonetheless, they will be equal to each other in a special case when a = 0. Thus, when the vertical axis intercept is zero, that is, if the consumption function passes through the origin, apc = mpc. Another good way of differentiating apc from mpc is to keep in mind that mpc relates to the ratio of 'changes' in consumption and income levels, while apc concerns itself with the ratio of those variables at a given value. (No changes involved). To clarify these things further, let us analyze a numerical example.

Suppose a consumption function of an economy is represented by an equation C = 150 + .6Y and the following queries are made:

a)   What is the value of autonomous consumption?

b)   What is the value of apc at income level 2000?

c)   What is the value of mpc?

By mere examination, one can see that autonomous consumption, the constant value in the consumption function is 150. To calculate apc we have to find the consumption at 2000 income. It can be done by the following:

$$
\begin{aligned}
C \; &= \; 150 + .6Y \\
&= \; 150 + .6(2000) \\
&= \; 150 + 1200 = 1350
\end{aligned}
$$

Hence, apc = 1350/2000 = 135/200 = .67 The value of mpc can be found easily because it is the coefficient of Y in the consumption function. Hence, mpc = .6.[1]

Other Determinants of Consumption: Just as price is the major determinant of the quantity demanded, income is the crucial determinant of consumption. However, there are certain

---

[1] An interested reader may formulize additional numerical examples with his/her own imagination to clarify these issues further.

determinants other than income which might cause people to consume more or less at each possible level of national income. Any change in these other determinants would cause the consumption function to shift from one position to another.

(a)   *Stock of assets*: In general, a stock of liquid or illiquid assets can change the consumption rate of the consumers. The higher the stock of assets, like bank deposits, stocks, bonds, etc. owned by consumers, the greater will be their willingness to spend out of their income. Hence, the consumption function is likely to shift to the right with higher stock of assets held by the consumers.

(b)   *Inflation rate or expected price level*: In case of an inflationary situation, the real consumption of the household is expected to go down. Hence, the price level (expected or actual) can affect the consumption. An increase in price level would be responsible for shifting the consumption function upwards. Changes in the price level also have an effect on the value of assets which again affect the level of consumption as mentioned above. Thus, the inflation rate is another determinant of the consumption rate of an economy.

(c)   *Stock of durable goods*: An economy which has consumed a lot before and has a high stock of durable goods is expected to consume at a lower rate currently than an economy which has a small stock of durable goods. Many households would not take any part in the consumption if they have had a stock of durable goods. A shift of the consumption curve to the left with higher stock of durable goods and to the right with lower stock of consumer goods is obvious.

(d)   *Consumer credit or indebtedness*: A higher amount of consumer credit would mean that consumers may be obliged to retrench on current consumption. Hence, the indebtedness of the consumer may affect, negatively, his/her consumption at the present time.

(e)   *Taxes*: The government can influence the consumption level of an economy by making changes in taxes. A higher tax burden would necessarily reduce the disposable income of people and, therefore, reduce their consumption. Income taxes, for example, directly affect income, which in turn, influences consumption. On the other hand, a lower tax rate is expected to boost the consumption and total expenditure of the economy.

In general, the above mentioned 'non-income' determinants of consumption are also important to determine the consumption behavior of an economy. Any change in the above determinants, as mentioned before, would cause the shift of the consumption function in Figure 7.2. This shift is known as 'movement of the curve.' On the other hand, with a change in income we may observe a movement from one point to another on the consumption function of Figure 7.2. This movement is known as 'movement along the curve.'[1]

Saving Function: With the help of discussion of the consumption function, we can also clarify the saving behavior. Saving is, in essence, the income that is not consumed. Hence, any saving behavior can be easily found by observing the consumption behavior. Initially, in algebraic terms, it can be done as follows:

$$\text{Saving (S)} = \text{Income (Y)} - \text{Consumption (C)}$$
$$S = Y - C$$

---

[1] Any change in the independent variable plotted on the graph, creates movement on the curve. Any change in other determinants of dependent variable creates 'movement of the curve.'

Substituting the value of consumption from the consumption function,

$$S = Y - (a+bY)$$
$$S = Y - a - bY$$
$$S = -a + (1- b)Y \text{————(3)}$$

Equation (3) is known as the saving function. Hence, if the consumption function is given as $C = a + bY$, the saving function is derived as $S = -a + (1-b)Y$. In numerical terms, if the consumption function is $C = 150 + .7Y$, then the saving function is $S = -150 + .3Y$ This obviously illustrates the idea that the saving function is the relationship between saving and income, just as the consumption function is the relationship between consumption an income. In geometric terms, from the consumption function, the saving function can easily be derived. Consider Figure 7.3, which has two parts. On the X axis of both parts we measure income, on the Y axis of the upper part we plot consumption (C) and on the lower part we measure saving (5). The upper quadrant is no different than Figure 7.2 except that in the former, we see an extra curve labelled as a 45 line. There is a special reason why we have drawn it there. As one of the characteristics of a 45 line, we know that all the points on that line are equidistant from both axes. In other words, at all points on the 45 line of the graph, the consumption level is equal to the income level. Obviously, the relationship shown by the 45° line (i.e., $C = Y$) is purely imaginary or hypothetical. But by using this hypothetical relationship, it is easy to derive the saving-income relationship in the lower part of Figure 7.3. Notice from the consumption function that at zero income, consumption is 'a' which means that saving is $-a$. Hence, we get one point, point K, on the lower quadrant which will be on the saving function. Also notice that at income level Y, consumption is equal to income (since at Y_0 income, the actual consumption, given by point E, is equal to income because point E is also on our hypothetical 45° line). This means that at income

Figure 7.3
Saving Function Derived from Consumption

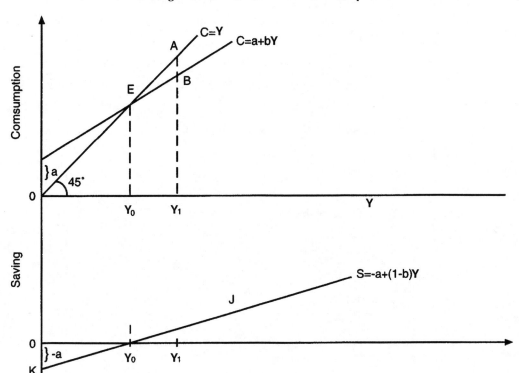

Y_0, saving is zero, which gives us point I on the lower graph. Now consider another GNP level, say Y_1. Consumption at Y_1 is given by the point B. Since point A is on the 45° line, we can also say that $AY_1 = 0Y_1$ which means that AY_1 is also income. Hence, with AY_1 as income and BY_1 as consumption, we can say that saving is AB. In the lower part of the graph, we can take point J in such a manner that $JY_1 = AB$. By joining the points, K, I, J we can draw the saving function.

From the saving function we can now define some other important concepts, like marginal propensity to save (mps) and average propensity to save (aps). Like mpc, mps is the slope of the saving function and is defined as the ratio of change in saving to the change in income and it is the coefficient of the income term in the saving function. But looking at the saving function we can say, mps = 1 − b, and b = mpc. Therefore, by definition, mpc + mps = 1. This is an important conclusion for any numerical example because if mpc is .7, we can immediately deduce that mps is .3.

Average propensity to save (aps) like apc is defined as the ratio of saving to income (S/Y = aps). By simple derivation it is possible to show that apc and aps also add up to unity. Let us define initial income as consumption plus saving.

$$Y = C + S$$

Dividing both sides by Y we get,

$$Y/Y = C/Y + S/Y$$

therefore,

$$1 = apc + aps$$

This is also an important result for numerical calculations because now if we know any one of these two, the other is easily calculated.

Among the non-income determinants of savings, the interest rate seems to be the most important one. The higher interest rate offered on the deposits, the higher will be the saving. The saving curve drawn in Figure 7.3 would shift from one place to another due to changes in the interest rate. One would also note that all the determinants of consumption are also the determinants of saving because saving is just income that is not consumed. Hence, these non-income determinants of consumption listed above also indirectly affect the saving behavior of the economy.

7.3   Investment and Multiplier Analysis

While consumption constitutes the most important part of total expenditure of the economy, the second most important part is investment. Investment, in real terms, is defined as one of the following three things: (a) buying of machinery, tools and equipment, (b) construction activities, and (c) changes in inventories. Inventories are the stocks of goods which are produced but are not sent to the market. The above definition of investment is peculiar and hence, quite important for our purposes. According to Keynes, the investment activity undertaken by the producers of goods and services would depend upon two 'rates.' One is the rate of expected returns from the use of that machine, popularly called, the marginal efficiency of capital (MEC). For instance, if the interest rate happens to be lower than the expected profit rate, then producers would realize that the rate which they would repay their loans from the bank would be less than the profit rate expected from investment. Obviously, the producer would go ahead and borrow from the bank and carry out the investment activity. Thus, under these circumstances, investment would go up. Investment in the economy would tend to go down if the expected profit rate happens to be less than the interest rate charged by the banks. As mentioned above, this expected profit rate in economic literature is referred to as the marginal efficiency of capital (MEC) or marginal efficiency of investment MEI). In practice, it is hard to measure this rate in numerical terms. In order to tackle that problem, Keynes defines this rate as "that rate of discount which would make the present value of the series of annuities given by the returns expected from the capital asset during its life just equal to its supply price." The relationship between marginal efficiency of capital and investment is seen to be inverse. With higher investment, the rate of profit is expected to decline.

Hence, in Figure 7.4, the MEC curve is sloping downwards from left to right. Assuming the constant interest rate charged by

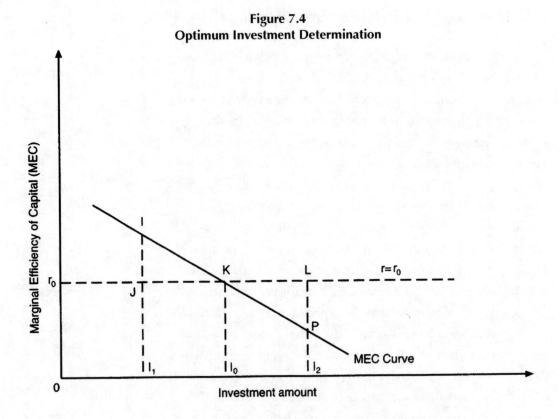

Figure 7.4
Optimum Investment Determination

banks ($r = r_0$), irrespective of the borrowed amount (or invest-ment), we can determine optimum amount of investment (I_0) at point K. I_0 is said to be optimum investment because at any other amount of investment there is inequality between MEC and the interest rate and therefore, a tendency of investment either to increase or to go down. For example, at investment I_1, MEC $> r$ and there is a tendency for investment to go up. Also, at invest-ment I_2, MEC $< r$, therefore investment would go down from I_2.

There are several factors in the real world that would have an effect on the value of MEC. Notable among these are (a) the expected revenues from an investment (b) taxes (c) cost of pro-duction and (d) expected inflation rate. All of these factors would be responsible for a shift in the MEC curve in Figure 7,4. For instance, a higher tax rate would force producers to increase the supply price of capital equipment and the discount rate (MEC) that makes the supply price equal to the present value would have to be lower. Hence, the MEC curve would shift downward determining lower investment than at I_0 as the optimum amount. The expectation of inflation (reduction in the value of money as Keynes sees it) has a similar effect on investment. In Keynes' words, "the expectation of changes in the value of money influences the volume of current output. The expectation of a fall in the value of money stimulates investment, and hence employment generally, because it raises the schedule of the marginal efficiency of capital, e.g., the investment demand schedule; and the expectation of a rise in the value of money is depressing, because it lowers the schedule of the marginal efficiency of capital."[1]

Now, it is crucial to realize that to a Keynesian mind, since investment is dependent upon the relationship between the interest rate and the marginal efficiency of capital, investment is independent of income. Hence, changes in GNP have no effect on investment. If we assume an economy which is closed (no international trade) and in which government plays no role, then aggregate demand in it is just consumption (C) plus investment (I). To draw such an aggregate demand curve in Figure 7.5 is easy because when autonomous investment is added to consumption, the consumption function will not change its slope. C + I curve lies to the upper side of the consumption curve by the amount of investment.

The C + I curve is also called the aggregate demand curve or total expenditure line. It is used to define another important concept of the equilibrium level of income. In order to determine the equilibrium level of income we must first understand its meaning. In general, the equilibrium level of income is defined as that level of income at which the aggregate demand (total expenditure) in the economy is equal to the aggregate supply in it. In notational

---

[1] Suggested Additional Reading: Keynes, John Maynard. *The General Theory of Employment, Interest and Money*, pp. 141-142.

Figure 7.5
Total Expenditure Curve

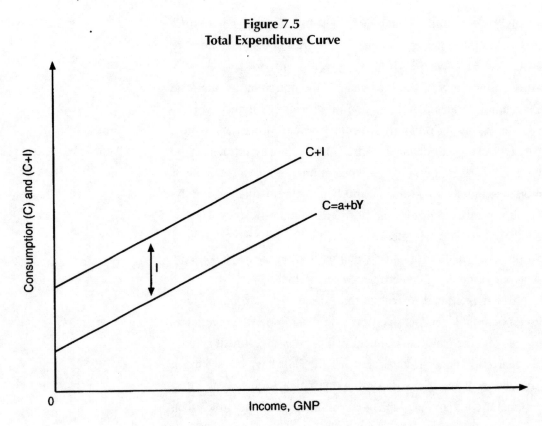

form, the equilibrium level of income makes C + I = C + S. Hence, in a closed economy, it is the level at which investment is equal to saving. There is yet another way of defining it. Investment is seen as an injection in the expenditure stream because any increase in it increases the total expenditure of an economy. On the other hand, saving is called a leakage from the total expenditure of an economy. From this approach, the equilibrium level of income is that level at which leakages in an economy are equal to injections.[1]

---

[1] Other examples of injections are government expenditure and exports, and other examples of leakages are taxes and imports, but because of our assumptions here, of inactive government sector and no international trade, we can ignore them for a while.

In the Keynesian system, in order to determine the equilibrium level of income, we use Figure 7.6 which has come to be known as the 'Keynesian Cross.'

In the above graph, C + I line is the same as we derived in Figure 7.5. Together with this (C + I) line, which we call the actual aggregate demand line, we would also plot a 45° line. In this graph, the 45° line represents those points at which aggregate demand is always equal to aggregate supply. However, at point E where both lines intersect, we have an equality of actual aggregate demand and aggregate supply.[1] Hence, point E decides the equilibrium level of income as Y.

In numerical form, the equilibrium level of income can be determined as follows: Suppose the consumption function of an economy is given as C = 250 + .65Y and the investment determined by MEC and the interest rate relationship is given as 500 currency units. A question of equilibrium level of income can be answered by noticing that equilibrium income levels need:

$$C + I = C + S$$
i.e., $\quad C + I = Y$

Equilibrium income needs:

$$C + I = Y$$
i.e., $\quad a + bY + I = Y$
i.e., $\quad 250 + .65Y + 500 = Y$
i.e., $\quad 750 = .35Y$
i.e., $\quad 2142.8 = Y$

Therefore, the level of income of 2142.8 currency units is the equilibrium level. The next issue we want to discuss is how changes in the equilibrium income can be caused by changes in investment levels.

---

[1] Income of an economy is nothing but its aggregate supply.

Let us suppose now that for some reason, investment increases from the level shown in Figure 7.6 to a higher level. (Let us call the original level of investment, I_0, and the new level of investment, I_1). In other words, investment increases by ΔI amount.

Figure 7.6
Equilibrium Income Determination

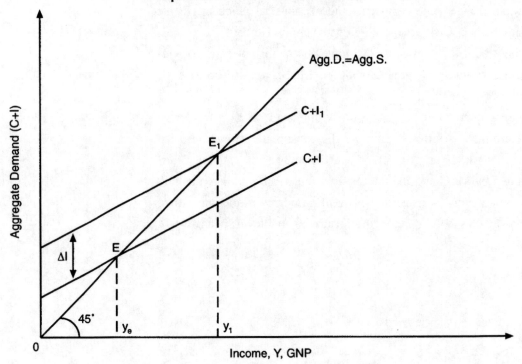

With higher investment in Figure 7.6, we may have to draw another aggregate demand line. Obviously, the new level of equilibrium income would be higher than Y_0, say Y_1. Let us denote this increase in income by ΔY. Thus, we can see from Figure 7.6 that with an increase in investment, equilibrium income increases.

A mathematical derivation is carried out in the following simple calculation.

Define

$$Y = C + I$$

substituting consumption's value as $(a + bY)$,

$$Y = a + bY + I$$

Rearranging:

$$Y - bY = a + I$$
or
$$(1 - b)Y = a + I$$
and
$$Y = (a/1 - b) + (1/1 - b) \times I$$

Totally differentiating the above, keeping in mind that 'a' and 'b' are constants, we get:

$$DY = \left(\frac{1}{(1 - mpc)}\right) \times DI = \left(\frac{1}{mps}\right) \times DI$$

The value of the factor $1/1 - mpc$ (or $1/mps$) is called the multiplier (or the investment multiplier) and is denoted by the letter K. Therefore, by definition, the investment multiplier is the multiple of change in investment which gives rise to the change in the equilibrium level of income. In algebraic terms, it is equal to the inverse of the marginal propensity to save (mps) or one divided by one minus the marginal propensity to consume. In numerical terms, the value of the multiplier would always be greater than unity because marginal propensity to consume (and also to save) is always less than one. This is because it is improbable (even if not impossible) that $\Delta C/\Delta Y$ can be greater than one. Obviously, this means that any change in investment would create a larger change in equilibrium level of income. A numerical illustration follows:

Suppose the consumption function of an economy is given as $C = 150 + .75Y$ and investment initially is 500. If the investment increases from 500 to 600, what is the change in the equilibrium income? A question like this can be answered by actually calculating income initially as:

$$
\begin{aligned}
Y &= C + I \\
&= 150 + .75Y + 500 \\
\text{or} \quad .25Y &= 650 \\
\text{or} \quad Y &= 2600
\end{aligned}
$$

and with new investment:

$$
\begin{aligned}
Y &= 150 + .75Y + 600 \\
&= 750 + .75Y \\
.25Y &= 750 \\
\text{or} \quad Y &= 3000
\end{aligned}
$$

Therefore, due to an increase in investment by 100, the equilibrium level of income increases by 400. This necessarily means that the value of the investment multiplier is 4, which can be doubly checked by $1/mps = 1/.25 = 4$.

Now we must understand why there is a multiple increase in equilibrium income when investment increases by a certain amount. When there is an investment activity, say of 100 units (of buying either machinery, tools, equipment, or construction activity) there is an increase in income of 100 units created in the first period. Those people who receive this income are obviously going to spend a part of it and save the remaining part. Their action of consuming more from the increased income will be dictated by the value of marginal propensity to consume (mpc). Hence, they would consume mpc x 100 in the next period which would become the income of someone else. In the economy as a whole, there is an increase in income of 100 + mpc x 100 up to this point. However, those who receive income of mpc x 100 would consume in the next round by mpc x mpc x 100 and the process would continue for the fourth, fifth, sixth, etc., time periods. All in all, at the end of the process, i.e., in equilibrium, the increase in income would be:

$$AY = 100 + mpc \times 100 + mpc \times 100 + mpc \times 100$$
$$= (1 + mpc + mpc + mpc + \ldots) 100$$

$$= \frac{1}{(1 - mpc)} \times 100$$

$$\Delta Y = \frac{1}{(1 - mpc)} \times AI$$

Thus, any increase in investment is responsible for a multifold increase in the income level. The multiplier principle works in both directions however. Any decrease in investment also causes a multifold decrease in equilibrium level of income. Also, the multiplier process can be ignited by change in any part of the total expenditure. Hence, similar to the investment multiplier, there is a government expenditure multiplier (and change in any part of aggregate demand creates a multiplier effect on the equilibrium level of income). In fact, as the multiplier process is started by a change in any autonomous factor, the multiplier is sometimes called the 'autonomous spending multiplier.'

7.4   Full Employment and Keynesian Analysis

The basic thrust of the Keynesian analysis is to determine the way to achieve full employment in the economy. Keynes was probably the first economist to emphasize the point that the equilibrium level of income may not be equal to the full employment income. This may be so, even for a simple reason that equilibrium level of income is defined as the income level at which aggregate demand and aggregate supply are equal, and the full employment level of income is defined as that level at which all persons in the economy who are willing to work can find a job. There is not 'a priori' reason why both these income levels may be the same. According to Keynes, classicalists erred in not realizing this point. Now the basic reason why the economy may not achieve full employment could be the lack of aggregate demand.

In other words, the economy on its own may attain Y level of income in Figure 7.6, but it is likely that full employment income could be greater than Y_e. Therefore, the economy, left to itself, does not have any mechanism leading to full employment. The government which is anxious to achieve full employment in the economy has a definite role to play under these circumstances. Its main task has to be to influence the aggregate demand structure and raise it to the appropriate level needed for full employment. Hence, we should now analyze the role of an active government. At the very instance the government becomes active, aggregate demand is defined as consumption (C) plus invest (I) plus government expenditure (G). Government expenditure, like investment, is autonomous, independent and exogenous of changes in income of the economy. Hence in Figure 7.7, the shape of C + I line would remain unchanged, only its location would change by the amount of government expenditure.

Hence, the new aggregate demand will be represented by C + I + G curve and a new equilibrium level of income would be given by point J (and its level is Y on the horizontal axis). Let us assume that the full employment level of income, as shown in the graph, is Y_j. In order to achieve that level, according to Keynes, the government must take the initiative in starting new social programs and raising the aggregate demand level to C + I + G' that is appropriate for full employment.

Figure 7.7
Aggregate Demand with Active Government

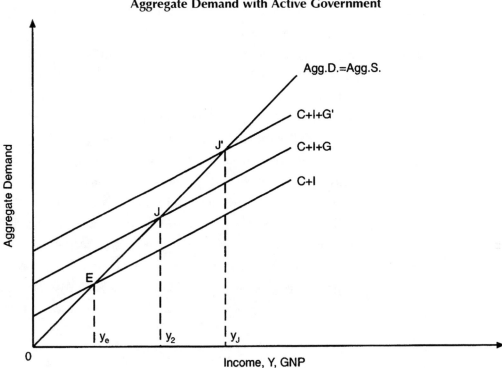

In Keynes' words, it can be pointed out, "The State will have to exercise a guiding influence on the propensity to consume partly through its scheme of taxation, partly by fixing the rate of interest, and partly, perhaps, in other ways. Furthermore, it seems unlikely that the influence of banking policy on the rate of interest will be sufficient by itself to determine an optimum rate of investment. I conceive, therefore, that a somewhat comprehensive socialization of investment will prove the only means of securing an approximation to full employment; though this need not exclude all manner of compromises and of devices by which public authority will cooperate with private initiative."[1] Nothing can be clearer than this quote. This distinctly shows the aim of

---

[1] Suggested Addtional Reading list: Keynes, John Maynard, *The General Theory of Employment, Interest and Money* (p. 378).

Keynes, to give a larger share of responsibility to the government for the attainment of full employment. The policy of the government which makes changes in taxes and the government expenditure is called fiscal policy. From the above quotation, it is also clear that Keynes regarded fiscal policy to be a very efficient policy. This was partly due to his belief in the multiplier process. When government expenditure is increased, he believed that the same multiplier process is put into action as the one after an increase in investment. Hence, fiscal policy is always effective in increasing real output of the economy. Thus, the message received from the commodity market analysis by Keynes is the one which emphasizes the active role of government for full employment. There was also another special reason why Keynes conceived the limit to the effectiveness of the monetary policy. In order to understand the why and how of this belief, we move to the next chapter on money market analysis in the Keynesian system.

Suggested Additional Reading for Chapter 7

1. Boyes, William. *Intermediate Macroeconomic Theory*, 3rd ed. Southwestern Publications, 1994. Chapter 3 and 4.

2. Gordon, Robert. *Macroeconomics*. 4th ed. Boston: Little, Brown and Company, 1994. Chapter 6.

3. Heilbroner and Thurow. *The Economic Problem*, 7th ed. New Jersey: Prentice-Hall Publication, 1984.

4. Hicks, John. "Mr. Keynes and the Classics: A Suggested Interpretation." *Econometrica 5*, April 1937: 147-59.

5. Johnson, I. C. and W. W. Roberts. *Money and Banking: A Market-Oriented Approach*. New York: The Hyden Press, 1982. Chapter 20.

6. Keynes, John Maynard. *The General Theory of Employment, Interest and Money*. New York: Harcourt, Brace and World, Inc., 1936. Chapters 1, 6, 8, and 10.

7. Mayer, J., J. Duesenberry, and R. Aliber. *Money and Banking and the Economy*, 2nd ed. W.W. Norton Co., 1984. Chapter 13.

8. Scott, R. H. and Nic Nigro. *Principles of Economics*. Boston: Macmillan Publishing Co., 1982. Chapter 21.

9. Smith, W. L. "A Graphical Exposition of the Complete Keynesian System" in W. L. Smith and R. L. Tergen, eds. *Readings in Money, National Income and Stabilization Policy*. Homewood, Illinois: Richard D. Irwin Publishers, 1974: 61.67.

10. Thomas, Lloyd. *Money, Banking and Economic Activity*. New Jersey: Prentice Hall Publications, 1982. Chapter 18.

The Keynesian System: Money Market

8.1 Introduction

The main aims of this chapter include the following: (i) introduction of some important Keynesian concepts such as the demand for money, (ii) analysis of the interest rate determination according to Keynes, and (iii) analysis of the effectiveness (or the lack of it) of monetary policy according to Keynes. In the Keynesian system, nominal or monetary factors have little importance. This is because with few exceptions, monetary factors are unable to influence the real factors like consumption, investment, etc. In the Keynesian view, the most important factor was obviously aggregate demand, and monetary forces were to be examined in accordance with their effect on aggregate demand. The real interest rate was thought to be the link between the monetary and the real factors. The interest rate, of course, being decided by the intersection of demand for money and the supply of money. The definition of demand for money was crucial because demand for money, unlike demand for any other good, was not given by the want of it but by the actual holding of it. Hence, demand for money is the amount of money people would like to keep in terms of cash at a given time period.

According to Keynes, there are three important motives (reasons) why people would keep money in cash or in non- interest bearing bank accounts. The types of money demand are transactionary demand for money, precautionary demand for money, and

Figure 8.1
Transactions Demand for Money

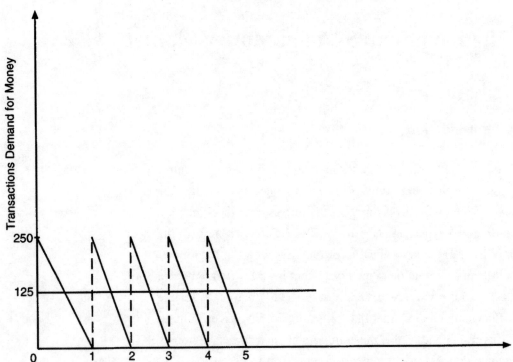

speculative demand for money. We first analyze these motives of demand for money in detail.

8.2   The Transaction Demand for Money

Since money functions as a medium of exchange, one of the important causes for holding money is having it available for making transactions. In Keynesian words, "one reason for holding cash is to bridge the interval between the receipt of income and its disbursement."[1] Depending upon how much money is received by a person and how long is the time available to disperse that income, one can always determine the transaction

---

[1] Suggested Addtional Reading list: Keynes, John Maynard, *The General Theory of Employment, Interest and Money* (p. 195).

demand for money. If we assume that uniform income is received every month and total payments are equal to total receipts, then by using Figure 8.1, we can determine the average transaction demand for money. The time interval for receipt of income and the income one receives per month can decide the amount of money demanded by the person. As the interval between the time income is received (and it is spent) is shortened, average cash balances held will decline.

In general, the transaction demand for money by a person who receives 250 money units of income would be 125 on the average over a month. The longer the time period is, the larger is the demand for money. A higher income would create a higher transaction demand for money. Thus, the transaction demand for money is primarily determined by the income level and the time interval between two income receipts.

8.3   Precautionary Demand for Money

The precautionary demand for money, as the name suggests, is the amount of money kept in cash for the precaution purposes. This money is needed "to provide for contingencies requiring sudden expenditure and for unforeseen opportunities of advantageous purchases, and also to hold an asset of which the value is fixed in terms of money."[1] The volume of this type of demand for money would depend upon the reward for holding money in any other substitute form (e.g., interest rate on bonds) and the risk of being illiquid. The higher the risk of being illiquid, and the higher the cost of getting additional cash, the higher the precautionary demand for money. To elaborate with an example, let us suppose you are traveling far away from your home (and back) and the cost of getting the cash is high (and the risk of being illiquid is high as well). In this situation, you would tend to keep more

---

[1] Suggested Additional Reading: Keynes, John Maynard. *The General Theory of Employment, Interest and Money*, p. 196.

Figure 8.2
Liquidity Preference Curve

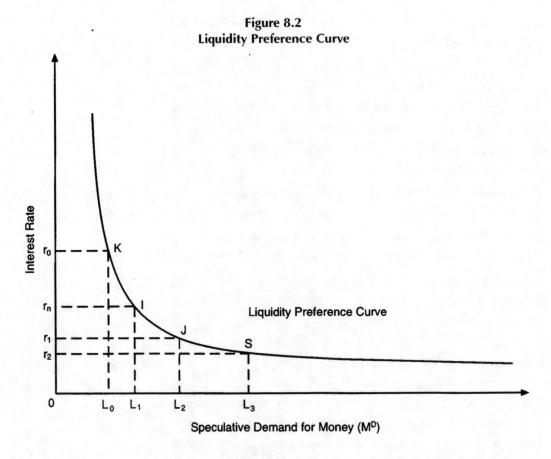

money in your pocket. That money is obviously the demand for money for precautionary purposes. Also, a higher interest rate on the substitutes for money would mean people would keep more of these substitutes and less of the money holdings. Hence, demand for money is inversely related to the yields on the substitutes of money.

8.4   The Speculative Demand for Money

The most important type of demand for money, according to Keynes, is the speculative demand for money. It is the amount of money people hold for making speculations in the bond market. If people have a choice of holding wealth in the form of either money or bonds, then the interest rate on bonds is the only determinant of the speculative demand for money. In general, people would have a preference for holding money to buying bonds, since money has the liquidity characteristics to a higher degree than bonds. This is known as 'liquidity preference.' It is only when the interest rate increases on bonds that people would be ready to buy more bonds and reduce their speculative demand for money. Hence, the higher the interest rate, more is the bond buying and less is the money held in cash for speculation of bond prices. This inverse relationship between the interest rate and speculative demand for money is depicted by the downward sloping curve from left to right, shown in Figure 8.2. Keynes called this curve the *liquidity preference curve.* "This component of money demand is highly volatile since it depends heavily upon the changing nature of the public's expectations. If the outlook for stock and bond markets becomes increasingly gray or cloudy, speculative demand for money increases as people seek to unload securities. As the outlook clears up and becomes more favorable, the speculative demand for money declines and people take the plunge and utilize money balances to purchase stocks and bonds."[1]

Furthermore, one should notice from Figure 8.2 that the shape of the liquidity preference curve becomes flatter at the lower interest rates. This is because Keynes believed that the interest elasticity of speculative demand for money increases as the interest rate declines. The lower the interest rate, the greater is the responsiveness of the demand for money for interest rate changes. This needs more explanation. According to Keynes, people always hold in their mind a certain rate of interest which they think should normally prevail. Hence, the 'normal' interest rate is the level toward which people expect the interest rate to gravitate. The normal interest rate in peoples' mind is generated from past experience. If the current interest rate is much below

---

[1] See Thomas, Lloyd in the Suggested Reading List, chapter 14, p. 342.

Figure 8.3
Equilibrium of Money Market

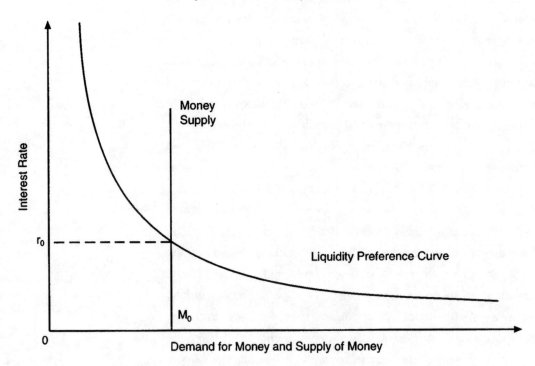

the normal interest rate, then people expect the current rate to move back to normal. This is because movements in the current interest rate do not make people substantially revise expectations to the level of the normal interest rate. Now, if the above theory applies to an individual, it also to a large extent, applies to the economy as a whole.

Thus, Thomas clarifies it by stating; "When one goes from the analysis of an individual to aggregate analysis, it is necessary to allow for the fact that different individuals have different conceptions regarding the 'normal' level of interest rates."[1] Keynes argued that the lower the current level of interest rate, the greater the number of people that will be convinced that the current rate is below the 'normal' rate and therefore, the greater the number

---

[1] Suggested Reading List: Thomas, Lloyd. *Money, Banking and Economic Activity*, Chapter 14, p. 342.

of people that believe the interest rate will rise and bond prices will decline. Therefore, according to Keynes, the lower the current interest rate, the lower will be the demand for bonds and the greater will be the demand for money." In terms of Figure 8.2, at interest rate r_0, the normal interest rate is lower than current, hence, demand for money for speculation is quite low. At interest rate r_1 the normal interest rate (r_0) is above the current rate, hence, people expect the interest rate to move up in the future.

Consider an extreme case when interest rate is currently very, very low like at r_2 level. All persons in the economy would expect that the normal interest rate level is r_0, and that the interest rate cannot go down further in the future. It is therefore, quite likely that in this special case no one in the economy would be interested in buying bonds.

The demand for money for speculative purposes would be very, very high, almost to infinity. Obviously, the shape of the demand curve for money would become horizontal in this special case. This horizontal part of the demand curve for money is given a special name by Keynes. It is called the 'liquidity trap.' When interest rates are very low (as they were in the Great Depression) Keynes could easily visualize the existence of the liquidity trap. But here the explanation of liquidity trap existence is not the main contribution of Keynes. Noticing the policy consequences of the existence of the liquidity trap is even more important. However, in order to understand that, we must explain money market equilibrium first.

8.5 Money Market Equilibrium

In the money market, the demand for money and supply of money interact to determine the price of money, namely, the interest rate. Equilibrium in the money market is defined by an equality of demand for money and supply of money quantities. Demand for money, as we have just seen in Section 8.1 is determined, in general, by national income (Y) and the interest rate. It holds a

Figure 8.4
Effectiveness of Monetary Policy: Keynesian View

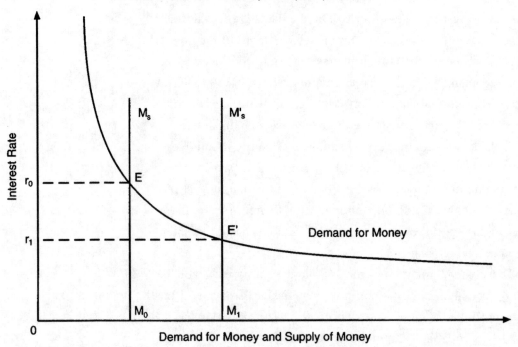

direct relationship with income and an inverse relationship with the interest rate. The supply of money is determined by the policies of the Central Bank in the country.

It is possible that their policies are dependent upon the levels of interest rate but there is no reason for us to know it 'a priori.' Hence, money supply is determined independently of the interest rate (or money supply is decided autonomously or exogenously). In Figure 8.4 we draw the downward sloping demand curve for money to show the inverse relationship between the interest rate and demand for money. The money supply is shown by a vertical straight line to indicate no relationship between supply of money and interest rate. At the point of intersection of these straight lines, at point E, equilibrium in the money market is established. If interest rates are sufficiently flexible, then in the long-run, r_0 is the only interest rate that would persist. This is because as we have seen in Chapter 6, at any interest rate above or below r_0

there would be pressure generated on the interest rate (by excess demand or excess supply) to move back to r_0 level. The paradox of flexibility has application here. If the interest rate is flexible, then it will stay at equilibrium.

8.6 Effectiveness of Monetary Policy According to Keynes

In the Keynesian mind, monetary policy is effective only if it is able to affect the aggregate demand. Effectiveness of any policy is measured in terms of the change in real GNP the policy can cause. In the Keynesian way of thinking, real GNP increases only if there is an increase in real aggregate demand. It is only through the multiplier process that any policy action can affect real GNP, after it is able to increase the real aggregate demand of an economy.

Monetary policy, which makes changes in the money supply, is responsible for the shifts in the vertical straight line in Figure 8.4. A higher money supply would create a rightward shift in the money supply curve and a lower money supply would create a leftward shift in it. Assuming the same demand curve for money, we may conclude that higher liquidity in the economy creates a lower interest rate as equilibrium moves from point E to E'. In the Keynesian system designed in this chapter and in Chapter 7, a lower interest rate would create a situation where marginal efficiency of capital (MEC) would be greater than r_1. In this situation, producers would realize that it would be profitable to carry out investment activity, hence, the investment level would increase. In terms of Figure 8.5, with interest rate r_0, the optimum investment was I_0 and with lower interest rate of r_1 the new investment would be I_1 that is higher than I_0.

Thus, in the Keynesian system, a higher money supply creates a lower interest rate which creates higher investment. This increased investment sparks the multiplier process which generates higher levels of real income. Thus, in notational form, a

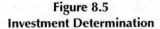

Figure 8.5
Investment Determination

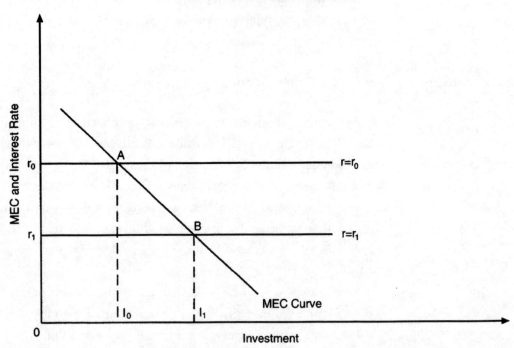

chain of events as ΔM causing Δr causing ΔI causing ΔY can be designed that is elaborated by Keynes. This chain of events sometimes is referred to as the *Keynesian chain*. According to Keynes, monetary policy is effective via the Keynesian chain alone. Having said so much about the effectiveness of monetary policy, now is the time to ask ourselves the question, "why is it that Keynes is popular for saying 'Money does not matter?'"

To answer this question we must consider a special case under which the Keynesian chain breaks down. This case is given by the existence of the liquidity trap.

In terms of Figure 8.6 let us assume that at a very low interest rate, like at r_3, a liquidity trap exists. When there is an increase in money supply before the liquidity trap, (say from M_0 to M_1 to M_2), the Keynesian chain explains the effectiveness of monetary policy. However, after the money supply has reached the M_2 level (or interest rate has become r_3), any expansionary policy ceases to be effective.

In other words, at point E_2, where interest rate is r_3 and money supply is M_2, any increase in the money supply is unable to reduce the interest rate, hence, it is unable to increase investment and real income. In Keynes' view, since the interest rate fails to decline, the increase in money supply will exert no impact on aggregate demand and GNP. The economy is stuck in what Keynes called the 'liquidity trap.' It is in this case when Keynes would whole-heartedly say that 'Money does not matter.' A situation like this was probably the reason why in the Great Depression of 1929-1933, no monetary policy could become effective.

To analyze the problems faced by the world in the Great Depression, let us examine a sample case of the U.S. economy by noting a few facts. From October, 1929 to March, 1933 the real

Figure 8.6
Liquidity Trap and Monetary Policy

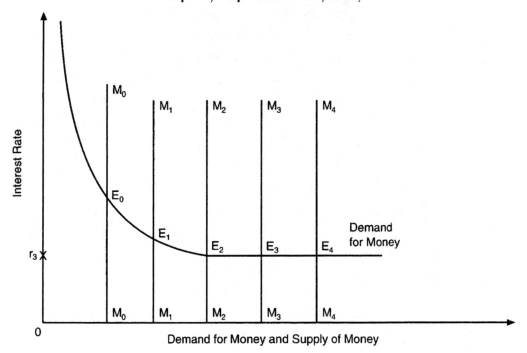

GNP fell about 30 percent, unemployment rate increased from less than 4 percent to 25 percent and the consumer price index fell about 25 percent. Money supply, defined as Ml or M2, showed a considerable decline, probably because of a large number of bank failures. Nonetheless, the monetary base, which is defined as bank reserves plus currency with the public and which is believed to be controllable by the Central Bank, showed an overall increase of 20 percent. If we extend the period through the end of 1935, the growth of the monetary base exceeded 75 percent. Observing the above facts, Keynes would argue that a policy of 'easy money' (increase in monetary base) was in fact instituted by the Federal Reserve but was unsuccessful. What was required in this case, according to Keynes, was massive fiscal actions such as an increase in government expenditure or tax reductions. Given these conditions, there was nothing the Federal Reserve could have done to extract the economy from depression.

Money market analysis developed in this chapter was the basic interpretation of Keynes regarding the demand and supply of money. We also have seen that due to the existence of a liquidity trap, monetary policy becomes completely ineffective. Hence, the best monetary policy can do is to keep money supply consistently at that level at which the interest rate is as minimal as possible. If the interest rate happens to be greater than r_3 in Figure 8.5, monetary policy should pump more money in to the economy to bring it down. This type of policy recommendation is known as 'pegging the interest rate.' According to Keynes, the optimum monetary policy will always follow the 'pegging the interest rate' policy recommendation, since the economy will eventually be stuck in the liquidity trap. In the liquidity trap, money does not matter, and the existence of the liquidity trap sets a limit to the effectiveness of monetary policy. This analysis clearly places fiscal policy above monetary policy. The former does not have any limit to its effectiveness as government expenditure changes directly affect the aggregate demand and real GNP of the economy by getting the multiplier process underway. Thus, fiscal policy should be the primary policy of the government which is anxious to take its economy to full employment. The monetary policy is subordinate, secondary and inferior to fiscal policy.

Having seen these special Keynesian feelings about government activism, our task is to move one step further and find out what could be the criticism of such a recommendation. But we take up that task in future chapters when we consider the monetarist analysis. Monetarists are a group of people who believe in very passive government compared to Keynes, and who rely on market mechanisms to solve the economic problems. They obviously disregard the Keynesian analysis of government activism on a theoretical as well as on a practical basis. However, before we take up the topic of the monetarist counter-revolution, it is important that we develop a new technique of IS-LM framework that was initially designed by Sir John Hicks of Cambridge University in England.

Suggested Additional Reading for Chapter 8

1.   Brunner, Karl and Allen Meltzer. "Liquidity Traps for Money, Bank Credit and Interest Rates." *Journal of Political Economy,* Vol. 76 February 1968: 1-37.

2.   Goldfeld, Steven. "The Demand for Money Revisited." *Brookings Papers on Economic Activity* Issue 3 1973: 577-638.

3.   Havrilesky, Thomas and John Boorman. *Monetary Macroeconomics*. Illinois: Harlan Davidson, Inc., 1973. Chapters 7 and 8.

4.   Jones, David. "The Demand for Money: A Review of the Empirical Literature." *Staff Economic Studies of the Federal Reserve System*, October 1965.

5.   Kaufman, George. "More on an Empirical Definition of Money." *American Economic Review*, Vol. 59 March 1969: 78-87.

6.   Keynes, J. M. *General Theory of Employment, Interest and Money*. New York: Harcourt, Brace and World, Inc., 1936. Chapters 13 and 15.

7.   Konstas, Panos and M. W. Khouja. "The Keynesian Demand for Money Function. Another Look and Some Additional Evidence." *Journal of Money, Credit and Banking*, Vol. 1, November 1969: 765-777.

8.   Laider, David. *The Demand for Money—Theories and Evidence*. 2nd ed. New York: Dun-Donnelly Publishing Corporation, 1977.

9.   Thomas, Lloyd. *Money, Banking and Economic Activity*. New Jersey: Prentice-Hall Inc., 1982. Chapter 14.

10.   Tobin, James. "The Interest Elasticily of TransactionsDemand for Cash." *Review for Economics and Statistics*, August 1956: 241-47.

IS-LM Framework and Stabilization Policies

9

9.1 Introduction

Chapter 7 concentrated on commodity market transactions and its equilibrium. The analysis of the commodity market can be carried out in real terms without much regard to monetary variables. In Chapter 8 we dealt with the money market equilibrium and the transactions in purely monetary or nominal terms. The link between the commodity market and money market is observed to be the real interest rate. The interest rate affects investment in the commodity market and the demand for money in the money market. Also, national income or aggregate supply of an economy influences the consumption in the commodity market and the demand for money in the money market. Sir John Hicks of Cambridge University developed a special technique called the IS-LM framework in the late 1930s to analyze the equilibrium of both markets simultaneously by emphasizing the equilibrium combination of the interest rate and income. In the present chapter we will develop the IS-LM framework and use it to analyze the effects of stabilization policies of an economy. Stabilization policies are any actions of a government to stabilize the economy from business fluctuations which supposedly take place in a free capitalistic economy. There are two basic stabilization policies, namely fiscal policy (dealing with government expenditure and taxes) and monetary policy (dealing with money supply and interest rate). In this chapter we will analyze the effects of these policies in terms of the IS-LM framework.

9.2   The Commodity Market Equilibrium and IS Curve

The commodity market, as analyzed in Chapter 7, is said to be in equilibrium when aggregate demand in an economy is equal to aggregate supply of that economy. This is the same condition as required to define the equilibrium level of income. If aggregate demand is greater than the aggregate supply, the economy experiences inflation and if aggregate supply is greater than aggregate demand, the economy suffers from a recession (or deflation). It is only when aggregate demand and aggregate supply are equal, there is neither inflationary nor deflationary pressure on the price level of an economy. Assuming two simplifying things; namely, the idle government, so that $G = 0$, $Tx = O$, and a closed economy so that $X = O$ and $M = 0$, the aggregate demand of an economy is defined as consumption (C) plus investment (I). The aggregate supply is total income which is equal to consumption (C) plus saving (S).

Hence, commodity market equilibrium is defined by the condition as follows:

$$C + I = C + S$$
$$I = S$$

Hence, if total investment in the economy is equally matched up by the total saving in the economy, we say that commodity market equilibrium is established. Obviously this condition also yields us the equilibrium level of income. Thus, IS curve is defined as the locus of combinations of interest rate and income (Y) at which the commodity market is in equilibrium. Investment, as we had seen in Chapter 7 is decided by the MEC and interest rate levels. The lower the interest rate, the higher will be the investment level and higher will be the equilibrium level of income. Hence, as interest rate goes down, investment increases and if we want saving to be equal to investment (i.e., define commodity market equilibrium) then we must consider a higher level of income. Only at a higher level of income do people tend to save more. Thus, the locus of interest rates and income levels which keep the commodity market in equilibrium is seen by the downward sloping line from left to right. In terms of a numerical example, let us suppose that the interest rate is 12% and at that interest rate investors decide to invest 100. The level of income that generates saving of 100 is (let us suppose mps = .2) 500. Hence, with an interest rate of 12%, 500 is the income level that keeps the commodity market in equilibrium. In Figure 9.2, the combination of interest rate of 12% and income of 500 is plotted by point K. Now let us assume that the interest rate goes down to 10% so that MEC becomes greater than interest rate (r). When MEC is greater than r, investors decide to invest more than 100, like 150. In order to consider saving to be 150 (so that the commodity market will again be in equilibrium) we must consider an income level of 750 (with assumed mps = .2).[1] Hence, the combination shown by point S in Figure 9.2 also establishes commodity market equilibrium. By repeating this procedure we can plot a few other points on the graph. By joining these points, the curve we get is known as the IS curve. At each point on the IS curve we have equality of investment and saving (therefore the name IS). If we relax the simplifying assumption that we made earlier, the IS curve might change its location but the inverse relationship it shows would stay the same. An active government, for example, adds government expenditure factor to aggregate demand and taxes to the income side. Hence, commodity market equilibrium requires:

$$C + I + G = C + S + T$$
$$\text{or} \quad I + G = S + T$$

---

[1] Initially with interest rate of 12% MEC must have been 12% because for optimum investment determination as we saw in Chapter 7, we need equality of MEC and r. Hence, as interest rate declines to 10% we find that MEC > r, so investment begins to increase.

Any factor that is responsible for changing investment (besides the interest rate of course) causes the shift in the IS curve.[1] For instance, if there is an increase in business confidence, there will be an increase in MEC and an increase in investment expenditure. At the same interest rate we would get higher level of equilibrium income, hence, all points of IS curve would shift to the right. An improvement in business confidence, thus, can shift the IS curve to the right.

If government decides to carry out an expansionary fiscal policy (an increase in G) then also we have an increase in equilibrium level of income and hence, all the points in IS curve would

Figure 9.1
IS Curve

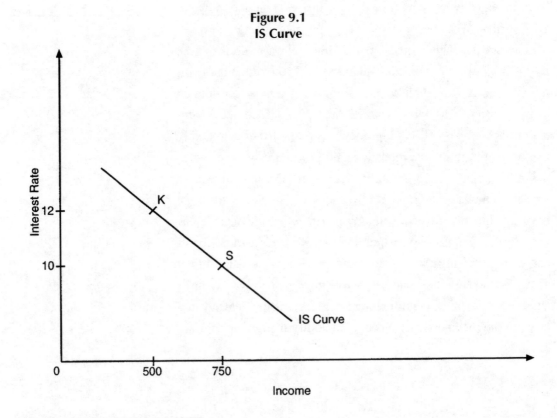

---

[1] Another factor that determines the slope of IS curve is the responsiveness of investment to the changes in interest rate. This responsiveness is also referred to as elasticity. A higher elasticity means with a small decrease in interest rate, there is greater increase in investment. That creates flatter IS curve. For mathematical treatment of this see Gordon in the reading list, Chapter 4, Appendix.

be achieved to the right of the old IS curve. Thus, an increase in G shifts IS curve to the right and a decrease in it shifts IS curve to the left. The value of the multiplier (K) which depends upon mps is capable of shifting the IS curve as well. A lower value of mps (that means higher value of multiplier) can shift the IS curve to the right. Strictly, the value of the multiplier also changes the slope of the IS curve. A higher value of K creates a flatter IS curve.

Any factor that influences saving behavior of the public can also cause the shift in IS curve. Suppose an improvement in consumer confidence induces reduction in marginal propensity to save. Saving would decrease in this case and IS curve should shift to the right because we have higher consumption. To summarize in Thomas' words, "an event which shifts I + G rightward (upward) or S + T leftward (downward) will shift the IS schedule rightward (upward) and thus exert an expansionary effect on GNP. Any event which shifts I + G leftward (downward) or S + T rightward (upward) will shift the IS schedule leftward (downward) and thereby exert a contractionary influence on GNP."[1]

9.3   The Money Market Equilibrium and the LM Curve

The money market as introduced in Chapter 8 consists of money supply and the demand for money forces. The money supply in general terms consists of coins, currency and demand deposits and is controllable by the central bank of an economy. It is therefore regarded as an autonomous or exogenous variable.[2]

Demand for money is hypothesized as in Chapter 8 to be a function of interest rate and income levels of an economy. It is positively related to income and negatively related to the interest rate as depicted in Figure 9.2. The money market is said to be in

---

[1] Suggested Reading List: Thomas, Lloyd. *Money, Banking, and Economic Activity*, p. 443.

[2] Recall that when there is a change in any one of the other variables (other than the one plotted on the Y axis) that can change the dependent variable, then there is a shift of the curve.

Figure 9.2
Money Market Equilibrium

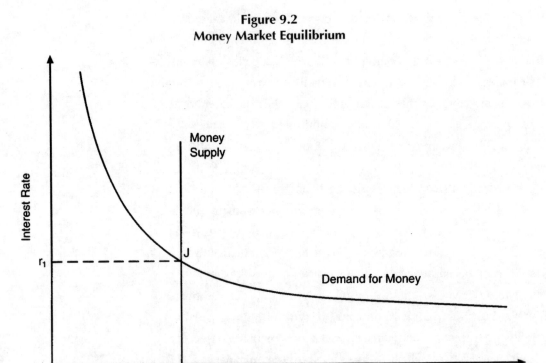

equilibrium when demand for money is equal to the supply of money as is the case with point J in Figure 9.2. However, note that when we drew the demand for money curve in Figure 9.2 (which shows the inverse relationship between interest rate and money demand) we had implicitly assumed a constant income level. Otherwise, as income changes the demand curve for money, it is likely to shift from one location to another. At higher income with the given interest rate, people tend to demand more money, hence, there would be a rightward shift in the demand for money curve.

The LM curve is defined as the locus of combinations of interest rate and income at which the money market is in equilibrium. As income increases, the demand curve for money in Figure 9.2 shifts to the right and with constant money supply the interest rate needed to achieve money market equilibrium is higher. Hence, there is a direct or positive relationship between income and interest rate levels that keep money market in equilibrium.

Let us suppose that at income 100 and interest rate 6%, we have demand for money equal to 60. Let us suppose the money supply as determined by the Central Bank of the economy is equal to 60. Hence, the given combination of interest rate and income is on LM curve. In Figure 9.3, that combination is shown by point A. As we consider an increase in income from 100 to 150, demand for money would increase from 60 to a higher level (say 85). Now if we desire to bring demand for money back to be equal to the supply of money, we must consider a higher interest rate than 6% (say 9%). Hence, the new combination of interest rate (9%) and income (150) would also keep money market in equilibrium. There are obviously infinite combinations of income and interest rates that can be found in this manner. The curve joining these combinations is called the LM curve.

The points on the lower left portion of the LM curve have a low level of income, hence, lower demand for money than that is needed for money market equilibrium. These points are characterized by an excess supply of money. Similarly, points on the right side of the LM curve show higher income, hence, higher demand for money than that is needed for money market equilibrium. These points show an excess demand for money in the money market. The slope of the LM curve depends clearly upon the responsiveness (or elasticity) of demand for money to the changes in interest rates. If this responsiveness is very high then even a small change in the interest rate will bring about a large change in the demand for money. Hence, a large increase in the interest rate would create money market equilibrium, giving a flatter shape to the LM curve. Obviously, in the reverse case when demand for money is inelastic with respect to interest rate, the LM takes a steeper shape. In extreme cases when demand for money is completely elastic with respect to the interest rate, the LM curve would be horizontal and when demand for money is

Figure 9.3
LM Curve

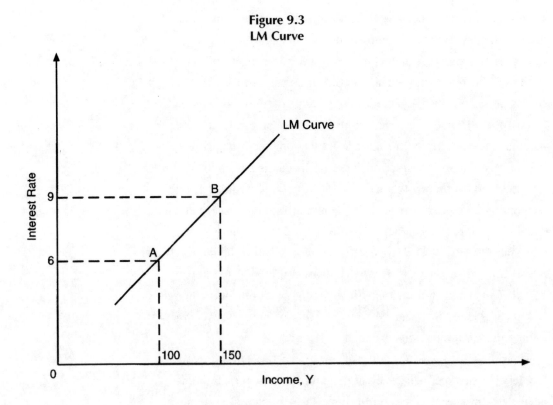

completely inelastic (absolutely non-responsive to interest rate changes) then the LM curve will be vertical.

Shifts in the LM curve may be caused by the actions of monetary authorities. An increase in the money supply, for example, would shift the vertical money supply curve to the right in Figure 9.2 and the interest rate required for equilibrium in the money market would decline. In Figure 9.3, the LM curve would shift to the right. Similarly, a decrease in money supply would create a leftward shift of the LM curve.

Another variable which causes shifts in the LM curve is the expected rate of inflation. If people expect higher inflation in the future (for whatever reasons, for example, an announcement from monetary authority to increase money supply in the future) then they would sell many of their securities and get ready to beat inflation by holding more money in cash. The demand for money would increase and the demand curve for money would shift rightward. At any given income level, we would observe a higher interest rate that would keep the money market in equilibrium. This causes a shift of all points on the LM curve to the left. Thus, an expectation of higher inflation rate causes a leftward shift in the LM curve and expectations of declining inflation in the future makes the LM curve shift to the right.

Having seen the derivations of IS and LM curves and the reasons for their shifts, we are in a position to use them for defining the general equilibrium of an economy.

9.4   General Equilibrium of an Economy

At all points on the IS curve we have shown the existence of commodity market equilibrium. At all points on the LM curve the money market of an economy is in equilibrium. IS and LM curves together would establish the equilibrium of the entire economy if we assume that there are only three markets in the economy.

At any point to the left of the LM curve we have excess money supply in the money market, and at any point to the right of the LM curve we may observe an excess demand for money. This is because at all points to the left of the LM curve, the interest rate is higher than that required for money market equilibrium. Hence, quantity of money demanded is lower than quantity of money supplied. At any point to the left of the IS curve we have excess supply of commodities. At all points to the left of the IS curve the interest rate is lower than that required for commodity market equilibrium (or for making investment = saving). Hence, at the lower interest rate, *investment* is higher than *saving*, leading to higher aggregate demand (C+ I) than aggregate supply (C+ S). This can be further explained as follows: Consider point J in Figure 9.4 where the interest rate is r_2 and income is Y_2. However, for commodity market equilibrium (or for point L on the IS curve) one needs Y_2 income, r_1 interest rate. Hence, the interest rate at point J is lower than that required for commodity market

Figure 9.4
General Equilibrium and IS-LM

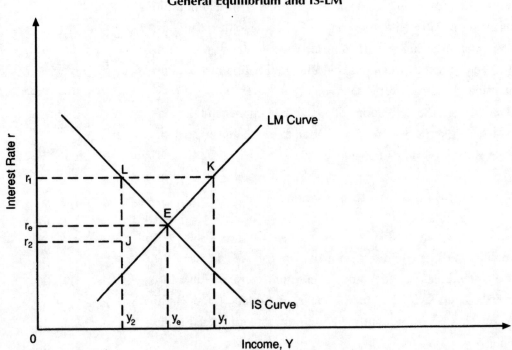

equilibrium. Hence, Investment at point J is higher than that required for commodity market equilibrium, leading to higher aggregate demand than aggregate supply.

The same logic can be used to determine excess demand (or excess supply) in the commodity or money markets at any other point that is outside the IS or LM curves.

At the intersection point of the IS and LM curves the economy has equilibrium in the commodity as well as the money market. Point E, in Figure 9.4 is called the *general equilibrium point*. Thus, the IS-LM framework yields us the unique combination of interest rate and income that achieves the general equilibrium. This is probably the biggest advantage of constructing the IS-LM framework. Another advantage of this framework is to explain how an economy possesses a built-in mechanism by which Point E would always be attained in the long run. Suppose the economy is experiencing Y_1 income level and r_1 interest rate and is at point K. With these levels of income and interest rate there would be equilibrium in the money market (K is on the LM curve) but excess supply of commodities in the goods market. Due to the lack of sufficient demand, inventories would accumulate, interest rate would start going down and also the income would start declining. As GNP declines, demand for money decreases and interest rate drops down further. The economy achieves levels of lower interest rates and income in this manner. This process is expected to continue as long as there is disequilibrium in the commodity market. In the long run, the combination of interest rate and income shown by point E, is established.

9.5 Monetary Disturbances and the IS-LM Framework

Another advantage of the IS-LM framework is its ability to analyze the effects of disturbances in the monetary as well as the real sector of an economy.

To analyze the effect of an expansionary monetary policy on general equilibrium, start off with a situation at point E_1 in Figure 9.5, with interest rate r_1 and income Y_1 With an increase in money supply there happens to be an excess supply of money in the money market and the LM curve shifts to the right. The increase in money supply that is created by buying government securities from the public increases the demand for securities and increases its price, lowering its yield. The interest rate therefore, is expected to go down due to the expansionary monetary policy. This reduced interest rate is responsible for an increase in investment in the commodity market. The increased investment due to multiple process raises the level of GNP of an economy. Hence, with LM curve shifting to the right, the economy attains a new equilibrium at point E, with interest rate r_2 lower than before and an income level higher than before.

Similarly, if people expect an increase in interest rates in the future (for whatever reason) then the demand for money may increase causing excess demand for money in the money market. This would shift the LM curve to the left because at the same

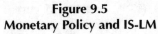

Figure 9.5
Monetary Policy and IS-LM

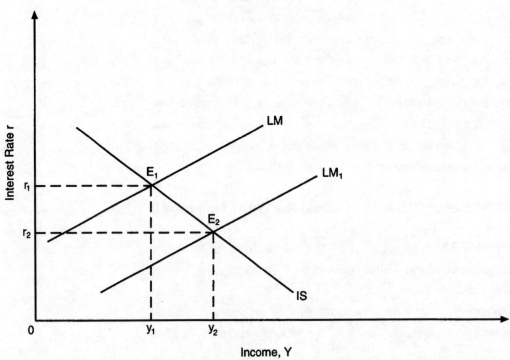

level of income there would be a higher interest rate that would achieve the money market equilibrium.

With LM curve shifting to the left, the economy may end up with lower income and higher interest rates in this case. In general, any event which increases (decreases) demand for money (money supply) causes an excess demand for money and becomes responsible for shifting the LM curve to the left. This event leads to higher interest rates and lower income in the economy. On the other hand, any event that decreases (increases) demand for money (money supply) causes an excess supply in the money market and thereby shifts the LM curve to the right. This event leads to lower interest rates and a higher income in the economy. Thus, the effectiveness of monetary policy can be observed by using the IS-LM framework

Figure 9.6
Effectiveness of Fiscal Policy and IS-LM

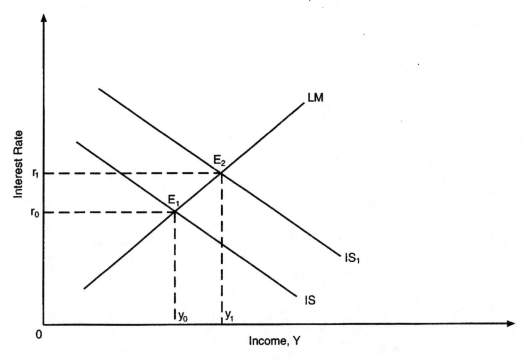

9.6   Disturbances in the Real Sector and IS-LM

The real sector disturbances are basically generated by government by making changes in fiscal policy. As mentioned before, changes in taxes as well as changes in government expenditure are responsible for shifting IS curve from one location to another. Suppose that government decides to increase the income tax rate. This would create lower consumption since disposable income of the economy would be reduced by higher taxes. An increase in income taxes, therefore, would lead to lower aggregate demand, hence, would shift the IS curve to the left. Similarly, an increase in corporate tax would create a lower expected profit rate for corporations. This may lead to lower investment and therefore may also cause a leftward shift of the IS curve.

Figure 9.7
Liquidity Trap and Demand for Money Curve

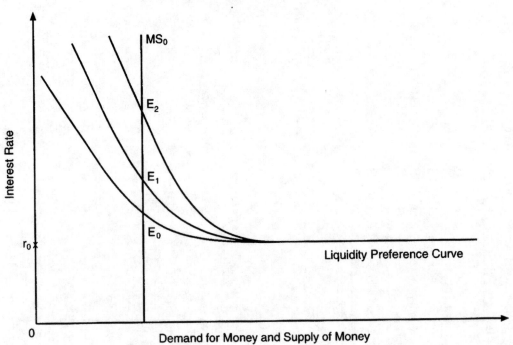

An increase in government expenditure (an expansionary fiscal policy action to be more general) can have an effect on the aggregate demand of an economy. An increase in government expenditure due to the multiplier process causes an increased expenditure that is financed by selling bonds to the public and creates an excess supply of bonds in the bond market which reduces the price of bonds, and increases the interest rate needed to be offered. Nonetheless, in this case, fiscal policy action is said to be effective because it leads to a higher level of GNP. The difference between effectiveness of expansionary fiscal and monetary policy is that the former leads to a higher interest rate while the latter leads to a lower interest rate. According to Keynes, if both policies are pursued simultaneously, then a constant lower interest rate is possible together with the economic growth and higher employment.

In an extreme (special) case of the existence of the liquidity trap, the ineffectiveness of monetary policy can be analyzed by simple modification in the IS-LM framework. When the liquidity trap exists, the shape of the demand curve for money becomes horizontal and it has repercussions on the shape of the LM curve. As long as the interest rate is very low, the demand curve for money is horizontal and therefore the LM curve is horizontal. When the interest rate is higher than the lowest possible level, the demand curve for money has a normal downward sloping curve.

Hence, at r_0 interest rate, the LM curve is horizontal. If the interest rate happens to be higher than r_0, the demand for money would have the usual shape and the LM curve is upward sloping as usual for all interest rates except the minimum level. Any expansionary monetary policy in this case would be unable to shift the horizontal part of the LM curve. (This is because there would always be a liquidity trap at the r_0 level of interest rate.) The monetary policy becomes completely ineffective due to the existence of the liquidity trap. Thus, in a liquidity trap, the Keynesian Chain breaks down. Given the downward sloping IS curve, however, there is no limit to the effectiveness of fiscal policy which causes a shift in the IS curve. An expansionary fiscal action for example, could always make the IS curve shift to the right and new general equilibrium will be achieved to the right of point J in Figure 9.8. Thus, ISLM framework is useful for analyzing the special problem like the liquidity trap. A unique characteristic of the IS-LM framework is that it considers equilibria of money and commodity markets simultaneously. As we just saw, it can be modified to show limitless effectiveness of fiscal policy and complete ineffectiveness of monetary policy in the case of a liquidity trap.

We can also analyze the other extreme case of classical economists' belief in the quantity theory of money and its effect on the shape of the LM curve. This is carried out with the use of Figure 9.9. Strictly speaking, the quantity theory equation of Chapter 6 emphasizes only the medium of exchange function of money.

Figure 9.8
Liquidity Trap and LM Curve

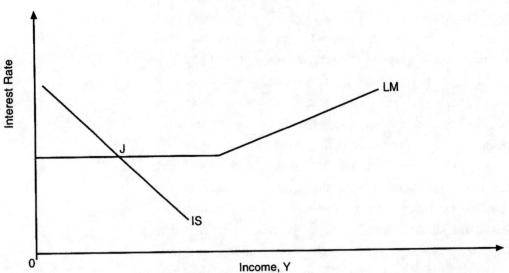

Figure 9.9
Classical Model and IS-LM

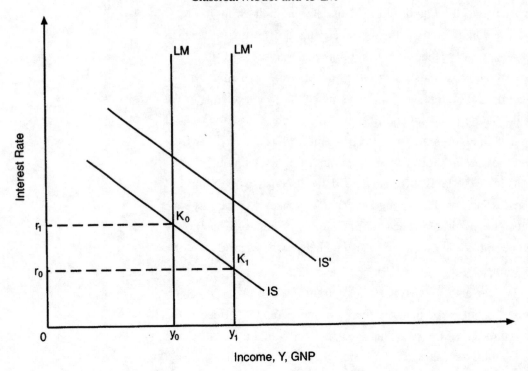

The demand for money is either not recognized by the quantity theory or is assumed to be independent of the interest rate. Hence, the demand for money is assumed to be completely nonresponsive (inelastic) with respect to interest rate changes. In this case, the demand for money is shown by a vertical straight line and there is only one income level that can achieve money market equilibrium. Obviously, given only one income level that keeps the money market in equilibrium, the shape of the LM curve is also vertical.

In this special case of a vertical LM curve, no fiscal policy action (the shifts in IS curve) can be effective to cause changes in income and employment of an economy. The monetary policy however, is able to shift the LM curve to the right (an expansionary monetary policy would create excess money supply) and to achieve another money market equilibrium by wiping this excess out, we must consider a higher level of income. Hence, as shown in Figure 9.8, LM curve shifts right due to expansionary monetary policy and can be effective in creating a higher level of income and employment. To classical economists' these actions are not desirable. They were advocates of laissez faire policy which means letting the economy function by itself and not intervening in the efficient market forces which are supposed to cure any disequilibrium situation.

Proponents of the IS-LM framework use it to analyze several other real world problems. A reader can make up problems of his/her own and examine their effects on the IS and LM curves to summarize their consequences on national income and the interest rate. In this book, our next task is to find out the lacunae in the Keynesian analysis. On a theoretical as well as a practical basis, Keynesian theory, despite its success in the nineteen-forties, fifties and sixties, was criticized, sometimes quite vehemently, by a group of economists known as monetarists. It is the work of the monetarists that forms the basis of our next chapter.

Suggested Additional Reading for Chapter 9

1.   Boyes, William J. *Macroeconomics: The Dynamics of Theory and Policy.* Cincinnati: South-western Publishing Company, 1984. Chapter 4.

2.   Dernberg, Thomas and Duncan McDougall. *Macroeconomics.* New York: McGraw-Hill Publishers, 1976. Chapters 8 and 9.

3.   Gordon, Robert. *Macroeconomics*, 3rd ed. Boston: Little Brown and Company, 1984. Chapter 4.

4.   Hicks, John. "Mr. Keynes and the 'Classicals: 'A Suggested Interpretation." *Econometrica 5*, April 1937: 147.

5.   McGee, Robert. "A Graphical Exposition of a More Complete Keynesian System." *Journal of Macroeconomics*, Fall 1984: 559-570.

6.   Mishkin, Fredric S. *The Economics of Money, Banking and Financial Markets.* 3rd ed. Harper/Collins Publishers, 1995. Chapter 23.

7.   Thomas, Lloyd. *Money, Banking, and Economic Activity.* New Jersey: Prentice-Hall Publishers, 1982. Chapter 19.

Revised Quantity Theory of Money: The Optimum Monetary Policy and the Monetarism

10

10.1 Introduction

Sir John Maynard Keynes was not only the most prolific contributor of monetary theory of the 1930s, he was also an influential practitioner of his advocacies. He traveled extensively to introduce the theories he developed to policy makers. He actively influenced the governmental authorities to practice his solution directly or indirectly in their policy actions and took a great share of policy making in the U.K. In several ways, he (and his followers after his death) became successful in their persuasion. On the political side, the Keynesian recommendations looked too attractive to avoid their practical implementations. In essence, Keynes advocated that an active government which undertakes the social projects of reconstruction is beneficial for economic growth and is a step forward in achieving the objective of full employment. Which government would deprive itself of an opportunity of spending more and being politically popular? Classic examples of governments which wholeheartedly approved of Keynesian philosophies are the governments of several industrialized economies including those of the United States, United Kingdom, Italy, France, the Netherlands, and Canada. Keynesianism was adopted by some developing countries such as India, Pakistan, Kenya, and Ghana. For several years the policy recommendations by Keynes were profitable in terms of achieving economic growth and prosperity. In general, for about 20 to 25 years the capitalistic government economies overwhelmed themselves with the gains of government activism and by the adoption of a new line of economic thought. Together with this increased governmental role in the economy, due to destruction created by World War II in the 1940s, due to continued industrial development, due to lower population than in the modern times, and due to availability of several unused natural resources, nineteen fifties and sixties were the most glamorous years of economic prosperity of the western world. However, by the late nineteen sixties, the prosperity era started coming to an end. As over-anxious government activism created an excessive growth in the money supply and government expenditures, economies started approaching a saturation point, population increased tremendously and inflation as well as unemployment existed simultaneously. The Keynesian advocacy of an active government sector started yielding greater harm than good to economies and the time started approaching when Keynesian economists could not find an answer to the mysterious phenomenon of simultaneous existence of inflation and unemployment popularly called stagflation. At this time, the University of Chicago gave birth to new economic philosophers who claimed that the answer to the question of stagflation lies in the disregard held by Keynesians to the quantity theory equation, and overactive governments all over.

A group of economists, now partly in the Chicago School and partly somewhere else, that regards excessive money supply growth as a basic reason for inflation is known as Monetarists, and Professor Milton Friedman of Hoover Institution in Stanford, (who finished substantial work at the University of Chicago) is considered to be the leader of this group. The economic theories monetarists believed in, are termed (initially by Professor Karl Brunner of Rochester University) as monetarism. Among several theories put forward by Professor Friedman before and after getting the Nobel Prize in Economics in 1976, the most relevant for the present chapter is the *revised quantity theory of money.*

10.2   Recent Developments of the Quantity Theory of Money

Even if Friedman's work was one of a pioneer's, developments of the quantity theory of money are also attributed to several other economists. Notable among these are Don Patinkin of Hebrew University who had his own statement of the quantity theory, Anderson and Jordon who showed the impact of money supply on income and prices, and Brunner and Meltzer who presented empirical evidence that demand for money is stable in a way that supports the quantity theory. Thus, monetarism has evolved not out of any single book, but from a variety of studies and theories supporting the basic fact that in the long run, extensive growth of money supply is the fundamental reason for economic problems. In general, the monetarists concentrate on the long-term effects of the policies while Keynesians believe that, "in the long run, we are all dead."

The main reason why Friedman feels that "all inflations always and everywhere are a monetary phenomenon" is his conception that the quantity theory equation, if correctly interpreted, is not a bad equation after all. From the quantity theory equation developed in earlier chapters and expressed as $MV = PY$, if the velocity of money is shown to be stable in the long run, then any increase in money supply (M) can either increase the general price level (P) or raise national income (Y) or raise both P and Y. When the economy is close to full employment, changes in Y are much harder and an increase in M leads to a higher increase in P than in Y. On the other hand, if the economy is far away from full employment, then an increase in Y is quite possible, hence, expansionary monetary policy leads to a higher increase in Y than in P. Hence, it is wrong to presume that 'Money does not matter.'[1] In fact, monetary policy is quite powerful policy, 'money does matter.' Hence, monetarists argue that if velocity of money

---

[1] This is a popular quotation from *The General Theory . . .*, which clearly summarizes the Keynesian belief.

is proved to be stable, then changes in the money supply are quite effective in making changes in P and/or Y. Moreover, anytime one observes an excessive increase in P (say inflation) the main cause of it is an excessive increase in the money supply.

Now, in the above analysis, the important part is to show the stability of velocity of money. It can be easily recognized that the unique determinant of velocity of money is the demand for money. If people wish to hold more money in terms of cash, the turnover rate of money declines, hence, velocity declines. Thus, the demand for money is negatively related to the velocity of money.

Therefore, to show the velocity of money to be stable we need to show the demand for money to be stable. Hence, the stability of demand for money became an important condition to show the effect of the money supply on the general price level. In the words of Peterson, ". . . we may characterize income-expenditure theory as a theory of the demand for output as a whole cast in the framework of the aggregate demand function (C + I + G, in a closed economy). By analogy, the modern monetarist theory can be characterized as a similar theory cast in the framework of a demand for money function that explains how the money supply affects the performance of the economic system. The demand for money is the fundamental behavioral relationship in monetarist theory."[1]

According to Friedman, the demand for money is a stable function of a set of variables that affects the demand for any other good. Moreover, the demand for money function is more stable than the multiplier (K) that Keynes has heavily put emphasis on and the effect of money supply is more direct and consistent (than the effect of investment) on the output and employment of an economy. By defining money as a "temporary abode for generalized purchasing power," Friedman claims that people demand

---

[1] Suggested Reading List: Peterson, Wallace C., pp. 373–377.

money for the same reasons they demand any other good. The most significant determinants of demand for any other good are (a) total wealth of the households or firm, (b) the opportunity cost of holding the good, (c) the tastes and preferences of the wealth holding unit.

The wealth of the household or business firm consists of the permanent level of income (Y) the household earns in a given time period and the ratio of nonhuman to human wealth (H). The permanent level of income, according to Friedman, is the level of income that is adjusted for the transitory changes like windfall losses or gains. Hence, omitting the sudden increase in income due to things like a Christmas bonus or lottery gain and the sudden losses like the ones due to natural calamities, the permanent level of income is defined. The second part of wealth, viz human capital, consists of an individual's inherited and acquired skills and training. In principle, the value of human capital would be equal to "the discounted value of the future income stream that an individual could expect to obtain from all of his education and training." Friedman believes that the holding of money balances, like the demand for education and recreation is seen as a luxury. Therefore, as the wealth, measured by permanent income, increases, the demand for money is expected to increase more than in proportion to the increase in wealth. In more technical terms, this means that the elasticity of demand for money with respect to wealth is greater in proportion than the increase in wealth. In more technical terms, this means that the elasticity of demand for money with respect to wealth is greater than one. Friedman essentially regards permanent income as the most significant determinant of the demand for money.

The second determinant of money demand is the general price level (P). The effect of the price level on nominal demand for money is positive and is straight-forward to explain. An increase in the price level will result in a proportionate increase in demand for money. This must occur if people wish to keep money balances constant in real terms. The general price level's effect is more important when price changes are larger than when they are but a few percentage points.

The direct cost of holding money is, of course, the rate of interest. To accept on a theoretical level that the interest rate is a determinant of demand for money is to align oneself with Keynesianism. As we saw while discussing the Keynesian theory of liquidity preference, the demand for money for asset purposes changes inversely with the interest rate. According to Friedman, the cost of holding money can also be seen in terms of an increase in the "expected" price level. An increase in it has an effect of making demand for money more costly, since the market value of other assets would rise if the demand for real balances is reduced.

Lastly, the third major determinant of demand for money as seen by Friedman is tastes and preferences. However, Friedman contends, "the tastes and preferences of wealth owning units . . . must in general simply be taken for granted in determining the form of the demand function . . . it will generally have to be supposed that tastes are consistent over significant stretches of space and time." Hence, the short-run changes in demand for money are not expected to occur due to habitual or taste changes of the money holding persons. All in all, Friedman sees demand for money to be a function of (a) wealth or permanent income, (b) the price level, (c) the rate of interest, and (d) the rate of increase in the price level. Amongst the four determinants above, the most significant is wealth or permanent income. The effect of the interest rate on the demand for money is negligible if at all. One reason for this low interest rate elasticity of demand for money is the definition of wealth which includes all assets rather than as done by Keynes to assume the choice between money and bonds. Monetarists' assets definition includes all assets including both producer and consumer durable goods. A low interest rate elasticity of demand for money results because given several (assets) options, people do not have the willingness to hold money as an asset. Hence, demand for money is less responsive to the rate of return being obtained on other financial assets, especially bonds. As we saw before, in Keynesian analysis, people do not have options for holding several assets but two: bonds and money. And when people have limited choices, the demand for money becomes very sensitive to changes in interest rates. In terms of Figure 10.1, the Keynesian demand curve for money is shown to be flatter than the monetarists' demand curve for money. This shows that money demand is more sensitive to changes in the interest rate in Keynesian analysis than in monetarists' analysis. In fact, in an extreme case of a liquidity trap, demand for money is very sensitive to changes in interest rates, making the elasticity of money demand with respect to interest rate changes to be equal to infinity.

Friedman and monetarists believe that since people have several financial assets to choose from, any excess money balances "will spill over directly into the spending stream for goods and services, primarily because the substitution effect between money and the range of financial assets available to the firm or the household is small." (See Peterson in the reading list, page 381.) Thus, monetarists believe that money demand is not very sensitive to the interest rate changes. When tested empirically, Friedman finds that the significant determinants of money demand are: permanent level of income and the price level. Since permanent level of income by definition is stable and since price level can be stable if the money supply is stable, the demand for money is inherently a stable function. And since demand for money is shown to be stable, the velocity of money is also stable. Thus, the main reason for revising the quantity theory of money was to show the stability of demand for money and therefore, in essence, the stability of velocity of money.

The next important question to ask the monetarists is "how does an increase in the money supply make changes in other economic variables?" In other words, what is the transmission

Figure 10.1
Demand for Money: Two Interpretations

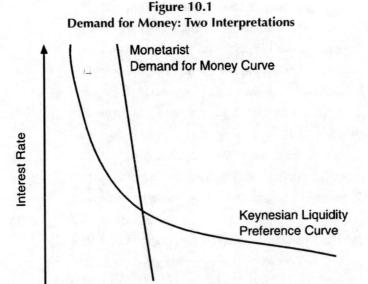

mechanism for the monetary policy change? That question can be answered in terms of Figure 10.2 in which money market equilibrium is at point J where the quantity of money demanded is equal to the quantity of money supplied. According to monetarists, the Keynesian view that with the increase in money supply there would be reduction in the interest rate is oversimplified. In Friedman's view, when there is an increase in money supply, the demand for money curve does not remain fixed but is likely to shift. There are three separate effects of a change in money supply upon the interest rate, viz, liquidity effect, income effect, and the price effect.[1]

(i)   *Liquidity effect*: Due to an increase in the money supply, the vertical line in Figure 10.2 representing money supply moves to the right. This establishes a new temporary equilibrium at point J_1 with a lower equilibrium interest rate of r_1. In common sense the result of lower interest rate due to

---

[1] Suggested Reading List: Friedman, Milton (1956), p. 8.

the liquidity effect can easily be explained. The increase in overall liquidity with the public would require banks to charge lower interest rates.

(ii)   *Income effect*: With higher liquidity available and with lower interest rates temporarily resulting from higher money supply, people tend to increase their spending on goods, services, securities, etc. There is also higher investment which results in higher national income. This higher national income becomes responsible for shifting the demand for money curve to the right.

In terms of Figure 10.2, the rightward shift of the demand for money curve establishes the new equilibrium, which also happens to be temporary, at point J_2 with a higher interest rate of r_2.

(iii)   *Price effect*: The increased money supply also has a positive effect on the expected inflation rate. As people expect a higher inflation rate, the demand for money curve shifts rightward one more time. The final equilibrium is achieved at point J_3 with interest rate r_3.

In Thomas' terms, "We thus have an initial liquidity effect which tends to reduce interest rates followed by an income effect and a price expectation effect, both of which exert upward pressure upon interest rates."[1] Friedman concludes that the net effect of money supply on the interest rate would be direct (instead of inverse) and an increase in the interest rate is more likely when monetary growth is rapid. In terms of Figure 10.2, the net effect on the interest rate would be decided by the strength of the liquidity, income and price effects. The strength of these effects would decide the extent of the shift of the demand for money curve. If the liquidity effect is greater than income and expected price effects taken together, then an increase in money supply would lead to a reduced interest rate. However, if price and income

---

[1] Suggested Reading list: Thomas, Lloyd, p. 371.

Figure 10.2
Money Market—Equilibrium

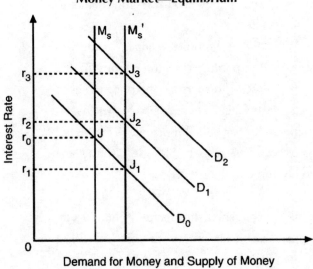

Demand for Money and Supply of Money

effects are greater than the liquidity effect, then an increase in money supply may lead to an increase in the interest rate. However, one thing has to be pointed out. Depending upon the state of the economy, there are time lags involved in completing the three effects discussed above. Even though they start taking place when money supply is increased, they may or may not be finished at the same time. Obviously, these time lags can determine the net effect on the interest rate of the money supply. The experience of the 1970s in several industrialized countries has proved the theory that when money supply changes are rapid, they may in fact lead to higher interest rates. In comparison to Keynesian theory, Friedman's explanation is much broader. While Keynes could see only the liquidity effect, Friedman's theory was the first celebrated attempt to recognize all three effects simultaneously.

10.3   Policy Implication of the New Quantity Theory

One of the main reasons why this theory has become extremely popular is its applicability to the experiences of several economies in the nineteen seventies. It was the decade in which economies experienced an increase in money supply simultaneously to the increase (not decrease) in interest rates. Keynesian explanation was too naive to analyze a phenomenon such as this, because Keynes could not recognize how an increase in money supply could lead to higher interest rates. Obviously, in Friedman's terms, it must be that the strengths of income and price expectation effects were greater than the liquidity effect which can lead to higher, not lower, interest rates. The possibility that a higher money supply can lead to higher interest rates, and the certainty that it would lead to inflation, especially when the economy has used most of its resources (and output level is inflexible), have led to monetarists' recommendation of following a monetary rule in the performance of the monetary policy.

The recommendation of monetary rule has basically emerged from Friedman's 1956 article and 1963 book on this topic.[1] Even if the exact percentage of increase in money supply that is recommended, is of little importance even to the monetarist, Friedman by analyzing the case of the U.S. economy has come up with 4% as the answer. He arrives at the monetary rule of four percent increase in money supply every year by making some assumptions about the behavior of four variables that form the equation of exchange $(MV = PY)$.[2] He argues that the velocity of money is expected to go down in the future because of his *luxury good* thesis. The *luxury good* thesis claims that demand for money is like a demand for a luxury good and has the income elasticity greater than one. Hence, as the demand for money increases, the velocity

---

[1] Suggested Reading List: Friedman (1956) and (1963).

[2] It means that the percentage increase in the demand for money is greater than the percentage increase in national income that causes it.

of money (V) it is expected to decrease at an average annual rate of 1 percent. The average annual growth rate of real GNP (Y) in the case of the U.S. is 3%. Hence, to have a non-inflationary U.S. economy (that is P being constant) the money supply (M) must go up with an annual average rate of 4%. Hence, the magic figure of "4 percent" growth in money supply is an ideal monetary policy to follow.

After Friedman wrote his article in 1948 about this monetary rule, the velocity of money measured by using M money supply definition in U.S. has not shown the expected decline. In modern times, several monetarists, including Friedman agree that an adjustment in the 4 percent is desirable.

To support the recommendation of the monetary rule, monetarists put forward several important points. First, they argue that an adoption of some kind of monetary rule may end the drastic and severe business fluctuations that are caused by the actual and expected monetary instability. The actual dramatic changes in the growth rates of money supply alter the spending behavior of the public. Also, the instability in the money supply growth rate causes people to expect future instability in money supply with business fluctuations as the obvious result. Friedman believes that if a constant money supply growth rule had been used by the Federal Reserve since its inception in 1914, the U.S. economy would have been spared all of the major inflations and depressions and some of the less severe fluctuations. It is alleged that the Federal Reserve on the balance has destabilized the U.S. economy and has thus been a negative factor in post-World War I U.S. economic history. Thus, according to monetarists, the business cycles will be drastically reduced in number (and in severity) if monetary rule was obeyed.

Second, monetary policy of an economy has only one objective to achieve and that is to stabilize the aggregate demand level of an economy. By implementing the monetary rule, the monetary policy would certainly be able to achieve that. However, in practice, monetary authorities of several countries try to achieve many more objectives than they can handle. For example, authorities assume that stabilization of interest rates, stabilization of exchange rate of domestic currency vis-a-vis foreign currencies, stabilization of business fluctuation and achievement of economic growth are their responsibilities. In the optimistic views like these, the monetary authorities let the money supply grow at a varied rate. Strictly speaking, they should concentrate on only one objective of stabilizing aggregate demand and if they do that then monetary rule is the best policy option to have.[1]

Third, by adopting monetary rule, the monetary authorities would interfere less in economic affairs. This would reduce the pressure on executive and legislative branches of government. Several governmental institutions can be wiped out in this fashion, reducing tremendous administrative cost. With added stability in the economic performance, the fiscal policy would also seem to be unnecessary and the number of bank failures would be reduced. In general, the proponents of monetary rule assert that there would be an overall stability in the economy allied to less governmental intervention. Therefore, the saving of administrative costs would result by following the monetary rule. It appears from the above that monetarists have a valid point in proposing the monetary rule as the desirable policy path for the monetary authorities. However, there are several points that can be made which may explain why monetary authorities of several countries were quite reluctant in accepting that as a policy guideline. One such problem of adopting monetary rule had already been pointed out. It originates from the inability of correctly estimating the behavior of the income velocity of money (V in the quantity theory equation).

As was shown later, Friedman incorrectly assumed velocity to decline by 1 percent annual rate in the future. Experience has

---

[1] Suggested Reading List: for more about this point see Thomas, Lloyd, p. 392.

evidenced no such consistent decline in velocity of money. More-over, the velocity of money does show several inconsistent cyclical fluctuations making it difficult to envision any constant growth rate of money supply desirable for policy. In the light of this monetary rule, it should be taken as a rule that suggests a moderate rather than constant growth rate of money supply. But even if we accept this new meaning of monetary rule there are practical problems in adoption. This leads us to the second point against the adoption of monetary rule which recognizes the difficulty in defining money supply itself. As we have seen in Chapter 3, there is just not one acceptable definition of money supply. The inability to arrive at a clear consensus regarding the proper definition of money supply raises severe problems. In words of Tobin, "Sometimes Friedman and his followers seem to be saying: We don't know what money is, but whatever it is, its stock should grow steadily at 3 to 4 percent."[1]

Another point the neo-Keynesians put forward is that in the modern times monetary policy is held responsible for a series of objectives. It includes the stability of the price level, interest rate, bond market and exchange rate fluctuations. In order to achieve all these objectives, monetary authorities need more, not less, discretion while changing money supply. The monetary rule does not allow monetary authorities to change money supply according to their discretion, hence, it is undesirable. Also, modern developments in research techniques—use of computers, more information and better forecasting methods have created a strong justification for a discretionary monetary policy rather than the one which applies the rule and does nothing. Because of all the above reasons, even if monetary policies have failed in the past, there is ample evidence to expect that they would do a better job in the future.

---

[1] Suggested Reading List: Tobin, James (1965), p. 647

Lastly, several economists were eager to point out that adoption of monetary rule by itself did not mean the end of the inflation era. This is because monetary rule can cure only one type of inflation, namely the demand-pull inflation. There is still another type of inflation, referred to as cost-push inflation, which occurs due to a decline in the aggregate supply of the economy that can be cured only by technological advancement, higher labor productivity and renewed availability of resources. The monetary rule, even if adopted, thus, is not going to end all inflation. This recognition of different types of inflation seriously questions the desirability and sufficiency of the monetary rule adoption. Taking all of the above points together makes a very strong case for rejection of the proposal of the constancy of money supply growth rate. In practice, no country has clearly adopted the monetary rule, but in the U.S., when inflation seemed out of hand in October, 1979, the Federal Reserve did make a shift in its objectives from the stability of the interest rate to the stability of monetary aggregates.

10.4   Crowding Out Hypothesis and Fiscal Policy

In the earlier section we have seen the monetarist views about the monetary policy effectiveness and their proposal of monetary rule. In this section we try to analyze the monetarist hypothesis about the effectiveness of fiscal policy. As mentioned before, fiscal policy concerns itself with the tax and government expenditure changes. Moreover, a pure fiscal policy is the one which carries out tax and government expenditure changes without changes in the money supply of an economy. When government expenditure is greater than tax revenues we say that the government budget is in deficit, if the reverse is the case, government budget is in surplus, and when government expenditure is exactly matched up by the tax revenues, the government budget is balanced.

As you may recall, Keynes and Keynesians were in favor of expansionary fiscal policy at least when there are unused resources in the economy. In other words, carrying out a deficit in the government's budget was something not only understandable but a desirable thing to do for Keynesians. Monetarists, on the other hand, hold the view that pure fiscal policy in the long-run is unable to increase GDP in the economy. National debt is created when governments sell bonds to the public to finance the expenditure that is incurred over and above the tax revenues. As the bonds are sold to the public, supply of bonds increases which reduces its price, and increases the interest rate. An increase in interest rate becomes responsible for lower investment especially when the interest rate is higher than the expected profit rate. What has been said, in brief, in the above chain is called the *crowding out hypothesis*. In Carlson and Spencer's words, "If an increase in government demand, financed by either taxes or debt issuance to the public, fails to stimulate total economic activity, the private sector is said to have been 'crowded out' by the government action."[1]

Crowding out initially was put forward by Anderson and Jordon (1968) indicating that an initial positive effect of expansionary fiscal policy is compensated by negative effects in the later quarters so that in the long run, an increase in government expenditure has almost zero effect on an economy's output. There are several explanations for such crowding out to take place on a theoretical basis. First is the simple classical case when demand for money is dependent upon income alone and is completely inelastic with respect to the interest rate. As in Figure 10.3, this creates a vertical LM Curve. Any increase in government expenditure or reduction in taxes will be able to shift the IS curve to IS_1 but such a shift will not be able to increase GNP of an economy. Thus, ineffective fiscal action is evident because of this classical case of

---

[1] Suggested Reading List: Carlson and Spencer, p. 128.

Figure 10.3
Crowding Out Due to Vertical LM Curve

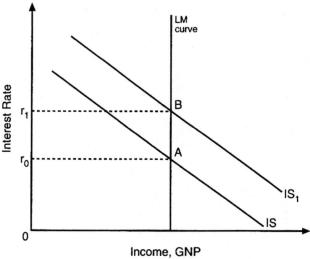

a completely inelastic demand curve for money. The second explanation of crowding out is presented by Friedman and others who stress that the vertical shape of the LM curve is not a necessary condition for crowding out to happen. According to Friedman, an "expansionary" fiscal action might first be reflected in a rise in output, but the financing of the deficit would set in motion contractionary forces which would eventually offset the initial stimulation effect. One of the main reasons why an offsetting effect can take place is the increased interest rate due to added supply of bonds that the government generates to finance the deficit.

One other interesting explanation of possible crowding out phenomenon is found in Keynes' *The General Theory* . . . itself. While Keynes was anxious to point out the expectations and confidence of the producers in determining investment, he was cautious enough to see the possibility that government spending could adversely affect the confidence of the private sector. To be more specific, one can easily find a sentence in *The General*

Figure 10.4
Keynesian Case and Crowding Out

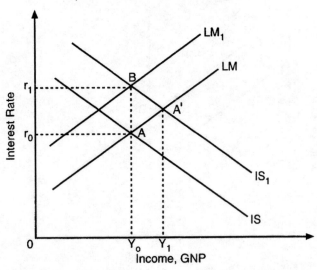

Theory... declaring, "With the confused psychology which often prevails, the Government programme may through its effect on 'confidence' increase liquidity preference or diminish the marginal efficiency of capital, which, again, may retard other investment unless measures are taken to offset it."[1] In terms of Figure 10.4 this can be explained by saying that an expansionary fiscal policy shifts the IS curve to IS_1 and raises initial output at new equilibrium point A. But due to an increase in the public's confidence, there could be higher liquidity preference (or shift of demand for money curve to the right in money market) which could shift LM curve to the left. It is possible that the shift of the LM curve is so great that it completely offsets the expansion in GNP from Y_0 to Y_1.

Lastly, there is an explanation of crowding out presented by David and Scadding (1974) which assumes that people (or households) hold ultra-rationality in their belief that corporate and government bonds are perfect substitutes. Appealing to Denison's

---

[1] Suggested Reading List: Keynes, John Maynard, pp. 119-120

law which says that the ratio of private saving to national income is stable, David and Scadding assert that increased bond sales by government necessarily displaces the private bond sales. Hence, the domestic investment reduces by an equal amount of deficit spending. If the ultrarationality assumption is really correct, then a complete crowding out effect is inevitable. A complete crowding out is said to have occurred when an increase in government expenditure is completely offset by a decline in domestic investment.

From the above, one can see that monetarists regard the monetary policy to be more direct in its effectiveness and fiscal policy to be of less importance because of the crowding out. To summarize this chapter we can make the case for monetarism by noting the following important points.

1.   Monetarists believe that demand for money is a stable function of the permanent level of income and is predictable, hence, velocity of money is stable and predictable.

2.   As a corollary of point 1, since velocity of money is stable, any excessive increase in money supply leads to increase in price level and therefore, inflation.

3.   Monetary policy has direct effects on the economy, hence, it should be carried out extremely cautiously. More specifically, monetary authorities should obey the constant money supply growth rate rule, called "monetary rule" for the stability of the inflation rate.

4.   Fiscal policy has a limited (or no) effect on the GNP of an economy because of the crowding out hypothesis.

Monetarism, thus, evolves from the strong belief in the above propositions. In modern times, including monetarists, economists were more worried about the phenomenon of inflation and/or stagflation. In the next chapter we intend to analyze this chronic phenomenon of consistent increase in the price level and its effects.

Suggested Additional Reading for Chapter 10

1. Anderson, L. C. and J. L. Jordon. "Monetary and FiscalActions: A Test of Their Relative Importance in Economic Stabilization." *Federal Reserve Bank of St. Louis Review*, November 1968: 11-24.

2. Ando, Albert and Franco Modigliani. "The Relative Stability of Monetary Velocity and the Investment Multiplier." *American Economic Review*, September 1965.

3. Carlson, Keith M., and R. W. Spencer. "Crowding Out and Its Critics." Federal Reserve Bank of St. Louis Review, December 1975. Reprinted in *Current Issues in Monetary Theory and Policy* by Havrilesky and Boorman: 128-153.

4. David, Paul and J. L. Scadding. "Private Savings; Ultrarationalily, Aggregation and Denison's Law." *Journal of Political Economy*, March–April 1974: 225-50.

5. Friedman, Milton. "The Quantity Theory of Money: A Restatement," in Milton Friedman edited *Studies in Quantity Theory of Money*. Chicago: Chicago University Press, 1956.

6. Friedman, Milton. "The Role of Monetary Policy." *American Economic Review*, March 1968.

7. Friedman, Milton. "Rules Versus Authority in Monetary Policy." *Journal of Political Economy*, February 1963: 1-31.

8. Friedman, Milton and David Meiselman. "The Relative Stability of Monetary Velocity and the Investment Multiplier in the United States, 1897-1958." Commission on Money and Credit Stabilization Policies. New Jersey: Prentice Hall, 1963.

9. Friedman, Milton, and Anna Schwartz. *A Monetary History of the United States 1867-1960*. New Jersey: Princeton University Press, 1963.

10. Goldfeld, Stephen M. "The Demand for Money Revisited." *Brooking Papers on Economic Activity*, Vol. 3 1973.

11. Peterson, Wallace C. *Income, Employment and Economic Growth*. 5th ed. New York: W. W. Norton and Company, 1984.

12. Rousseas, Stephen. *Monetary Theory*. New York: Knopf Publishers, 1972: 160-180.

13. Thomas, Lloyd. *Money, Banking, and Economic Activity*. New Jersey: Prentice Hall, 1979.

14. Tobin, James. "The Monetarist Counter-Revolution Today—An Appraisal." *Economic Journal 91*, March 1981: 29-42.

15. Tobin, James. "The Monetary Interpretation of History." *American Economic Review*, June 1965:647.

16. Wood, John H. "Money and Output: Keynes and Friedman in Historical Perspective." *Business Review*. Federal Reserve Bank of Philadelphia September 1972: 3-12.

17. Wrightsman, Dwayne. *An Introduction to Monetary Theory and Policy*. New York: Free Press Publications, 1971.

Inflation: Causes, Consequences and Cures

11.1 Introduction

Among the most puzzling of economic difficulties is the existence of inflation and/or unemployment in an economy. It seemed several times in history that inflation, once started, kept on increasing. Inflation has resisted or at best, has responded only sluggishly to traditional restrictive policies. There are numerous questions to be answered. What is an inflation? What accounts for its persistence? Why is it regarded bad? Is there any silver lining to the black cloud of inflation? To answer the above and similar other questions we address the problem of inflation in this chapter.

11.2 Inflation and Its Causes

One of the intricate problems is to try to define what is really meant by inflation. In a strict sense of the term, "inflation" means, "a consistent increase in the general price level of an economy." But this creates problems because the general price level is defined in at least three ways viz, consumer price index (CPI), producer price index (PPI), and GNP deflator. An economist can define inflation as a consistent increase in any one of these price indexes. Obviously, we now have three ways to calculate inflation and all are equally acceptable. Once inflation is measured one has to mention the method of calculating it. The most popular way in which inflation is measured is by using the consumer price index. Secondly, inflation generally refers to a consistent increase in the price level which evidently disqualifies the one-shot increase in the price level. How long a price level has to be increasing to be referred to as inflation is also up to the discretion of the interpreter. This gives another reason for misinterpretation of inflation. In general, an increase of 1–2 years in the general price level should be taken as an inflationary phenomenon. The third important point about the incidence of inflation is the realization that since inflation only means a consistent increase in the general average price level of all goods, it is perfectly possible that some goods have increased in their price much more than some others. Also, it is perfectly possible to pinpoint certain goods which experience a decrease rather than an increase in their prices in inflation. Hence, do not feel surprised to see certain goods which, in spite of inflation, are experiencing a decreasing price.

Another way to look at an inflationary situation is to define it by the stage of an economy where there is excess aggregate demand for goods and services in relation to their supply. Any time aggregate demand happens to be higher than aggregate supply, irrespective of their absolute levels, the tendency of the general price level is to go up. Hence, if the situation of excess aggregate demand occurs for a long time inflation may result. There are basically two sets of causes for inflation if inflation is seen as a stage of excess aggregate demand. One set is of the causes that raise the level of aggregate demand and make it greater than aggregate supply. The causes which do this and make the inflationary situation occur, are called demand-pull factors. By its very nature, a demand-pull factor creates a demand-pull inflation. To name a few demand-pull factors, one can point out the excessive increase in money supply, the government budget deficits, increase in export earnings, etc.

The other set of causes of inflation include the cost-push factors. These factors are responsible for an increase in cost of production and therefore, reduction in the aggregate supply of an economy. The reduced aggregate supply, if aggregate demand is constant, can cause inflation of cost-push nature. Then, of course, the crucial question is to find out a way to differentiate and recognize correctly what type of inflation an economy is experiencing at a given point. An important indicator of that is the rate of unemployment. Generally speaking, a demand-pull inflation is associated with lower unemployment rates than the cost-push inflation. This is logical because cost-push type of inflation affects the aggregate supply of the economy while demand-pull does not. A lower aggregate production would not need as much employment of the labor force in the economy; hence, cost-push inflation arrives simultaneously with the labor unemployment.

The increase in aggregate demand that causes inflation in the economy can occur because of several reasons. However, the increase in aggregate demand of an economy hardly occurs in the private sector as the private sector is not capable of generating autonomous shocks to aggregate demand. As we have seen before, consumption cannot, and does not, change vehemently unless there is a change in GNP. Also, private investment, which constitutes a small part of aggregate demand and its growth is self-limiting and probably produces only a minor increase in demand. That leaves only the public sector to generate any consistent increase in aggregate demand. Indeed, government does possess power to tax the public, increase money supply infinitely, finance wars, and run deficits in its budget. For this control, and for the use and abuse of its power, government is seen as a sole creator of the demand-pull type of inflation. A government that runs a deficit in its budget adds to (C + I + G) of an economy at two levels: direct and indirect. The direct impact of increased government expenditure is obvious. As G increases by a certain amount, so does (C+I+G), since G is part of aggregate demand.

The indirect effect comes about with different degrees in its impact, depending upon the way in which the deficit is financed. There are basically two ways in which the deficit is financed. First, government can sell bonds to the central bank and receive the money from the central bank. This is no different than asking the central bank to print more money supply to finance the deficit. This process of monetization (due to an increased money supply) has a maximum effect on the price level. As mentioned in Chapter 10, monetarists believe that this is the basic cause of inflation.

The second way of financing the deficit is by selling bonds to the public. This creates national debt and, hence, the current burden of excessive expenditure by the government is transferred to future generations. Nonetheless, if a creation of national debt does not raise the interest rates excessively and if the monetary policy, as carried out by the Central Bank of the country, does not increase the money supply to cure the increased interest rates, then this way of financing the deficit has a smaller impact on the general price level of an economy. This process we have already discussed earlier. The basic cause of demand-pull inflation is, therefore, a consistently occurring deficit in the government's budget.

The second basic cause of demand-pull inflation is an increase in population either because of a high birth-rate or because of immigration, legal or illegal. Obviously, increased population broadens the list of needs of an economy, and if these needs are backed up by increased purchasing power, they appear in increased aggregate demand. Thirdly, the changes in expectations about future inflation can also cause inflation to actually take place. Consider, for example that policy makers are only discussing a policy of increasing money supply in the future. When the information is widely available and when the general public knows that an actual implementation of an expansionary monetary policy leads to inflation in the economy, the public expects prices to go up in the future. In order to beat the increasing prices, individuals would rush to the supermarkets and start buying goods and services as early as they could in this case. There is an increase in aggregate demand despite the fact that no policy action has actually taken place. Thus, expectations play a vital role in the behavior of the price level and economists have been paying greater attention to this issue since the mid sixties. But more about that, we will consider in the future.

Lastly, a decreased tax rate which is able to generate higher disposable income can create a demand-pull inflation. As the tax rate decreases, people realize a higher income to use for purchases of goods and services. As the aggregate demand increases, the demand-pull type of inflation may occur. Turning to the cost-push type of inflation, one can point out that it occurs due to increased cost of production and/or decreased aggregate supply of the economy. The cost of production can increase for several reasons. An evident scapegoat is activity of the trade union which demands higher wages. When producers are forced to pay higher wages, they interpret that as an increased cost and pass it on to the consumers by raising the price of the product. Secondly, the prices of raw materials used in the production, the depleting stock of natural resources can also be responsible for the increased cost of production. The OPEC price increases of 1973 and 1978 were two examples of increased price of raw material, namely, gasoline used extensively in the aggregate supply of an economy. In the case of the United States, the gasoline is an important input in almost all productive activities. The impact felt by the U.S. economy in terms of decreased aggregate supply was the greatest. Thirdly, cost-push inflation can also arise because of the natural calamities like heat waves, floods, tornadoes, diseases, and several others. All of these natural events are responsible for a decreased supply in the economy and therefore, a shortage of goods and services.

Thus, inflation can be caused by several demand-pull and several cost-push factors. In reality, most of the inflationary phenomenon arise because of some factors happening from both types we mentioned. It is therefore hard to pinpoint any inflation completely demand-pull or completely cost-push type. In other words, factors causing both of these types of inflations occur simultaneously.

11.3   Consequences of Inflation

Before we can find out the real costs of inflation we have to see some of the imaginary costs of inflation. The imaginary costs of inflation come from the misconceptions held by the general public about inflation. For example, many times non-economists think that inflation worsens the standard of living of an economy. From the historical review of the data, this contention is just not true. Many economies that have experienced inflations have shown a consistent increase rather than decrease in their standard of living. Secondly, it is also incorrectly thought that inflation by itself creates unemployment. Actually, when inflation rises and producers are not initially forced to pay higher wages to compensate such inflation, the expected profit rate becomes high. As expected profit rate or Marginal Efficiency of Investment (MEl) increases and becomes greater than the interest rate, producers find out that it is profitable to undertake additional investment. As investment increases, the multiplier theory from Chapter 7 tells us that the GNP of an economy would increase by a larger amount. Assuming that higher GNP needs more employees to be employed, the increase in GNP leads to increase (rather than decrease) in total employment of our economy. This is the theoretical background of a special theory called the *Phillips curve hypothesis* to which we are going to visit in future chapters. The very analysis of the Phillips curve holds that inflation and unemployment over the long-run have shown a permanent trade-off between each other, as one increases the other decreases. Hence, the conception that higher inflation creates unemployment in the economy is baseless. Thirdly, a layman may take pride in claiming that inflation is always beneficial for the rich and costly to the poor class of a society. This is not always true either. Assuming that the rich community is the one that holds a lot of stock, bonds, and equities, one should not waste any time in pointing out that in inflation, the real value of all of these financial assets would decline. The rich creditors, because of the declining value of money in inflation, are the losers in it while debtors, or those who have borrowed from others are the gainers in inflation. If we think in this aspect, then the general belief which overwhelmingly supports that rich people are beneficiaries in inflation seem untrue. Observing, however, that the government sector is the biggest debtor, in reality there is no doubt that government gains in inflation in terms of the reduced burden it has to pay to the private sector.

Then the logical question is, "What are the real costs of inflation?" Let us observe the real costs one by one. First, any inflation, if left unchecked, exhibits a danger of running away. This is because in inflationary situations the expectations of future inflation become destabilized. Everyone makes guesses in his/her own way about the future inflation. If further inflation is expected in the future, then people increase the present demand for goods and services.

As the demand increases, the prices tend to go even further up and inflation worsens. Also, in inflation, to compensate for the declining value of real wages, the employees, either organized or unorganized, fight for higher wages. If their demands are satisfied by the employers, the recipients get higher purchasing power and the general price level of goods and services goes up further. Inflation, therefore, is seen as a cottonwood tree; once it is planted, it keeps on increasing. A high level of inflation undoubtedly is worse for the economy in terms of real costs than the inflation of small doses. This is because as inflation becomes severe, expectations are more destabilized and runaway inflation is more probable. Runaway inflations as experienced by Argentina, Israel, Mexico, and Brazil in 1980s, are catastrophic to the economy. In these cases, the economic policy makers cannot visualize the correct solutions for the situation. Thus, in the words of Heilbroner and Thurow, "inflation holds the threat of 'running-away'—of quickening its pace until finally the value of money drops to zero and we have a complete social and economic collapse. Even though actual runaway inflation (or hyperinflation) have been very rare, and in all cases the consequence of previous military or social disasters, the specter of such a possibility is profoundly unsettling. This is probably the main reason we perceive inflation to be a danger: It is not so much for what it is, but for what it might become."[1]

Secondly, as briefly mentioned before, inflation lowers the value of monetary assets. The money kept in bank accounts, bonds, insurance policies, stock, etc., lose their value and the families holding these assets are in danger of losing their saving in real terms. Nonetheless, one has to point out the increase in the value of real assets because of the inflation. Anyone who likes to use uncertainty to make profits, would switch from the financial investment to the real investment for using his/her wealth. This gives us a consequence of inflation in terms of redistribution of the resources.

From the social point of view, inflation is seen as an evil because in it, the value of money declines and even if employees make the same amount of money, their wages in real terms go down. Now, consider two classes of wage earners; (a) organized labor, who is aggressive via trade unions and similar organizations, and (b) non-organized labor who has no one to represent in wage negotiations, like minorities, poor, teenagers, and other laborers who cannot make their voices heard. In case of inflation

---

[1] Suggested Reading List: Heilbroner and Thurow (1984), p. 517

the organized labor always gets compensated for the cost of living index or by going on strikes they make employers pay them more. Non-organized labor on the other hand, has no one to represent it, hence, cannot get its money wages raised. Thus, inflation transfers income from non-organized labor which is basically poor and socially repressed, to organized labor. In this regard there is no doubt about the evil cost of inflation because it benefits only organized labor at the cost of non-organized labor.

Lastly, as modern times inflations have shown us, there is a danger of inflation being accompanied by a high rate of unemployment, creating what is popularly called the "stagflation" problem.

How inflation is transferred to high unemployment is not very clear. There are several explanations for stagflation though. One view perceives that high inflation creates high interest rates because the demand for loans from the banks is very high when the price level is rising. As interest rates become higher, there is a possibility that in spite of higher expected profit rate they become greater than the Marginal Efficiency of Investment. In this situation, as we have learned in earlier chapters, the volume of investment will be lowered, creating a lower real GNP growth rate. A lower GNP growth rate necessitates the laying off by the employers giving rise to the high unemployment in the economy. This is a probable channel in which inflation can be the reason for high unemployment. Secondly, some people also believe that when expectations of the employees are formed in which they ask for higher wages as soon as they envision a possible inflation, then stagflation can take place. More specifically, high inflation leads to high wage demands which increase the cost of production. When the cost of production goes up, the aggregate supply of the economy declines as less is being produced with the increased cost. A lower aggregate supply of the economy can create unemployment, thus, inflation can cause higher unemployment in the economy. Lastly, some economists may seem to hold inflation responsible for making policy makers realize that the cure for it is to create unemployment. Hence, the policy makers who would believe in restrictive stabilization policies as a cure for inflation problems would be ready to accept the high unemployment. If their policies are unable to be effective on inflation and unemployment, then both can exist simultaneously.

Thus, inflation which inherits the imaginary as well as real cost, can have some undesirable consequences on other economic variables like GNP and employment. Let us conclude this discussion by emphasizing that there are some severe costs of a very high inflation but small doses of inflation do not hurt the economy, instead they are desirable and beneficial. Also, one has to remember that just like there are some real costs of inflation, there are some imaginary costs as well. In the next section we will consider some points about cures for inflation.

11.4   Cures for Inflation

Just like economists differ in their view about what causes inflation, they also differ about what cures it. No one, however, doubts that a severe depression stops any severe inflation. The problem is therefore not just stopping inflation but returning to economic growth without getting a severe price increase. The first solution comes from the concept that since deficit financing by the government creates basic inflationary pressure, the cure lies in balancing the government budget. Hence, a balanced budget is a good remedy for inflation if at all government is able to balance its budget. But balancing the budget necessitates either increase in taxes or reduction in government expenditure or both. All these solutions are politically unacceptable, therefore the balanced budget solution even if it seems plausible, has limited applicability and acceptance by governmental authorities.

The second solution for inflation comes from the monetarists' idea of monetary rule or adopting a tighter monetary policy. Since monetarists believe that too much money chasing too few goods is the only probable way to describe inflation, the solution of inflation lies in putting brakes on the flow of the money supply generated by the monetary policy. The policy of tight money can be a very effective anti-inflationary policy if it is carried on with relentless persistence. Many times as the price level comes down because of the reduced growth rate of the money supply, monetary authorities celebrate the success by pumping more money into the system. This overambitious response can adversely affect the expectation of the public and may discredit the success already achieved. Moreover, when the government sector is incurring a debt because of its deficit financing, the money supply cannot be held in check for a long time. As we described earlier, a non-monetized debt only leads to an increased interest rate, as the government competes with the private sector for borrowing money. As the interest rate increases, there is more pressure on the monetary policy to ease up on the money supply of the economy. Nonetheless, tight monetary policy as a tool to solve the inflationary problem is widely accepted and several countries have paid the price of a recession to solve the excessive price increase.

The third solution of inflation is seen in terms of what is popularly referred to as incomes policy. This involves either voluntary or mandatory price and wage controls. In case of voluntary wage and price controls, government announces guidelines for the employers to obey to voluntarily check the wage-price spiral. The wage-price spiral is the vicious circle held by the increase in wages that is responsible for increasing aggregate demand and cost of production making it necessary for producers to charge the higher prices. As prices go up there is more demand for increased wages. Income policy that requests producers to voluntarily control wages and prices is effective if all employers agree to it. Obviously when inflation is of a high degree, income policy's effectiveness is limited.

When inflation is out of hand and governments do not have any other resort to apply, they tend to consider mandatory price controls which involve an announcement of prices of certain goods and an implementation of administrative machinery to oversee the allocation of the announced prices. Price control, in fact, can solve the problem of inflation instantly. If governments take charge and compulsorily ask producers to obey the guidelines, then inflation should come under control. However, as Arthur Lewis puts it, "Price control is a delicate instrument, easily misused." To justify his statement there are several points. First, price controls cannot be a long-run phenomenon because if they tend to be so, then there is a 'resource allocation effect.' One has to be aware that price controls are not needed for luxury goods as opposed to necessary goods. The prices of luxury goods should go up, that is what any government would want, because as prices increase, the quantity demanded goes down; and considering that luxuries are not very necessary, that is exactly desirable for an economy. Hence, price controls when adopted, would be used only for the necessities. If price controls tend to be of a long-run nature, producers of luxuries would make profit at a higher rate than those of necessities.

There would obviously be an incentive for producers to switch their resources from the production of necessities to the production of luxuries. In the long-run, this is certainly not beneficial for the economy. Secondly, if price controls are to be implemented for a short-run, then there is a bubble-effect for the prices. The producers, in order to cover up the losses, would increase the prices a lot higher when price control policy is discussed by the policy makers. Also, a short-run price control would encourage hoarding of goods and services creating an artificial shortage leading to increase in price and adding to the bubble-effect. Hence, the government has to decide beforehand the length of time price controls are to be implemented. Thirdly, since price controls are always used to reduce prices, they mandatorily lower the prices of goods and services from their natural levels. At any price below the natural price, there is a higher quantity demanded by the consumers and a lower quantity supplied by the producers.

To adopt the policy of price control is to create a deliberate shortage. Obviously, there would be individuals who would like to buy more at the lowered price which can create supply problems. Hence, price controls should always be backed up by quantity controls. Quantity controls (or rationing) have an administrative cost because they require able and efficient administration which is exactly what many countries lack. Fourthly, there are some individuals who would need the commodity more than some others. For example, gasoline is a commodity consumed and needed more by the people who commute to their work place than by those who do not. Hence, it is perfectly possible that some people would be ready and able to offer a price higher than other people would be ready and able to. This creates an illegal market for that commodity which puts even further burden on the administrative machinery. Lastly, price controls can influence the quality of the product if they are allowed to prevail for a long time. Especially in food items, quality of the product is hard to measure and when producers are told that they cannot charge more than the specified amount for certain food items, the easiest way for them is to reduce the quality of that product. Hence, price controls need to be backed up not only by quantity controls but also by quality controls. This is therefore a circle where one can easily get in but one would find it hard to get out.

In general terms, we may conclude by stating that even if price controls are an attractive weapon to be used, they require tremendous administration and they cannot be of a long-run duration. One has to be very cautious in using this delicate instrument. Having said so much about the cures of inflation, we have come close to an end of this chapter. To reiterate, we discussed the causes of inflation in demand-pull and cost-push types; we talked about the imaginary and real costs of it and we also summarized the most popular solutions for it. In the next chapter, our aim is to analyze the inflationary and recessionary rounds the economy occasionally has to suffer. These cycles are called business fluctuations and they create a constant headache for the policy makers who presume that solving these fluctuations is their responsibility.

Suggested Additional Reading for Chapter 11

1. Birch, Dan E,, Alan A. Rabin, and L. B. Yeager. "Inflation, Output and Employment: Some Clarifications." *Economic Inquiry*, Vol. 20 April 1982: 209-221.

2. Federal Reserve. "Federal Reserve Readings on Inflation." Federal Reserve Bank of New York. February 1979.

3. Frisch, Helmut. "Inflation Theory 1963-1975: A Second Generation Survey." *Journal of Economic Literature*, December 1977.

4. Glahe, Fred R. *Macroeconomics*, 3rd ed. Harcourt, Brace, and Jovanovich, 1985. Chapter 13.

5. Gordon, Robert. *Macroeconomics*, 3rd ed. Little Brown Publishers, 1984. Chapters 8, 9, 10.

6. Gordon, Robert. "The Theory of Domestic Inflation." *American Economic Review*, Vol. 67, February 1977: 128-134.

7. Heibroner and Thurow. *The Economic Problem*. 7th ed. New Jersey: Prentice-Hall, Inc., 1984. Chapter 32.

8. "Inflation: Long-Term Problems." Edited by C. Lowell Hariss. New York: Praeger Publishers, 1975.

9. Lewis, Arthur. Principles of Economic Planning. 1968.

Business Fluctuations and Their Theoretical Explanations

12

12.1 Introduction

Any capitalistic economy shows some duration of prosperity and some other periods of recession and even depression. These cyclical fluctuations in the economic activity of an economy are referred to as business fluctuations, or business cycles. Theoretically, one can term each segment of the business cycle separately as recovery, prosperity, recession and depression. In this chapter, we intend to survey these stages of a business cycle and investigate some of the explanations of their occurrence. Starting from William Jevons in the nineteenth century, there have been several economists who attempted to explain the causes of business cycles. In modern times, governmental authorities are more aware of the adverse effects a recession or depression can have on the economy. The policies designed to solve the problem of business cycles are called stabilization policies. The big question discussed quite often in economic literature is whether government should intervene in the economic affairs and try to adjust the economy or not. Those who believe in the intervention are called interventionists who basically consist of Keynesians and neo-Keynesians. Those who claim that government intervention is unnecessary and undesirable are called non-interventionists, and they consist of monetarists and new classical economists. In this chapter we also intend to review the controversial arguments of these groups.

12.2   What Are Business Cycles?

In order to explain the meaning of a business cycle, let us assume for simplicity that a systematic cycle appears as shown in Figure 12.1, in the given duration of time. Also assume that without cyclical fluctuations, the real GNP of an economy would grow at a constant percentage as shown by the horizontal line. Real GNP measure is the primary measure of economic activity— the final goods and services transactions. Hence, fluctuations in real GNP is a reliable proxy for measuring the business fluctuations.

One can observe that assuming a cyclical growth of actual real GNP of an economy, in Figure 12.1 in the time period t_0 to t_1, the growth rate is declining. This means that the economy is suffering the loss of resources, decreased productivity, increased unemployment but stable or declining prices in this period. The segment of the business cycle in this time period, AB, is referred to as the 'depression.' Point B is called the 'trough' because at that point, the growth rate of real GNP is the lowest. This is obviously the worst situation an economy can experience in terms of employment opportunities, social disorder and the general performance.

After point B however, the economy starts picking up its growth path as more jobs are offered. The growth rate of real GNP increases and from time t_1 to t_2, a 'recovery' stage of the business cycle prevails. In this stage the economy recovers from the lowest point of growth, still, the growth rate of actual real GNP is not as high as the growth rate that would have prevailed without the existence of the business cycle.

After the recovery stage has been completed, the economy experiences an increase in real GNP at a faster rate than the constant real GNP growth rate. In the economy, a faster growth of real GNP means more jobs are opened, more transactions are done, and the economy is using its capacity at the highest rate.

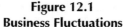

Figure 12.1
Business Fluctuations

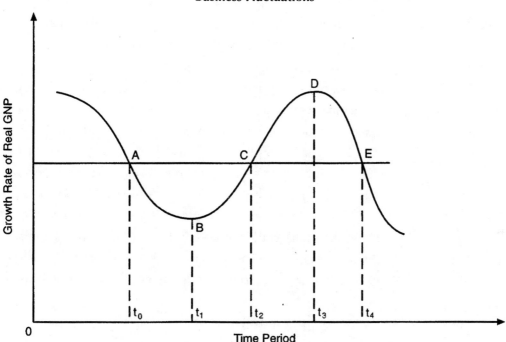

This can also mean that the prices are increasing in certain sectors of the economy. This is likely to happen because some sectors would use their resources earlier than others and if the demand for the products produced in these sectors keep increasing, then the prices in those sectors would rise faster. Using all the available resources and increasing the production at the highest rate means the economy is experiencing 'prosperity.'This stage is shown by time period from t_2 to t_3 in Figure 12.1. After some time of prosperity, the economy approaches the 'peak' point of the cycle. At the peak point, growth of the economy occurs at the highest rate, and the economy tends to employ all the resources available.

For the reasons that we are going to discuss later, after the peak point the economy starts growing at a slower rate. The productivity is high but declining in this time period. This stage is depicted in Figure 12.1 by the time period t_3 to t_4 and is called 'recession.'

The recession stage is similar to depression except that in it, the actual real GNP growth rate is higher than that of the GNP that increases at the constant rate. The prices tend to be stable in this time period and the unemployment is increasing.

Two points should be clarified about the definition of the stages of the business cycle. First, even if Figure 12.1 shows a systematic cyclical path of the growth of real GNP of an imaginary economy, in practice, no country is expected to or has experienced such a systematic cyclical path. The durations of each stage are likely to change according to the case under consideration. Second, the very fact that the business cycles do not appear as shown in the Figure 12.1, makes it necessary to correctly predict the future path an economy is likely to take and apply the policy options to adjust for the stabilization. These jobs are performed by the forecasters and the policy makers, respectively.

12.3   The Causes of Business Fluctuations

Among the theoretical explanations available, the foremost is the one given by an economist of the nineteenth century, William Jevons. According to Jevons, the business fluctuations can occur because of the natural condition that can change because of the kind and (sometimes unkind) weather. Obviously, when Jevons was writing, the main sector of production in the economy was the agricultural sector. As the weather favored the production in the agricultural sector, the economy prospered with a great speed, and there was visible prosperity in the economy. When the weather was not that cooperative, the prosperity was not as evident and the economy suffered from the recession and depression. Hence, the basic cause of business fluctuations according to this theory, was mother nature or the sunspots. As a result, this theory of Jevons' is called, the 'sunspots theory.'

The second explanation of the reasons of business cycle occurrence can be found in the celebrated theory of Joseph Schumpeter. In his mind, Schumpeter visualized that the growth of an economy basically takes place because of the work of some important class of people whom he refers to as innovators. Innovators are the persons who are responsible for the improvement in technology, who carry out research and development activities, who are production oriented and whose activities are the key for the growth of an economy. The main reason for the business cycles in the economy, according to Schumpeter, is the psychology of the innovators. If innovators expect the economy to prosper in the future with a good speed then they work hard and carry out the inventions with the zest and intensity that are higher than what they would if they had no expectations about the prosperity in the future. As the innovator decides to carry out investment activity, he borrows money from the bank and the process of the money multiplier takes place. Other innovators are offered similar loans and the economic activity is enhanced. This is the reason prosperity occurs in the economy. When the innovators do not expect a bright future, then the borrowing is not carried out with the same speed as before and the stage of recession begins. Hence, it is the expectation level of the innovators that gives the main impetus to the economy for the growth in the future. The idea of the class of innovators in Schumpeter's theory puts a great amount of credit to the producers class as compared to the agriculturist class in the Jevons' theory. Nonetheless, in modern times, with an increase in the industrial sector to a degree of the prime importance, what Schumpeter advocated seems logical. It is undoubtedly true that the main source of modern time growth in the economy is the innovation in that economy. No wonder Schumpeter's theory of business cycles is considered to be the major convincing explanation of the fluctuations in the economic activity.

Another popular theory of the business cycle is offered from the *secular stagnation hypothesis* by Alvin Hansen of Harvard University. The idea used in this hypothesis is strictly Keynesian in a sense that it perceives the decline in the marginal propensity to consume of an economy when the economy becomes richer. As Keynes had argued before Hansen, when the economy prospers and gets richer, the propensity to consume becomes less; which as you may recall, affects the value of the multiplier process, this increases the GNP of an economy and there is a growth of the country. As this process of growth continues for a while, the economy becomes rich, and the rich economy has a lower propensity to consume than a poor economy. Obviously, this means the value of the multiplier (the investment multiplier, of K in Chapter 7) goes down because of this. Any increase in investment would not create as much increase in the equilibrium GNP if the multiplier is smaller than before. Naturally, this would cause a smaller growth of the economy in the next round. Thus, the propensity itself is responsible for a slower growth of an economy according to the *secular stagnation hypothesis*. When the economy is in the downturn of the business cycle, exactly opposite changes would take place. As the economy progresses with a negative growth, it becomes poorer, and the poor economies would experience an increase in the value of the marginal propensity to consume. Thus, the business cycle may occur because of the natural tendencies of the MPC value to change, as the economy becomes prosperous or poorer.

The third explanation of the business cycle fluctuation is obtained in the theory of another great economist, Paul Samuelson. Samuelson's theory is based on the same idea as the *secular stagnation hypothesis*, but it goes one step further in recognizing another important concept called an accelerator. The accelerator shows us the effect of an increase in GNP on the investment level of an economy. To obtain the value of the accelerator in notational form, let us suppose that the total stock of capital in the economy is K and the output of the economy is Y so that K/Y represents the capital including all the physical capital like the buildings, furniture, land, forests, real estate, and other property.

The value of the capital output ratio is a lot greater than one. Let us denote this ratio by 'a.'

$$\text{Therefore, } a = K/Y \text{ or } K = a * (y)$$

assuming that 'a' is constant, any change in the capital stock is caused by a change in the output level, Y. Hence, $\Delta K = a * Y$, but a change in the capital stock of an economy is no different than the investment undertaken in that economy at any given time. Therefore, the left hand side of the above equation can be replaced by investment, I. This gives us, $\Delta I = a * \Delta Y$.

We now have a relationship between the investment of an economy and the GNP of that economy. Comparing this with the multiplier equation of Chapter 7, which shows GNP, Y, to be dependent of the investment, I, we can get the basic two equations of the accelerator-multiplier theory of Samuelson as follows:

$$\Delta I = a * \Delta Y \qquad \text{accelerator equation and}$$
$$\Delta Y = k * \Delta I \qquad \text{multiplier equation}$$

Now let us suppose that there is an initial increase in the investment of an economy, this would create an increase in the GNP via the multiplier process as shown in the multiplier equation. As the level of GNP increases, it creates a further increase in the investment of the economy. This again increases the investment and the chain continues. This is obviously the explanation of the stage of prosperity of the business cycle in that economy. Then the big question is why does this process of increase in investment and the output slow down? To answer that question, consider an application of the *secular stagnation hypothesis*. As the economy becomes prosperous, the value of mpc declines and the multiplier becomes smaller. In that case, an increase in investment does not cause a great change in output. Since the output does not cause a great change by a large amount, the investment does not increase by a large amount either. Leading to the same process as before, there is no growth in the economy. This is an explanation of the recession or depression in the economy. Considering the natural tendencies of the economy of the multiplier and accelerator processes, this theory does sound very convincing.

Another explanation of the business cycle is seen in the political steps taken by the administration in an election cycle. In other words, a change in an administration cycle makes it necessary that a business cycle occurs. For example, let us suppose that a new administration has been elected and the policies are not exuberant so that the process of the multiplier and accelerator discussed above are not underway very vigorously. But when the time of re-election comes, the concern is to stimulate the economy so that adventurous projects are undertaken, money supply is high, infrastructure is built and unemployment is low. Such policies tend to affect the level of output and employment first, the price level with a somewhat longer lag. If the timing is right, the inflation will not show up until after the election is safely decided. Again, when the inflation does appear after the re-election, it can be solved by paying the price of a recession. Thus, the political changes themselves cause the business fluctuations and the government is the most responsible party for it. The last explanation of the business cycle points out that man-made causes like wars, revolutions, strikes, and lockouts are the basic cause of the fluctuating supply of the economy. Obviously, when one accepts the reality of the man-made disturbances in the economy, one does not need any other explanation for a business cycle. The next point we want to consider is the relevance of the responsibility of the government sector to adopt the policies that can cure business fluctuations. There are believers of the explanation that business cycles are caused by the government, hence, it has no control or authority or capability to cure them. The class of economists, namely the monetarists, strongly advocates that the government should not try controlling the business cycles of the economy.

However, monetarists form only the vocal minority and the economists and politicians alike have for a long time argued that the government should and could try to stabilize the economy from the business fluctuations. This, therefore, sets a stage for a controversy that has been debated in the economic literature very strongly by both sides. Those who argue that government intervention is desirable are referred to as interventionists and those who object to the increased role of the government sector are called non-interventionists. In the next section we will consider both sides briefly.

12.4   Is the Government Interference Desirable?

To consider the controversy, let us first analyze the point mentioned by the non-interventionist. As mentioned before, non-interventionists claim that the interference by the government sector is unnecessary and undesirable. To support their belief they put forward the permanent income hypothesis constructed by Professor Milton Friedman which states that consumption spending, which is the largest part of the aggregate demand, is the stable function of the permanent level of GNP of an economy. As a consequence, this means that the level of spending, excluding the minor changes in the investment, is basically a stable concept. Another basic stabilizing factor according to non- interventionists is the flatness of the IS curve due to a special reason as follows: Monetarists claim that investment is just a part of the total demand that depends on the interest rate. If it is so, then investment is more interest sensitive than Keynesians claim. This creates a flatter IS curve because as we saw in Chapter 8, the slope of the IS curve depends upon the interest sensitivity of the investment function.

The second point non-interventionists put forward is the fact that the price level is flexible and before the government could correct output from the drastic fluctuation, the price level would have come to an equilibrium level and the policy in this case would have been unnecessarily too late. In other words, the stabilization policies need some time to be effective and the price level is not very rigid to stay at the level for all that time. There are at least three time lags recognized by the non-interventionist. The first one is called the 'recognition' lag which is the time needed for a policy authority to recognize the need for a policy change after a disturbance in the economy has taken place. Let us suppose for example, a natural disaster like a flood occurs in a part of the economy. This can create a supply shock for the economy and therefore, can be considered as a disturbance that needs a correction from the government. It would still take about a week for governmental authorities to realize the situation is serious enough to take an action of correction. This one week is the recognition lag in this case. Secondly, even after the need for a policy action is recognized, policy authorities take time to implement the policy change. This time is called the 'implementation' lag. Generally speaking, monetary policy has a brief implementation lag as compared to the one needed for fiscal policy. Nonetheless, both the above mentioned lags are under the control of the governmental authorities. Hence, together they are called 'inside lags.' The third lag is outside the control of the government, hence, is referred to as the 'outside lag.' This is the time needed for the policy action to show its effects on the economy. Effectiveness of any policy action is measured by the increase in the GNP level it can cause. The higher is the increase in the GNP, the more is the effectiveness of the policy.

Every policy change needs certain time to show its impact on the economy. Moreover, monetarists as we saw before, believe that the impact lag for the fiscal policy is infinite because of the complete crowding out, and the impact lag for the monetary policy can be infinite if the economy is very close to the full employment stage. In Chapter 15 we discuss these lags in greater detail.

The third point that is made by the non-interventionist relates to the harm that the policy action can do to the economy in spite of the fact that the price level and aggregate demand are inflexible. They claim that the forecasting ability of the economists is too limited so that they cannot correctly perceive what change has to be made for a permanent solution of the instability. Further, uncertainty in the policy effectiveness adds an additional source of disturbance that makes the economy less stable than would occur without any changes in the policy decision.

Lastly, non-interventionists also proclaim that in the long-run, the stability of the private sector is more guaranteed than in the short-run because of the higher price flexibility in the long-run than in the short-run. Therefore, they advocate that the monetary policy follow a monetary rule and the fiscal policy be conservative and carry out only very necessary services such as maintenance of law and order.

Interventionists, on the other hand, have several points that they like to put forward in support of government intervention in economic affairs. First, they claim that the forecasting ability and the theoretical underpinning is at a higher level in modern times than in the past. Economists can have more information, they can use better econometric techniques and they have more experience with policy activism than before, which gives us a strong reason to continue government intervention rather than curtail it. This increased forecasting ability has been emphasized by several neo-Keynesians including Modigliani, Tobin and Gordon. Moreover, they make an observation that stabilization activism has taken the economy out of trouble more than it has gotten it into disorder. Also, the time lags mentioned before are likely to be shorter in the modern time than in the past because of the increased predictive power. Secondly, the interventionists do not agree with the monetarists' belief that the markets are basically stable. Due to a lack of information everywhere and due to the lack of capability of the individuals to use the available information, it is inconceivable that the market would be perfectly stable by itself. It is therefore not appropriate that the government stop its stabilizing efforts.

Lastly, but most importantly, many economists just do not agree with the non-interventionists on the grounds that government passivism is an impractical thing in the modern times. In most of the free world the government sector has become so widespread that everywhere we go there is something involved with government action. The public sector offers several thousand jobs, it owns huge amounts of capital, it controls the day-to-day transactions of several businesses and therefore, in general, it is just not possible to get rid of the government presence in the next few years. Hence, several economists look at government interference as a fixture of the permanent existence and therefore, do not agree with the non-interventionists that there should be no active role by the government in the economy.

Then the question still remains, why is it that government intervention of any degree has not eliminated business fluctuations from the modern free economies?

One reason for that is the failure of the forecasters. And there are several reasons for the forecasting errors. Forecasters make their forecasts by assuming several policy instrument settings. Often, this assumption proves to be unrealistic. Also, there are many non-policy exogenous changes that occur and the forecasts about the future economic events have to be revised. For example, the OPEC nations' increase in the price of gasoline in 1973 (and 1979) was pretty much unexpected. Hence, forecasters at that time failed to correctly forecast any of the economic events past 1973. Obviously, the government policy actions that were based on the forecasts that did not recognize the exogenous event like the increase in the price of gasoline, was liable to fail in achieving its desired target. To solve this problem in modern times, forecasters and others have started making forecasts for different scenarios. Secondly, the econometric models used for making the forecast have become comprehensive in their nature only in the recent past. Use of computer technology has greatly increased the reliability of these models, hence, the interventionists see much hope for future success in the government activism.

Lastly, as a compromise to the debate of the desirability of the government activism, we may state an obvious fact about the popular rule called 'Effective Market Classification' rule. This rule states that the number of policy instruments must be matched by the number of targets a policy is trying to achieve. For example, if we want to move to another place by a bus then the bus engine is the instrument to move in one direction and the bus driver's wheel is the instrument to move in another direction. Therefore, any place on the map can be accessible by rotating these two instruments. Hence, the target of moving in two directions can only be satisfied by having two instruments to get to those targets. Moreover, EMC rule claims that the instruments should be used for that target on which it has the maximum effect. If monetary policy has an effect on the price level and also on the exchange rate of the domestic currency, then it should be used to control only price level if it is more effective for making changes in the prices rather than the exchange rate. In more general terms, there are two things government authorities have to keep in mind. First, they should not try to achieve any more targets than the available number of instruments. Second, they should assign the policy instrument for that target on which it has the maximum effect to satisfy the condition of the Effective Market Classification rule.

After having said so much about the controversy between two groups of economists, our next concern is to find out more about a theory that is the cornerstone of our time—increased role of the government sector in the free economies. That theory is the product of a hypothesis put forward by an economist named Arthur W. Phillips. To discuss the Phillips curve hypothesis is the main aim of our next chapter.

Suggested Additional Reading for Chapter 12

1.   Clark, J. M. "Business Fluctuations and the Law of Demand." *Journal of Political Economy*, March 1917: 217-235.

2.   Ekeland, Robert B. Jr. and Robert Tollison. *Macroeconomics*. Boston: Little Brown and Company, 1985. Chapter 17.

3.   Hayek, Friednich A. *Monetary Theory and the Trade Cycle*. New York: Harcourt Brace and Jovanovich Publishers, 1932.

4.   Heilbroner and Thurow. *The Economic Problem*, 7th ed. New Jersey: Prentice Hall Publishers, 1984. Chapter 18.

5.   Hicks, John R. *A Contribution to the Theory of the Trade Cycle*. Oxford: Oxford University Press, 1950.

6.   McConnell, Campbell R. *Economics*, 9th ed. McGraw Hill Publishers, 1984. Chapter 10.

7.   Schumpeter, Joseph. *Capitalism, Socialism, and Democracy*, 3rd ed. New York: Harper and Row Publishers, 1950: 81-86.

Phillips Curve Hypothesis: Old and New and Effectiveness of Macro-Policies

13

13.1   Introduction

No other theory in the sixties about policy activism was more influential than that of Arthur William Housego Phillips, originally of the London School of Economics, but who wrote a celebrated article from the Australian National University in 1958 about the empirical observations he made of the U.K. economy. His theory developed into what is popularly referred to as the *Phillips curve hypothesis*. Many economists and politicians around the world held views for or against the advocacy of the Phillips curve, and it became a very dominant philosophy in the making of policy. In the United States, the Kennedy and Johnson administrations were clearly influenced by this way of thinking, and in general, all over the free world governments engaged in adventurous activism because of the impetus offered by the Phillips curve hypothesis.

By late 1960s however, the monetarists school vehemently attacked the recommendations of the Phillips curve as too much government intervention led to high inflation all around the world. There remained several faithful neo-Keynesians who still supported the message offered by the Phillips curve hypothesis. By 1970 this issue emerged as yet another reason for controversy between the two groups of economists: monetarists and neo-Keynesians.

Our main purpose in this chapter is to review the Phillips curve hypothesis and investigate further recent developments in this theory. Naturally, we also intend to analyze the controversy that surrounds the hypothesis.

13.2   What is the Phillips Curve Hypothesis?

Phillips observed the data of the U.K. economy for the 96 years from 1861 to 1957, regarding the percentage increase in the wage rate and the unemployment rate (unemployment rate here was taken as an index of the degree of excess demand of 'labor shortage' in the labor market). He found that there had been a trade-off between these two variables in the long-run. This means that whenever money wages increased faster, the unemployment rate declined. Hence, on the outset, the Phillips curve hypothesis is just an observation that the money wage rate and the unemployment rate of the economy have an inverse relationship. This relationship is shown in Figure 13.1. There was obviously nothing revolutionary about finding a relationship like this, what was clearly prolific was Phillip's explanation of this relationship. He argued that there can be two economic reasons that are responsible for the trade-off.

Secondly, as the wage rate went up, the higher purchasing power was created that led to a higher aggregate demand. This higher aggregate demand was thought to be responsible for the increased price level and the improved expected profit rate. This higher expected profit rate must have caused higher investment in the economy. Increased investment via the multiplier process creates higher output and employment. To Phillips, it did not seem completely evolutionary and illogical to post an inverse relationship between the increase in the money wage rate and the unemployment rate.

After Phillips produced his results for the U.K. economy, there happened a string of other studies, some of which clearly supported the observations of the Phillips trade-off and some

Figure 13.1
The Original Phillips Curve

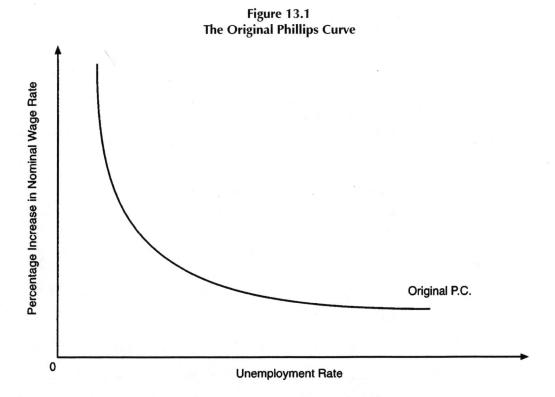

others disputed them. Developments and repetition were also accompanied by modifications. In recent years, economists began to interpret the original Phillips relationship in terms of inflation and unemployment rather than wage rate increase and the unemployment rate as Phillips did. The substitution of the inflation rate for the percentage increase in wage rate was logical since the inflation rate is proportionately related to the increase in the wage rate. In order to show this mathematically, let us assume that the wage rate is determined by the value of the marginal product of labor. As you may recall, the marginal product of labor is the increase in the total product and the product of labor is the increase in the total product due to employment of the last labor unit. The value of the marginal product is the product of the price of the product and the marginal product of labor.

Obviously, a producer would be willing to employ labor up to that point at which the value of the marginal product of labor is

equal to the wage rate the labor is earning. In mathematical nota-
tions we can write:

wage rate = price of the product * marginal product of labor,
or,
$$W = P * MP$$
Where W = money wage rate, P = price level and
MP = marginal product of labor

Assuming that the marginal product of labor is constant, and
totally differentiating the above equation,

$$\Delta W = \Delta P * MP + \Delta MP * P$$

Since MP is constant, MP is zero. Therefore, we have:

$$\Delta W = \Delta P * MP$$

Dividing both sides of this equation by W, we get the desired
result:

$$\frac{\Delta W}{W} = \frac{\Delta P * MP}{P * MP} = \frac{\Delta P}{P}$$

The percentage increase in the wage rate is exactly equal to the
percentage increase in the price level. Hence, it is possible to
view the Phillips curve relationship in terms of the trade-off
between the inflation rate and the unemployment rate. Figure
13.2 shows such a trade-off about which we can say the following
things.

The Phillips curve in Figure 13.2 is the curve made popular by
several empirical studies carried out in the early and middle sixties to prove the point that there is a trade-off between inflation
and the unemployment of the economy. By itself, a trade-off of
this sort means that the governmental policies cannot solve both
the problems of the economy simultaneously. The policy makers

Figure 13.2
Modern Times Phillips Curve

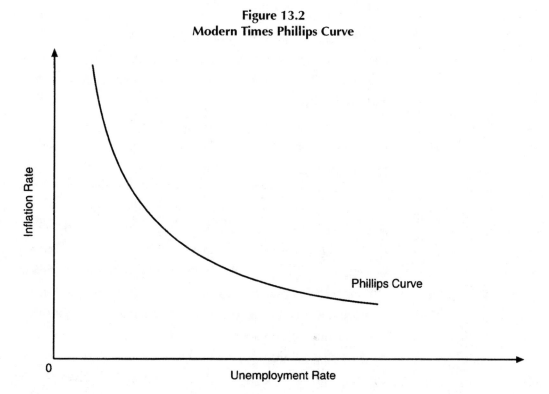

have to be ready to pay the price of inflation to solve the unemployment and vice versa. The position of this curve determines the available combinations of the inflation and unemployment. Any combination on the right of this curve is unfavorable for the policy makers as they represent worsening of both the evils in the economy. Any combination on the left of this curve is preferable to the one on the right of it, but it is unattainable by any policy change. Hence, the combinations on the left of this curve would be socially acceptable but practically impossible for the policy makers to arrive at. Nonetheless, policy makers have an option to select any combination on the curve that they find socially bearable. This type of thinking based upon assistance offered by the Phillips curve was dominant in the industrialized countries in the sixties. Policy makers did not hesitate to adopt the expansionary policies when they thought the unemployment in the economy was too high.

The readiness for paying the price of inflation to solve the problem of unemployment was widespread in the sixties, and at least in the short-run we did witness significant growth in these economies. The Phillips curve hypothesis looked very impressive and extremely practical.

The experiences of the late sixties and seventies, however, did not repeat the success achieved by the earlier policy changes, and the economies of most of the industrialized world were beset by the simultaneous existence of inflation and unemployment popularly labeled stagflation phenomenon. Besides claiming that the stagflation implied points off the Phillips curve to the right side, there was no theoretical explanation in existence. Some economists argued in favor of even more policy activism by pointing out that the Phillips curve has shifted to the right and an economy in modern times must be ready to pay a higher price of inflation to solve the same amount of unemployment as before. They believed that the main reason for this increased sacrifice was the closeness of the economy to the full employment level. As the economy uses most of its available resources, it becomes difficult to employ further labor and this is the reason for the requirement of higher prices in terms of inflation to solve the same problem of unemployment as before. This explanation, however, did not convince many other economists, especially the monetarists. However, before we examine the monetarist analysis, let us consider the shape of the Phillips curve under special Classical and Keynesian beliefs.

On the theoretical levels, the shape of the Phillips curve can be significantly different when we consider these special thoughts of Classicals and Keynesians. The Classicals believe that there is always full employment in the economy because of the complete flexibility of the price level, wage rate and the interest rate. Given this belief, no amount of unemployment can be reduced by any amount of inflation. Therefore, in classical analysis, the shape of the Phillips curve would be vertical. Second, in the Keynesian analysis, in the short-run there was a complete flexibility of the aggregate supply of the economy. Keynes did not see any price and wage flexibility because of his observations of the trade unions activity. This belief could lead to a horizontal aggregate supply curve and a horizontal Phillips curve in the Keynesian analysis. Keeping aside these extreme cases, we have considered the Phillips curve of downward sloping from left to right and have discussed the policy options of it. Now we must consider the facts of the late sixties and the early seventies concerning the simultaneous existence of inflation and unemployment in several developed economies.

The existence of stagflation created doubts about the shape of the Phillips curve. According to the standard Phillips curve analysis of the 1960s, one would have expected an increasing inflation rate of the late sixties to accompany a declining unemployment rate. In the late sixties, none of these things happened. Far from purchasing lower unemployment, escalated inflation evidently was required to keep the unemployment rate fixed. The second reason for the increased skepticism of the Phillips curve trade-off, as Humphrey (1973) sees it, was the increased evidence that the relationship shown by the Phillips curve might not be as stable or as consistent as was commonly believed. In fitting the Phillips relationship empirically, there was a large degree of dispersion, or variance of the actual inflation-unemployment about the fitted values. In Humphrey's words, ". . . two-variable Phillips relationship was shown to be very loose and inexact." These findings ultimately led an increasing number of economists to question the consistence, uniqueness and stability of the short-run Phillips curve. However, questioning the logic of the Phillips curve hypothesis did not come on the empirical basis alone.

On the theoretical side, Milton Friedman, of the University of Chicago, and Edmond Phelps, of the University of Pennsylvania established the *accelerationist theory*, or what is popularly referred to as the *natural rate hypothesis (NRH)*. This hypothesis

Figure 13.3
Accelerationists' Phillips Curve

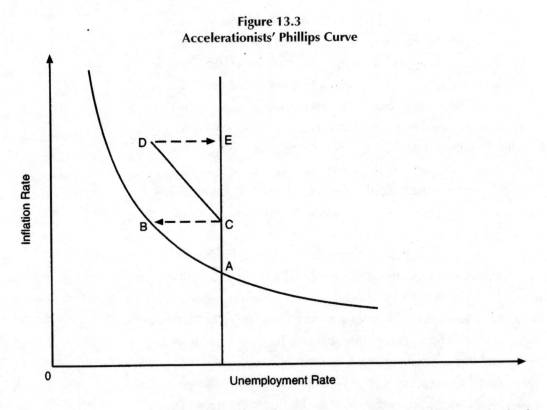

claims that the expectations about future inflation are the basic cause of nonexistence of the trade-off between inflation and unemployment at least in the long-run. In a nutshell, their view holds that the policy makers cannot solve the problem of unemployment in the long-run no matter how much inflation they are ready to offer as the price of unemployment. This implies a vertical shape for the long-run Phillips curve. In order to understand the accelerationist's hypothesis, consider a chain of events that would take place in terms of Figure 13.3. Let us assume that the economy is at point A initially where there is large unemployment and relatively low inflation. Looking at the possibility of reducing the unemployment at the cost of inflation, the policy makers should be tempted to implement expansionary policies, the situation in the economy can be explained by a northwest movement on the Phillips curve from point A to point B. Point B shows a reduction of unemployment at the cost of additional inflation in the economy.

Accelerationists claim that people would, in the long-run, at point B, realize that their real income is less than at point A because of the inflation. When the price level goes up, the real wage, defined as the ratio of nominal wage and the price level, would go down. As the people realize the loss of their real income, they could react in at least two ways. First, they would ask for higher money wages to compensate for their loss of real wage and if the employers do not agree to their demands, that can lead to wide-spread layoffs. Second, if they do not ask for the higher wages, the employees would start looking for another job that would pay them more. As additional persons begin to search for the new jobs, the unemployment in the economy would increase. The situation in the economy in the long-run would be expressed by a horizontal movement from point B in Figure 13.3. Notice that there is no reduction in inflation when this increase in unemployment is occurring.

Obviously, the job search of the people who realized the loss of their real income, continues as long as there is the same wage rate and the same amount of unemployment as before. Hence, the economy would be in a stable situation only at point C. Again, noticing that there is an increase in the unemployment in the economy, the policy makers would be anxious to take the economy in the northwest direction by carrying out another round of expansionary fiscal and monetary policies. This type of reaction by the policy makers would be explained by the movement from point C to D in Figure 13.3. Again, at point D in the long-run, people would realize the loss of real income and their response to that realization would be the same as before. This creates the movement from point D to point E on the horizontal plane.

When we consider long-run equilibrium, then only points A, C, and E would be observed, resulting in a vertical shape for the Phillips curve. Hence, the accelerationists argue that in the long-run, no government action can be successful in creating a permanent decline in the unemployment of the economy. In the long-run there is no trade-off between inflation and unemployment that tends to persist in the economy and the one that cannot be cured by any payment of inflation, is called the natural rate of unemployment. The accelerationists hypothesis that claims the existence of a natural rate of unemployment, is called the *natural rate hypothesis*. In terms of the policy consequences, the monetarists and the accelerationists would prefer to see no activism on the part of the government, since no amount of activism is going to permanently cure any amount of unemployment.

However, not all the economists agree with the position taken by the accelerationists. Basically, they differ on the shape of the long-run Phillips curve. While accelerationists argue for a vertical shape, the non- accelerationists insist that the long-run shape of the Phillips curve is only steeper than the shape of the short- run Phillips curve. As long as there is a downward slope to the curve in question, there are trade-off opportunities for the policy makers. Moreover, for the long-run policy options, a steeper Phillips curve only means that the policy makers should be ready to pay a higher price in terms of the inflation to solve the problem of unemployment. In terms of Figure 13.4, there is a clockwise movement in the horizontal direction but the movement is not as complete, even in the long-run, as the accelerationists claim.

Obviously, the accelerationists would disagree with the charge made against them. More specifically, they put forward the argument about the natural tendency of the market forces to cure its own problem and therefore, there is no need for the changes in the governmental actions. Nonetheless, the controversy between the monetarists and the non-monetarists is as intense as ever about the desirability of the policy options and actions from the government sector. As we are going to concentrate on this topic in future chapters, suffice it to say here that the detailed analysis of the thought of these economists on this particular issue is very

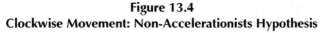

Figure 13.4
Clockwise Movement: Non-Accelerationists Hypothesis

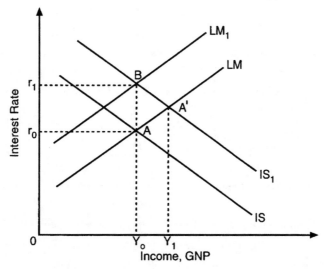

important. Also, the simultaneous existence of inflation and unemployment in the industrialized economies in modern times needs additional tools of the economic theory called the aggregate demand and the aggregate supply schedules. There is also a basic hypothesis about the behavior of the labor market of the economy which we have omitted so far. In the next chapter we will concentrate on that issue and try to analyze the modern problem of stagflation by using the aggregate demand and aggregate supply schedules.

Suggested Additional Reading for Chapter 13

1. Friedman, Milton. "The Role of Monetary Policy." *American Economic Review*, March 1968: 1-17.

2. Gegg, David. *The Rational Expectation Hypothesis in Macroeconomics*. Baltimore: John Hopkins University Press, 1982.

3. Humphrey, Thomas. "Changing Views of the Phillips Curve." *Federal Reserve Bank of Richmond Monthly Review*, July 1973: 1-13.

4. Lahiri, Kajal. "A Joint Study of Expectations Formation and the Shifting Phillips Curve." *Journal of Monetary Economics*, No. 3 1977: 347-357.

5. Lipsey, Richard. "The Relation Between Unemployment and the Rate of Change of Money Wage Rates in the United Kingdom, 1891-1957: A Further Analysis." *Economica*, February 1960: 1-13.

6. Phelps, Edmond. *Inflation Policy and Unemployment Theory*. New York: W. W. Norton, 1972.

7. Phillips, Arthur W "The Relation Between Unemployment and the Rate of Change of Money Wages in the United Kingdom, 1861-1957." *Economica*, November 1958: 283-299.

8. Rees, Albert. "The Phillips Curve As a Menu for a Policy Choice." *Economica*, August 1970: 227-238.

9. Solow, Robert. "Down the Phillips Curve with Gun and Camera," in David Beaseley edited, *Inflation, Trade and Taxes*. Ohio: Ohio University Press, 1976.

Aggregate Demand and Aggregate Supply Analysis

14

14.1 Introduction to Aggregate Demand and Aggregate Supply as a Tool

In this chapter we venture to derive another useful tool for the monetary analysis for the problem of inflation and unemployment. A need for such a tool is felt because as you may recall from earlier chapters, the IS-LM framework is insufficient to deal with the inflation problem of the economy. This is because IS-LM framework expresses all variables in real terms and assumes price level to be constant. The 1970s phenomenon of stagflation necessitates the introduction of the aggregate demand and the aggregate supply approach. Aggregate demand of the economy is made up of the consumption, investment, and government expenditure of the economy, and is related inversely to the price level. As the price level changes, there are reflections of the aggregate demand that we would consider by looking at the equilibrium of the commodity and money markets as given by the IS-LM framework. The relation of the price level and the equilibrium GNP is known as the aggregate demand schedule of that economy. In the initial part of this chapter we will consider the derivation of this schedule.

The aggregate supply is determined by the total product of the economy as produced by the available labor force. This brings us to another important market, the labor market, that we have ignored so far. There are labor demand and supply forces which are determined by the wage rate of the economy and are used to determine the aggregate supply curve. Having derived the

aggregate demand and the aggregate supply curves, we can deal
with the price level changes that create inflation in the economy.

14.2   Derivation of the Aggregate Demand Schedule

As mentioned before, one needs to consider the equilibrium of
the commodity and the money markets by looking at the IS-LM
framework and the effects of the price level changes on that
framework. Before we do that however, let us make some simplifying assumptions. Let us assume that the price level change does
not make any effect on the commodity market equilibrium so that
due to a price change, there is no change in the location of the IS
curve. This can be a rational assumption if we consider that the
variables in the commodity market are expressed in real terms
and they do not change when there are mere price changes.

Obviously, due to the price change, the real consumption, the
real investment and the real government expenditure values do
not change if there is no money illusion existing among the public. Money illusion is the illusion held by the public that lets the
real values be influenced by the changes in the nominal variables
such as the price level. For example, if the boss guarantees a
worker a raise of 10% in the next pay check and gives him only
the raise of 5% in actuality, then the worker may think that he had
been cheated. Such a feeling of the worker is termed as the
money illusion. Illusion, because in spite of the 5% raise he is
getting, he is thinking of the cheating. The same thing may happen in a macro sense as well.

When the economic agents possess a money illusion, the real
variables in the economy are affected by the mere price changes.
For the derivation of the aggregate demand schedule, assume that
there is no money illusion in the commodity market. Second,
observe that the demand for money, as it is measured in real
terms, in the absence of a money illusion, is unaffected by the
changes in the price level. This means that when there is the price
level change, in a money illusion free economy, the only variable

that would be affected is the real change inversely to the changes in the price level. As the price level goes up, the real money supply, M/P, would go down and vice versa.

We are now in a position to define what the aggregate demand schedule really stands for. It is the locus of combinations of the price level and the GNP level at which the commodity and money markets are in equilibrium. Given the above assumptions, an increase in the price level would create a shift of the money supply curve in Figure 14.1 on the previous page. Starting with the initial money market equilibrium at point J, suppose the price level goes up from P to P'. The new money supply would be lower, and the money supply curve would shift to the left. The new money market equilibrium rate would be higher than before at point J'. In terms of the IS-LM framework, the increase in the

Figure 14.1
Money Market Equilibrium and the Price Change

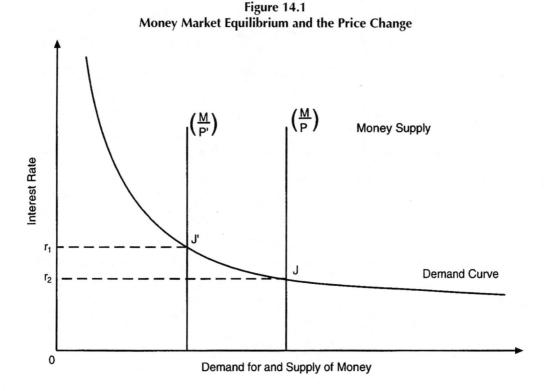

Figure 14.2
IS-LM Framework and the Price Level Change

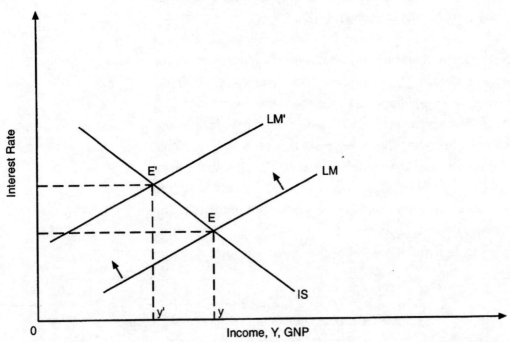

price causes a lower real money supply and shifts the LM curve
to the left. As we have seen in Chapter 9, the decrease in money
supply creates the leftward shift in the LM curve.

In terms of Figure 14.2, starting with the original general equilibrium at point E, due to the shift of the LM curve to the left, the
new equilibrium is achieved at point E' with a higher interest rate
and lower equilibrium GNP. Thus, a higher price level via money
market changes and the shift of the LM curve to the left, creates a
lower level of equilibrium GNP in the economy. When we concentrate on the combinations of the price levels and the GNP levels in the above discussion, so far we know at least two
combinations of the price level and the GNP level at which commodity and money markets are in equilibrium. Those combinations are P and Y and P' and Y' where P < P' and Y > Y'.

When we plot these combinations on another graph with the price level on the vertical axis and the GNP or Y on the horizontal axis, we can get two points viz K and K' in Figure 14.3.

Figure 14.3 includes some additional equilibrium combinations that can be obtained in the same fashion. That is, consider another change in the price level, determine the shift in the LM curve, and finally the change in the equilibrium GNP. The several points of Figure 14C can be joined by a curve sloping downwards from left to right. Thus, as the price level goes up the equilibrium GNP goes down. This inverse relationship between the price level and the GNP level, is called the aggregate demand schedule. This is shown in the following graph.

The main characteristics of the *aggregate demand schedule* are as follows: 1) The curve shows all the possible crossing points of a single commodity market equilibrium and the various money market equilibria at different price levels. Every point on this

Figure 14.3
Derivation of the Aggregate Demand Schedule

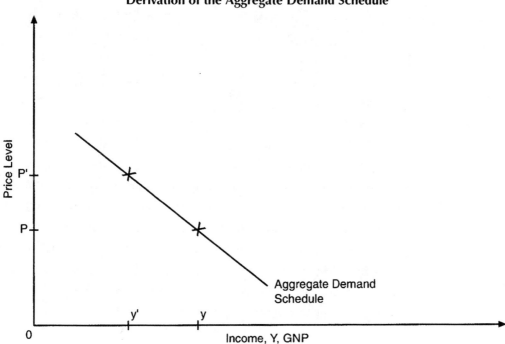

curve shows the general equilibrium in the economy. 2) The distance between any point on the aggregate demand schedule and the vertical axis is the value of the total expenditure in the economy. Hence, any change in the values of consumption or investment or the government expenditure would make this curve shift. 3) The slope of this curve depends upon the slopes of the IS and LM curves. Hence, the factors responsible for the slope changes in these curves would be the same factors that would cause the changes in the slope of the *aggregate demand schedule*. It should be obvious that steeper is the IS curve, steeper will be the *aggregate demand schedule*.

The slope of the IS curve depends upon the responsiveness of the investment to the changes in the interest rate, or specifically, the elasticity of investment with respect to the interest rate. The higher is the value of this elasticity, flatter will be the IS curve and flatter will be the aggregate demand schedule.

For the LM curve the story is different. A flatter LM curve would create a smaller change in the equilibrium GNP due to a shift in it. This would give us a steeper aggregate demand schedule. Hence, the steeper is the LM curve, the flatter will be the aggregate demand schedule and flatter is the LM curve, the steeper will be the aggregate demand schedule. You may recall that the slope of the LM curve depends upon the responsiveness of the demand for money with respect to the interest rate. The higher is this elasticity, the flatter will be the LM curve and steeper will be the aggregate demand schedule. Also, in the special case of the classical analysis, when it was expected that demand for money is completely inelastic with respect to the interest rate changes, the LM curve becomes vertical. In this special case, the aggregate demand curve is also a horizontal straight line. This means that due to price changes, there is no change in the value of the equilibrium GNP and the aggregate demand curve is a vertical straight line.

Shifts in this curve are caused by policy changes by the government. If government decides to adopt an expansionary fiscal policy, it initially would create an upward shift in the aggregate demand schedule, but as there is a decrease in the private sector investment due to crowding out, there is a downward shift in that curve and the effect of the fiscal policy is nullified. The exact shift of the curve would be decided by the degree to which the crowding out takes place.

14.3   Derivation of the Aggregate Supply Curve

Together, with the aggregate demand schedule, we must now investigate the behavior of the aggregate supply of the economy. Considering that the aggregate supply of the economy is made up of the total production or the total product in that economy, we should examine how the total product of the economy is determined. Assume that labor is the main factor of production. Higher production needs higher employment of the labor and vice versa. Hence, the total employment of labor in the economy decides the total product produced in that economy. Now the question is, how does the economy decide the optimum employment of labor? Obviously the producers demand labor and they are the ones who would determine how much employment for labor is offered in their firms. Let us suppose that they make their decisions depending upon the wage rate and the productivity of the labor. Thus, in the labor market, there are two decisions to be made: 1) how many workers would be demanded at different wage rates as decided by the producers; and 2) how much labor to be supplied at the wage that is offered by the producers as decided by the labor. Now let us make some simplifying assumptions: a) let us assume that the labor is the homogeneous factor of production and is perfectly devisable; and b) let us also assume that the producers face the situation where they are offering a constant wage rate to the homogeneous labor.

Figure 14.4
Labor Market Analysis and the Optimum Employment

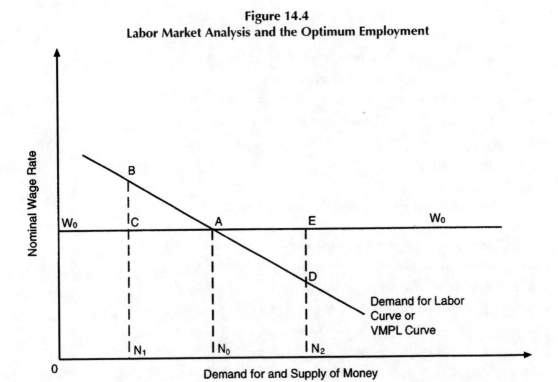

Now let us consider a few things about the production process. When the producers have a choice of deciding their volume of production, and when they enter into a production process, they would initially face the increasing marginal returns, then the constant marginal returns, and then the diminishing marginal returns. This is called the law of changeable returns and it has a universal applicability as it is a very logical law. When all other factors of production are constant in their employment and when an employer is adding more units of labor, initially he would experience an excess capacity, therefore the productivity of the labor would also be increased so that the returns of production would also be increasing. However, as capacity of the plant is utilized more and more, the additional employment of labor does not bring about as much productivity as before so that the returns would become constant and then eventually decline. When all other things are constant it also makes sense that an employer would continue hiring more labor when the returns are increasing. Hence, the producer would always produce in that stage of the production in which there are declining returns (or, to put it in other words, where the marginal productivity of labor is declining). In terms of Figure 14.4, as the labor employment is increased, the marginal product of the labor declines, hence, the marginal product curve is downward sloping from left to right.

Now let us define a new concept called the *value of the marginal product of labor*, or VMPL. VMPL is nothing but the product of the price of the good and the marginal productivity of the labor. If we assume a constant price of the product, then the VMPL curve would also be downward sloping from the left to right in Figure 14D. Producers, if they could have it their way, would like to decide the wage rate that is exactly equal to the VMPL. This is because if VMPL> Wage Rate (W), then producers would know that the value of the marginal product of the labor (or the value of the change in the total product caused by the last unit of labor) is greater than the wage offered to the labor, hence the producers would be happy to employ some more labor. As the producer does that, the VMPL would decline since the higher employment brings lower marginal product of labor. Exactly the opposite would happen to VMPL <Wage Rate. In equilibrium, the producers would prefer to offer the wage rate that is exactly matched by the VMPL. Additionally, we should consider that the wage rate in the economy and the supply of the labor would have a direct or positive relationship. As the wage rate goes up there would be a higher number of people ready to work, or the same number of people would be happy to work longer. Hence, the supply of labor curve is sloping upwards from left to right.

The downward sloping demand for labor curve and the upward sloping supply of labor curve are shown in Figure 14.5. The demand for labor curve is also called the VMPL and the wage

Figure 14.5
Equilibrium of the Labor Market

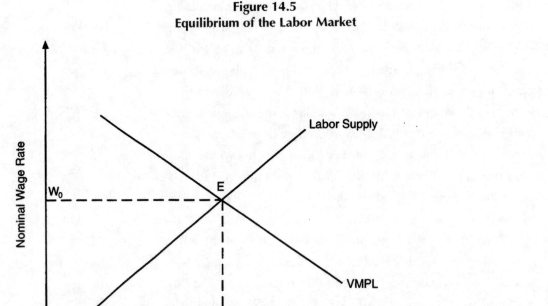

rate that decide the willingness of the producers to hire more or less laborers.

Now, knowing the positions of these two curves we can determine the optimum level of employment in the economy as given by the intersection point of these two curves. The intersection point is called the point of equilibrium in the labor market and the wage rate decided by this equilibrium point is the equilibrium wage rate.

Given the optimal level of employment in the economy from the labor market analysis, we can determine the total product that can be produced by this amount of employment by using total product that can be produced by this amount of employment by using the total product curve in Figure 14.6. With labor employment on the horizontal axis and the total product on the vertical axis, Figure 14.6 shows the application of the law of changeable returns. Initially with an increase in employment of labor, the marginal product of labor increases, so the total product increases at a faster rate. (Notice that the marginal product is the slope of the total product curve, or the rate of increase in the total product.) When the marginal product of labor becomes constant, the total product curve becomes a straight line and when the marginal product of labor is declining, the total product curve becomes concave. It is therefore important to understand why the total product curve takes the special shape as shown in Figure 14.6. Since the total product is the GNP of the economy, by observing its behavior we can derive aggregate supply of that economy. Now let us analyze the effect of the price changes on the aggregate supply of the economy. As the price level goes up, there is a shift of the VMPL curve in the labor market graph, (Figure 14.5), since VMPL stands for the product of the price of the good and the marginal product of labor. As the VMPL curve shifts to the

Figure 14.6
Aggregate Demand and Aggregate Supply Curves

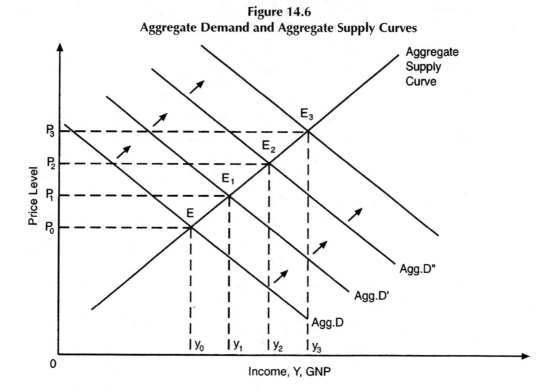

Figure 14.7
Aggregate Demand and Aggregate Supply Curves

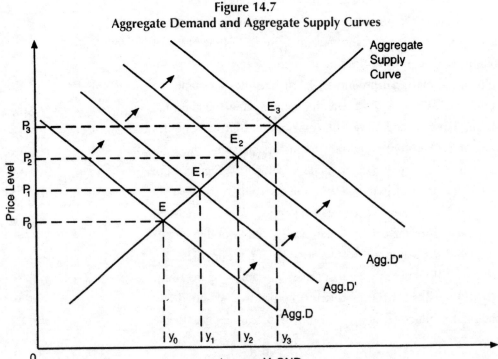

right, with the upward sloping supply of the labor curve, we find a new equilibrium in the labor market with the higher wage and higher employment. As the employment increases, the total product of the economy increases (which also means an increased aggregate supply in that economy).

Thus, as the price level increases, under normal circumstances, there is an increase in the aggregate supply of the economy. Hence, in the graph that follows, the relationship between the price level and the aggregate supply is shown by the upward sloping curve from left to right.

We are now in a position to talk about the equilibrium price level of the economy by observing its aggregate demand and aggregate supply curves together. This is done in Figure 14.7. Remember that the aggregate demand schedule shows combinations of the price level and income levels at which both money and commodity markets are in equilibrium. The aggregate supply curve, on the other hand, shows how much an economy would be ready to produce at different price levels. Together these curves would decide the unique combination of the price level and income level at which the money and commodity markets are in equilibrium. Their intersection point, therefore, is called the equilibrium point. Besides defining the equilibrium point in the above manner, this framework is also useful in analyzing the problem of inflation. But before we analyze the inflation problem let us first define it. As you may recall from the earlier chapter on inflation, inflation is the general price level. In terms of Figure 14.7 it means a continuous increase in the variable on the vertical axis.

Hence, unless we observe an increase in the price level in Figure 14.7, we will not be able to analyze the inflation phenomenon. To do that, let us examine the shifts in the aggregate demand and the aggregate supply curve. Consider for example, an adoption by the government of an expansionary fiscal or monetary policy on a continuous basis. This would create continuous upward shifts in the aggregate demand curve in Figure 14.7 leading to a continuous increase in the price level and the income level. Hence, the policy would be regarded as effective but inflationary. Thus, inflation can be caused by a continuous increase in the government budget deficit or the money supply. The inflation that takes place due to continuous shifts in the aggregate demand curve, is labeled as demand-pull inflation. This is however not the only way in which inflation can occur. Consider the increase in the cost of production due to say, an exogenous increase in the input price. This can create a leftward shift in the aggregate supply curve causing an increase in the price level and the decline in the GNP for the economy. A continuous occurrence of this type of phenomenon would lead to an inflation problem of the economy. Also observe that a decline in income of the economy is the same as reduced employment of the labor. Hence, a shift in the aggregate supply curve not only causes inflation but also is

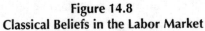

Figure 14.8
Classical Beliefs in the Labor Market

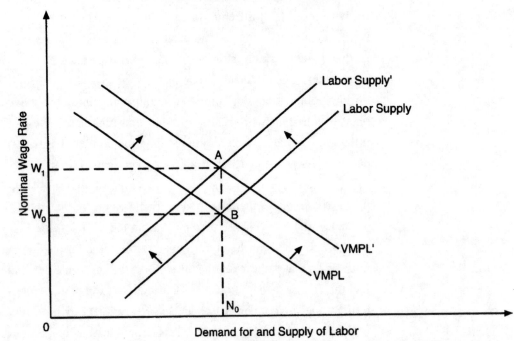

responsible for unemployment and is referred to as stagflation as we have seen it several times before.

On the theoretical basis one can analyze the possible changes in the shapes of the aggregate demand and aggregate supply curves according to the special beliefs held by classical economists and the Keynesians.

a)   *Classical economists and aggregate demand and aggregate supply framework*: Recall that the classicals believed in the quantity theory of money and the perfectly flexible prices, wages, and interest rate levels. Also, they did not recognize the phenomenon of money illusion so that they believed in perfect foresight on the part of the public. Hence, when the price level goes up and the VMPL curve shifts upwards, classicals believed that the public would realize the loss of real income due to the increased price level. When the wage rate is perfectly flexible, they would try to compensate for this loss by supplying less labor up to that point at which their real wage rate is the same as before. In terms of Figure 148, starting with the original equilibrium in the labor market at point B, when there is an increase in the price level due to the loss of real income, the supply of labor curve shifts to the left. The shift in labor supply would occur up to that point at which the real wage remains the same amount as before and the money wage goes up by the same amount as the increase in the price level. The same real wage rate gives the same amount of labor employment in the economy. Hence, the price level increase in the classical model does not lead to an increase in the employment. This obviously means that the increase in the price level does not lead to any increase in the total product and therefore, GNP of the economy. As a consequence, classicals believe that the shape of the aggregate supply curve is perfectly vertical. With a completely vertical aggregate supply curve, the policy of the government has an interesting reflection.

When any expansionary fiscal or monetary policy is undertaken by the government, as we have seen before, there is a rightward shift of the aggregate demand curve, as shown in Figure 14.9. But due to a vertical aggregate supply curve with an expansionary monetary or fiscal policy, there is a higher price level and no change in the GNP level of the economy. Thus, we can use this framework to reach the same conclusion as we had seen several times before, that the classicals believed in completely ineffective government policies. Starting with the initial equilibrium at point E, when the government adopts an expansionary policy, there is a shift of the aggregate demand curve giving us a new equilibrium point E_1 where there is a higher price level and the same level of income.

Figure 14.9
Classical Beliefs and the Aggregate

Demand and Supply Curves

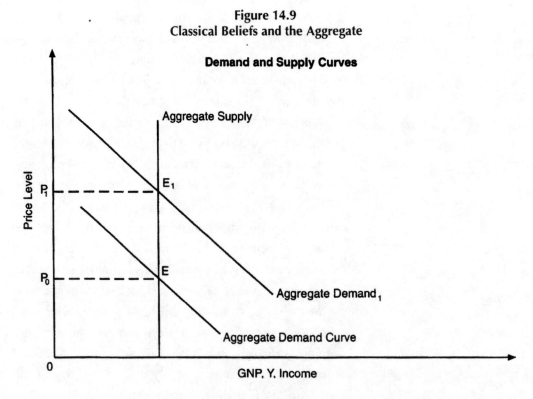

b)   In the similar fashion we can also incorporate the special Keynesian feeling about the shape of the aggregate supply curve and the effectiveness of the policies. As you may recall from our earlier chapters, Keynes believed in an active role by the government.

In terms of the labor market analysis, Keynes observed that in reality, the wage rate is constant at a certain level. This is because Keynes observed that the trade unions do not agree to wage cuts unless they are threatened with the loss of jobs. This makes rigid wages in the downward direction. On the other hand, when the producers are free to demand any amount of labor at the given wage rate, it is unlikely that they would voluntarily increase the wage rate level. Hence, according to Keynes, the wage rate can be taken as fixed at a certain level. Therefore, as a consequence of his observation of reality, Keynes believed that the wage rate in the economy would be perfectly inflexible. To show this let us draw a horizontal line in Figure 14.10 at a certain wage rate say W_1.

When there is an increase in the price level under these circumstances, the VMPL curve shifts to the right. Also, if people have the money illusion, they do not supply any less labor than before and the supply curve stays at the same location. However, if people do not have the money illusion, the supply of labor curve shifts to the left since they realize the loss of real income and start supplying less labor. In either case, with the constant wage rate, the employment of labor increases due to the increase in the price level that we started out with.

Thus, in the Keynesian analysis, the increase in price level leads to an increase in labor employment. This increased labor employment obviously means more total product from the total product curve and the higher GNP level,. Hence, the aggregate

Figure 14.10
Keynesian Analysis and the Labor Market Equilibrium

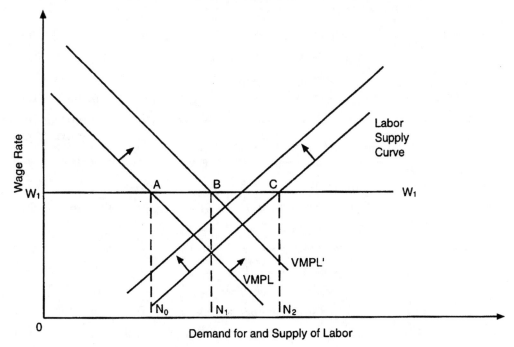

Demand for and Supply of Labor

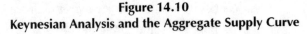

Figure 14.10
Keynesian Analysis and the Aggregate Supply Curve

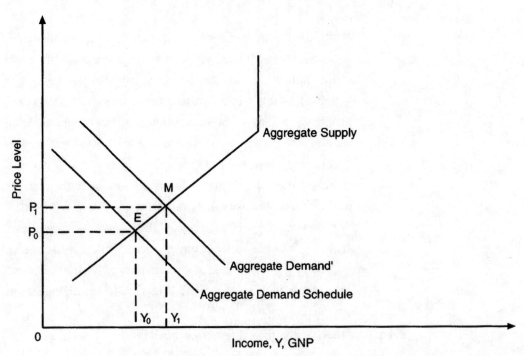

supply curve in Keynesian analysis is upward sloping from left to right. The policy consequence of such a shape is obvious. With the increased government expenditure and/or money supply, there is a rightward shift in the aggregate demand schedule. In terms of Figure 14.11, it means a shift of the original equilibrium to a new point like point M where we have higher GNP than before the policy activity. Hence, in the Keynesian analysis we can see that the government policy is effective but in the case of the classical analysis the effectiveness of the policies is none. Thus, aggregate demand and aggregate supply curves can be used to show the special assumptions and analysis of classical economists and those of Mr. Keynes.

Notwithstanding these opposing views and realizing that in reality, wages are neither completely flexible nor fully rigid, we can see that the policy effectiveness depends upon how quickly people realize the loss of real income due to the inflation caused by the expansionary policies, and how long a time they take to supply less labor as a result of this realization. If they are slow in realizing this, the policies can be effective longer. On the other hand, if they are smart enough to realize that the expansionary policies caused higher price levels and therefore less income for them, then the policies are not effective for very long.

Therefore, it essentially reduces to the statement that the policy maker should be clever to fool people into not noticing the inflationary effects of their policies, and if they are successful in doing that, their policies would be effective longer. In this regard we must also pay attention to the process in which people have expectations of future prices. This is because if people believe that the future price level is going to be higher than the present one, then they would supply less labor and the GNP of the economy can be reduced. On the other hand, in spite of an expansionary policy, if people are made to believe that inflation is improbable, then the policy can be effective for a long time. It is therefore almost mandatory that we pay more attention to the expectation formation process of the public. In the next chapter an analysis of the expectations hypothesis and the public's expectation formation process will be reviewed.

Suggested Additional Reading for Chapter 14

1.   Boyes, William. *Macroeconomics*, 1st ed. Ohio: Southwestern Publishers, 1984. Chapter 7.

2.   Christ, Carl E "A Model of Monetary and Fiscal Policy Effects on the Money Stock, Price Level and Real Output." *Journal of Money, Credit and Banking*, No.1, 1969.

3.   Clower, Robert and Axel Leijonhufvud. "The Coordination of Economic Activities: A Keynesian Perspective." *American Economic Review*, May 1975.

4.   Froyen, Richard T. *Macroeconomics: Theories and Policies*. New York: Macmillan Publishers, 1983.

5.   Gordon, Robert. "Recent Developments in the Theory of Inflation and Unemployment." *Journal of Monetary Economics*, Vol. 2, 1976: 185-219.

6.   Gordon, Robert. *Macroeconomics*. 3rd ed. Boston: Little Brown Publications, 1984. Chapter 6.

7.   Hough, L. "The Price Level in Macroeconomic Models." *American Economic Review*, Vol. LXIV, June 1954: 269-286.

8.   Leijonhufvud, Axel. *On Keynesian Economics and the Economics of Keynes*, 1st ed. New York: Oxford University Press, 1968.

9.   Samuelson, Paul and Robert Solow. "The Problem of Achieving and Maintaining a Stable Price Level: Analytical Aspects of Anti-Inflation Policy." *American Economic Review*, May 1960: 177-194.

Other Problems for Macro Policy: Expectations Hypothesis

15

15.1   Introduction

We concluded the last chapter by saying that government stabilization policies will be ineffective if the public correctly perceives their inflationary effects. That is not the only problem a monetary authority faces. Non-interventionists are eager to point out the time lags involved in the operation of the monetary or fiscal policy, and there are also the critics who believe in the adaptive expectation hypothesis and in rational expectations theories in the simplest forms and then examine the consequences thereof for the effectiveness of the governmental policies.

15.2   Effectiveness of the Policy

To recollect, let us briefly summarize the economic events that normally would take place due to an expansionary monetary or fiscal policy. In Figure 15.1, starting with the original equilibrium at point J, let us suppose that the government decides to increase money supply or the government expenditure. There will be an increase in the aggregate demand due to these policy actions and a shift of the aggregate demand schedule to the right. The new equilibrium would be attained at point L with a higher GNP and the higher price level. Since the GNP level is increased by the policy action, we could conclude that the action was effective. But the effectiveness of the policy action could be short lived

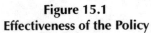

Figure 15.1
Effectiveness of the Policy

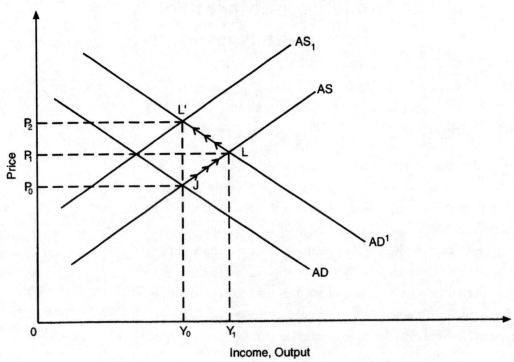

Income, Output

depending on the speed at which expectations of the public are adjusted to the higher price level at point L.

As we have seen in Chapter 14, the slower the rate of adjustment to expectations of future prices, the longer the effectiveness of policy action. If people become aware of the fact that there is a loss of real income due to a higher price level at point L, and if they set their wage contracts for the short-run durations as opposed to the long-run durations, then they would immediately ask for higher wages to compensate the loss of real income. As a result of these demands for higher wages, the cost of production would increase causing the supply curve in Figure 15.1 to shift to the left. This would obviously nullify the effectiveness of the policy. Moreover, one may note that even expectations about future inflation are as effective as the actual increase in price level in creating a leftward shift of the supply curve. Now the big question is, "How do people form the expectation of future prices?" Also, what are the consequences of the mechanism of the expectation formation on the effectiveness of the policy? One theory that claims the possession of the answers to these questions is the adaptive expectation theory.

15.3   Adaptive Expectation Theory

Originated in writing by John Muth in 1961 but as elaborately developed by Phillip Cagan of Columbia University, in the 1970s, the adaptive expectation theory claims that people, when they form an expectation of the future inflation rate, learn at least partly from their old mistakes. Hence, if they have learned from their past experience that an expansionary policy creates inflation, then an expansionary policy of this time period would make them expect at least some inflation in the future. In mathematical terms, it means that when expectations of future inflation are formed, the following equation is used:

$$p^e_t \;=\; p^e_{t-1} + j(p_{t-1} - p^e_{t-1}) \;\text{———————} \; (1)$$

where

p^e_t =   expected inflation rate of the current time period.
p^e_{t-1} =   expected inflation rate of the last time period.
p_{t-1} =   actual inflation of the last time period.
j =   coefficient of adjustment with its value between zero and one. $0 < j < 1$.

Depending on the value of the coefficient j, we have several scenarios to predict. Let us suppose that the value of j happens to be zero. By plugging in the zero value for j, from equation (1), it means that $p^e_t = p^e_{t-1}$ and people do not adjust their expectations at all to the actual value of inflation. Keeping in mind that this type of behavior is unrealistic, in terms of Figure 15.1, there would be no change in the location of the aggregate supply curve in this case. This is because if people expect inflation in this time period in the same way as they expected it last year, they would not ask for any higher wages, the cost of production would remain unchanged and the aggregate supply curve would stay at the same location as before. The policy would be effective permanently. On the other hand, if j is equal to one, the expected inflation rate is always set equal to what actually occurred in the last year. If people correctly perceive the actual inflation occurring at point L in Figure 15.1 to form their future expectations, then they would obviously ask for higher wages in the future contract, the cost of production would go up instantly and the aggregate supply curve would shift to the left creating lower GNP and higher unemployment in the economy.

Barring aside these extreme cases, the value of j always remains between zero and one and it is referred to as the speed of adjustment to the changes in circumstances. The speed of adjustment determines the effectiveness of the policy action. the closer the value of j to unity, the lower the effectiveness of the policy action. In general, adaptive expectation theory claims that depending on the value of the coefficient j, the effectiveness of policy action is decided. It is perfectly possible that the policy is effective at one time period and is completely ineffective in the other since the value of j is liable to change. In terms of empirical evidence, the policy actions were more effective in the initial stages when the government started becoming ambitiously active in the 1940s and 1950s. However, as people learned from their old experiences, the policy actions in the 1960s and 1970s were much less effective.

Hence, the adjustment process for the future expectations of the inflation rate does create a problem for the monetary policy effectiveness. There are, however, other economists who claimed in the late 1960s that the effectiveness of the policies is essentially zero especially when people have what they call 'rational' expectations.

15.4   Rational Expectations Theory

A crucial implication of the adaptive expectation formation was that the variable must change before individuals begin to anticipate further changes. For example, the public must observe an actual decline in the inflation rate in this period to expect a reduced inflation in the next period. The rational expectation theory goes one step further than this. This theory was created by Thomas Sargent and Wallace of the University of Minnesota and is further extended by Robert Lucas of the University of Chicago. It claims that the public in modern times is exposed to more information via TV, radio, newspaper, etc. This free information enables every economic agent to form a special model of his/her own to analyze the economic changes. Moreover, as the information in the future changes, everyone feeds that information in his/her forecasting model so that any policy announcement immediately affects the expectations about the future changes in the economy. Hence, in case of the rational expectations, people already know what would be the effect of an expansionary policy. Also, if people have observed in the past the inflationary consequences of an increase in the money supply, then in the current times, even when the policy makers are discussing an adoption of an expansionary monetary policy, the public, by looking at their rationally built model, correctly anticipates the upcoming inflation.

This obviously has a severe problem for the effectiveness of the policy. As people correctly anticipate the inflation, they ask for higher wages as soon as the policy is enacted (or some times even before enactment of the policy). Their demands for higher wages creates a shift of the supply of labor curve in the labor market diagram reducing the employment and output, and the effectiveness of the policy is nil. As Johnson and Roberts put it, "The implication of the rational expectations is that expectation would be reformulated sooner than under adaptive expectations based on observations of actual changes in the variable alone. For example, the rate of increase in prices would not necessarily have to decrease before individuals anticipated that prices would be rising at a slower rate. All that would be necessary for the reformulation of expectations is the realization of a change in monetary or fiscal policy that would lead to a reduction in the rate of increase in prices."

Thus, the rational expectations theory succeeds in putting a serious question in front of policy makers. As opposed to the Phillips Curve hypothesis that claimed at least partial success in solving the two main problems of the economy, viz, inflation and unemployment, rational expectations hypothesis offers no incentive for the policy activism. From the policy makers point of view, several lessons can be learned from the rational expectations theory. First, never announce the policy beforehand, because if it is announced previous to its enactment, then people already expect what is coming up in the economy and change their acts to compensate for the anticipated change. Secondly, do not be honest in accepting the fact that you are trying to trade off inflation for unemployment and vice versa. Because if people know it for the fact, then they would anticipate an expansionary policy in the case of high unemployment and a restrictive policy in case of severe inflation. Policies lose their effectiveness if people are able to anticipate the actions in advance. Thirdly, the key for the success of the policy activism is in the success of not letting people know what the future changes in the policy would be.

In terms of Figure 15.2, an expansionary policy effectiveness can be seen when people have adaptive and rational expectations. The movement from point A to B is very quick when people possess rational expectations giving zero effectiveness to the policy change. The next question naturally is, do people in fact possess the rational expectations? The answer is obviously no, not at least

when we are considering the general public in the whole economy. Even when information is abundantly available, people do
not always use it for making the expectation of the future prices.
How many people in reality are interested in building an economic model and watching every policy change? Very few. People hardly ever realize the meaning of the policy changes let
alone the working of them. Hence, in a complex world with many
individuals of different attitudes and tastes, it is irrational to
expect that people have rational expectations. This means that a
policy activity can have at least a limited effectiveness in reality.
These practical limitations give a ray of hope for the policy activism. However, the rational expectations hypothesis cannot be
completely ignored. Also on the micro-economic basis the rational expectations can have application in certain markets like the
stock market where the dealers are very attentive to the everyday

Figure 15.2
Expectation Hypothesis and Policy Effectiveness

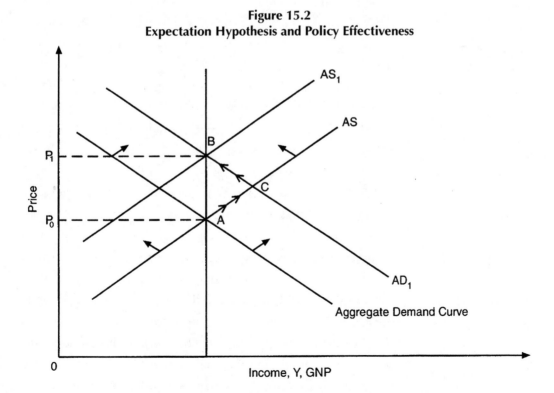

changes in the policy activity and they in fact use certain rationality in their expectations of the future variables.

As far as the problems for the monetary policy are concerned, the expectations hypothesis makes it clear that the policy effectiveness is hampered by the information available to the public and the rationality of their expectations. Policy makers have to keep a close check on these expectation formation processes if they are to succeed in their actions.

15.5   Lags in the Operations of the Policy

The second set of problems for the monetary policy is created by the time lags involved in the operation of it. For any policy change there are several time lags, like the time involved in implementation, recognition, etc. which can create delays in the effectiveness of the policy action. In the early 1960s, economists started paying special attention to these time lags because these lags happened to be another point on which the non-interventionists could rest their case for non-activism on the part of the government.

There are basically two major types of lags. The wages which naturally occur but are under the control of the government, are called inside lags, and those which are outside the control of the policy makers are called outside lags. In turn, there are three inside lags and two outside lags.

The first inside lag is called 'data lag.' It is the time involved in getting information about an economic disturbance once it has occurred. For example, let us suppose there is an occurrence of a disturbance in the economy like a heat wave in a certain part of the economy. Obviously it would take time to correctly analyze the severity of the heat wave and the loss that would be incurred because of it. This time involved is called the data lag. Secondly, even when government has obtained the information about the heat wave, many times policy makers may think of it as a short-run disturbance and one which does not call for any policy action.

If governmental authorities take a certain amount of time to make up their mind about the need for a policy change to correct the disturbance, then that time is called the 'recognition lag.'

The third lag is called the 'implementation lag.' It is the time involved in implementing the policy change once the need for it has been realized. For example, the fiscal policy change has to be approved by several committees in the governmental structure once a change is decided. In this respect, the monetary policy is in a better situation because generally, the monetary policy actions are implemented more quickly than the fiscal policy change. Note that all of the above lags are under the control of the policy makers. If they have to, in the case of emergencies, they can reduce the length of these time lags very easily. For example, the recognition lag can even be negative if the government correctly anticipates the disturbance well ahead of time. For this reason, these lags as mentioned before, are called the inside lags.

The outside lags are two: transmission lag and the impact lag. The transmission lag is the time interval between the policy decision and the actual implementation of the policy change. This again, is more relevant to the fiscal policy than to the monetary policy. Once the policy change is decided, the monetary policy activation takes less time than the fiscal policy change like the tax change. And lastly, the most interesting lag is the impact lag. It is the time needed for the policy change to show its effects once it has been activated.

The effectiveness of a policy change is measured by the amount of change it can cause in the real GNP of the economy. If the policy change can cause no change in the real GNP, then it is termed as ineffective. What is the impact lag for the fiscal policy? The answer to this question would depend on whom you are asking. For example, the monetarists would point out the complete crowding out phenomenon and would conclude that the impact lag for the fiscal policy is infinite. On the other hand, Keynesians would explain the multiplier process and would conclude that the impact lag is the time involved in finishing the chain of multiplier that we discussed in the earlier chapters. This, they would assert, is a shorter lag than the impact lag of the monetary policy.

The effectiveness of the monetary policy, according to the Keynesians, occurs only via the Keynesian chain that we discussed before. Remember that the Keynesian chain is the only way in which Keynes and the Keynesians claim the monetary policy can be effective. Hence, according to their thinking, it takes longer for monetary policy to be effective than for the fiscal policy. This gives them another reason to believe that the fiscal policy is superior or stronger than the monetary policy. Monetarists, on the other hand, insist that the monetary change does not need the Keynesian chain to be effective. Its impact is more direct via the quantity theory of money. According to the monetarists and especially Friedman, it takes about sixteen months for any monetary policy action to show its effects on the economy. Sixteen months is a long time for sure, but in case of fiscal policy change, the things are even worse since the impact lag (because of the crowding out) is infinite.

To summarize, we can show a hypothetical movement of the real GNP of an economy in Figure 15.3 and specify the time periods for each lag we mentioned above. The main contention of all of the above discussion is that the policy effectiveness does involve several lags and the policy makers should be aware of those.

Besides the time lags and the expectation hypothesis, there are also some other beliefs which claim that policy activism has problems. One such theory is called the *credibility hypothesis* as given by William Fellner, an ex-Yale University Professor, but now with American Enterprise Institute. According to Prof. Fellner, when the public has come to believe the governmental policy makers have a tendency to adopt only expansionary policies, then a restrictive policy adopted by them does not get a desirable result very easily. In other words, a restrictive policy with an objective

Figure 15.3
Time Lags in Policy Actions

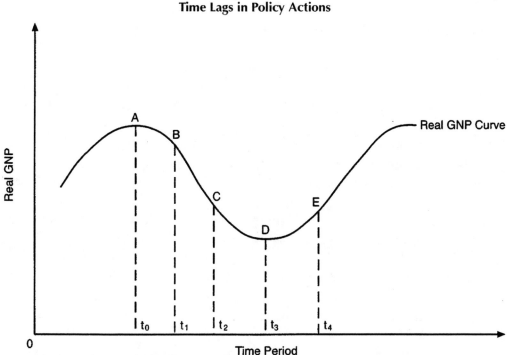

of controlling inflation would not do so if the public knows or expects that the government has a usual tendency to adopt expansionary policy again. The government, therefore, has limited credibility with the public and as a result, the policy effectiveness can be restricted. The credibility hypothesis does put the policy makers in a strange situation. They would find it hard to make changes in the direction of the policy activism.

We have, in this chapter, found out the problems involved in the policy making of monetary or fiscal changes. Because there are these problems, the policy makers should be cautious about the over-activism and unnecessarily unattainable objectives. Moreover, there are international effects of any policy change, fiscal or monetary, that we have not considered so far. We will devote our next chapter for that purpose.

Suggested Additional Reading for Chapter 15

1.   Anderson, L. C. "An Evaluation of the Impacts of Monetary and Fiscal Policy on Economic Activity." 1969 Proceeding of the Business and Economic Statistics Section. District of Columbia: American Statistical Association, 1969: 223-240.

2.   Ando, A., E. C. Brown, Solow Robert, and I. Karekan. "Lags in Fiscal and Monetary Policy." Commission on Money and Credit, Stabilization Policies. New Jersey: Prentice Hall Publishers, 1963.

3.   Cumbertson, J. M. "Friedman on the Lag in Effect of Monetary Policy." *Journal of Political Economy*, December 1960: 617-621.

4.   Friedman, Milton. *A Program for Monetary Stability*. New York: Fordham University Press, 1960: 87-89.

5.   Hamberger, M. J. "The Impact of Monetary Variables: A Survey of Recent Econometric Literature." Essays in Domestic and International Finance. New York: Federal Reserve Bank of New York, 1969: 37-49.

6.   Mayer, T., J. Duesenberry, and R. Aliber. *Money, Banking and the Economy*. Norton and Norton Company.

7.   Mayer, T. "The Lag in Effect of Monetary Policy: Some Criticisms." *Western Economic Journal*, September,1967: 324-342.

8.   Smith, W. L. "On the Effectiveness of Monetary Policy" *American Economic Review*, September 1956: 588-606.

9.   Thomas, Lloyd. *Money, Banking and Economic Activity*. 3rd ed. Prentice Hall Publication, 1985, Chapter 22.

10. Warburton, C. "Variability of the Lag in the Effect of Monetary Policy, 1919-1965." *Western Economic Journal*, June 1971: 113-115.

Macro-Monetary Theory in Open Economy Setting

16

16.1

One may have observed that so far this book has dealt with only the analysis of a closed economy. It is however a grave mistake to think that monetary theory does not worry about economy's openness and there is little to talk about monetary theory in an open economy setting. In fact in the last few decades few other areas of economic science have developed faster than the area of open economy's monetary theory. In this chapter therefore we start with a few important definitions of such concepts as the balance of payments of an economy, foreign exchange market and equilibrium of the external sector of the economy. By using the external sector's equilibrium one can also discuss the general equilibrium idea with the help of IS and LM curves of Chapter 9.

16.2 Balance of Payments

Any discussion of the balance of payments (BOP) needs a clarification of some of the procedural points about it. First, balance of payments in general is defined as a record of international transactions of an economy with the rest of the world. Clearly international transactions are of two basic types: transactions of goods and services and transactions of financial assets such as bonds, stocks etc. To keep some order to recording the balance of payment it is divided into different balances that concentrate on the recording of specific exchanges.

Second, for balance of payment recording only the permanent residents of a country are considered to be the domestic residents. Hence, such persons as visitors, temporary workers, foreign students, or diplomats are seen the same as foreign nationals. In fact, the purchases of these individuals are same as an export from a country. A payment to these individuals is also seen as a capital outflow from the country.

Third, any activity that leads to an increase in purchasing power of domestic residents is recorded as a credit on the balance of payment and any activity that results in a decline in purchasing power of the domestic residents is recorded as a debit on the balance of payment.

Fourth, on balance of payments, each transaction is recorded twice by keeping in line with a "double entry book-keeping."

Fifth, contrary to the general belief, just like a deficit in balance of payment does not necessarily indicate a lost of economy's welfare, a surplus in balance of payment does not necessarily mean a reduction in economy's welfare. Therefore, it is not true that a country that has higher exports than imports is better off than a country that has higher import than export. One of the famous and witty economists, Herbert Stein, once made an interesting comment about the balance of payment deficit and surplus in the following way: he said, "last year I went to Paris, and spent a lot of money on shopping. This essentially created a large deficit on US balance of payment, but I loved every minute of it!" Hence one has to recognize that activities that create a deficit in balance of payment deficit do not necessarily lower economy's welfare.

Also, consider another case of a purchase of domestic properties by foreign residents. Clearly when foreign residents buy domestic properties, one may think that this should lead to lower economic welfare. However, for balance of payment recording, this only means a capital inflow and therefore a credit on the capital balance leading to a surplus in balance of payment. In any country's balance of payment records, there are basically four major balances.

1) *Balance on goods and services account*: This account records the transactions of goods and services as reported by Department of Customs or Foreign Trade. This balance gets a credit entry when goods leave a country and transactions that make foreign goods and services enter the country are recorded as a credit. Hence exports are a credit and imports are a debit. Surplus on this account is popularly called *net exports*.

2) *Balance on current account*: This account records all transactions of the balance on goods and services account and adds to it the special transactions referred to as the unilateral transfers. As the name suggests unilateral transactions are those that are said to be "one way traffic": those that leave the country without any expectation of repayment. Hence such payments as foreign aid, retirement payments to retirees abroad, foreign base payments and military personnel expenditure, etc., are classic examples of unilateral transactions. Current account thus records all exports and imports and adds to it the unilateral transactions.

3) *Capital account balance*: This balance is reserved for recording all capital transactions. Hence when foreign residents buy domestic financial assets like bonds, stocks, government securities, etc., there is a capital inflow into the economy. These transactions are recorded as a credit on capital account. When domestic residents purchase foreign financial assets there is a capital outflow and these transactions are recorded as a debit on the balance of payment. Thus a surplus on capital account occurs when there is a greater capital inflow than outflow.

4) *Official reserve settlement balance*: This balance records all transactions that occur at the governmental level or at the central bank level of a country. Clearly when central

bank has a greater amount of foreign reserves in its possession, there is a credit on this balance. Of course all central banks have reserves of foreign currencies, Special Drawing Rights (SDRs), gold stock, and such weighted currencies as European Currency Unit. Special drawing rights are issued by the International Monetary Fund which is a fund of approximately 184 countries. Each member country is required to contribute to this fund as per an accepted formula that depends on the size, population, GDP of a country. If a certain country wants to contribute to the IMF more than this formula requires, the IMF issues to this country a special drawing right (SDR). Thus when a country has a large stock of SDRs, there is a credit on the official reserve balance of the balance of payments.

Therefore balance on goods and services, current account balance, capital account balance and official reserve settlement balance are the four major balances of the BOP. The main economic variables that influence the balance of payments changes are three: GDP (Y), Exchange Rate and interest rate. When there is higher GDP. there is a higher capacity of the economy to import from the outside world and imports increase. Thus there is a positive relationship between GDP and imports (M). An equation that shows this positive relationship is called import function and a typical import function is represented as follows:

$$M = m0 + m1Y$$

where $m0$ = constant in import function, or the amount of imports when GDP is zero or that part of import which is independent of GDP levels, $m0$ is also called autonomous import. Coefficient of Y, $m1$, represents the slope of import function or it is measured by the ratio of change in import over change in GDP. Hence, m1 is also called the marginal propensity to import (mpI).

Effect of interest rate change is more on the capital account than on the current account. As domestic interest becomes higher than the foreign interest rate foreign residents will tend to purchase domestic financial assets and there will be a capital inflow creating a surplus on the capital account of the BOP. Similarly a reduction in domestic interest rate can create a capital outflow as domestic residents will tend to buy more foreign financial assets. Exchange rate change can also have an effect on balance of payment by making import or export change. When the exchange rate increases (and domestic currency depreciates) then imports become more expensive and if the import demand is elastic then there is a reduction in import. (Similarly there is an increase in export with increase in exchange rate)

5) *Foreign exchange market*: Foreign exchange represents a bunch of foreign currencies. In fact unless one has a common unit of measuring foreign currencies, one can treat foreign exchange only as a theoretical concept rather than a practically measurable thing. But we can talk about only one foreign currency when we treat an exchange rate of domestic currency in terms of one foreign currency and analyze the foreign exchange changes. Thus in foreign exchange market consumers purchase foreign currencies and suppliers supply them. When the prices of foreign currencies are expressed in terms of domestic currency they are called exchange rates. There is a separate exchange rate for each foreign currency, but all the exchange rates are determined by supply and demand forces of the foreign exchange.

In practice foreign exchange transactions can occur on the streets of Mumbai or Mombasa, or they can take place in a plush bank in Singapore. Nonetheless the volume of foreign currencies bought and sold on a daily basis is as high as one trillion US dollars. Clearly foreign exchange market is the largest market, and is the one that never closes. Traders in it can be individuals, banks, other financial institutions like investment companies, multinational corporations (MNCs) and governments.

6)   *Equilibrium of foreign exchange market*: In the foreign exchange market, there is a force of demand for foreign exchange and a force of supply of foreign exchange. These two forces decide the exchange rate of a currency. The demand for foreign exchange is created by domestic residents when they want to import more from outside of an economy. On the other hand, a supply of foreign exchange is created by foreign residents when they desire to import from us, leading to higher quantity of our exports. For our analysis, let us define an exchange rate as the ratio of number of domestic currency unit per foreign currency unit. Hence, as the exchange rate goes up, more domestic currency is available for foreign currency, so that there is a devaluation of domestic currency. On the other hand, as the exchange rate goes down, more foreign currency is available for the same amount of domestic currency, so that there is revaluation of the domestic currency. In terms of the demand for and supply of foreign exchange, at a higher exchange rate, when the value of domestic currency is lower with respect to foreign currency, there is higher demand for our products from the foreign residents which creates a higher supply of foreign exchange. In terms of Figure 16.1, there is a direct relationship between the exchange rate and the supply of foreign exchange. (This is a simplified explanation of the real derivation of the curve. An advanced textbook would make it clear that, depending

upon the value of elasticity, it is possible to have a backward bending supply curve for foreign exchange.)

When an exchange rate is higher, and when value of domestic currency in terms of foreign currency is lower, domestic residents reduce their demand for the foreign products. This is because with the new lower value of domestic currency, the foreign products are more expensive. Hence, our imports go down leading to a lower demand for foreign exchange. In terms of Figure 16.1 the demand for foreign exchange curve slopes downward from left to right because of this inverse relationship between the exchange rate and the quantity demanded of the foreign exchange.

At a point where demand for and supply of foreign exchange curves meet each other, the equilibrium of foreign exchange market is established. The exchange rate at which these demand and supply forces are equal is called the equilibrium exchange rate.

At any exchange rate above the equilibrium exchange rate, there is higher quantity of foreign exchange supplied than demanded leading to a surplus in balance of payments. At a lower exchange rate there is a deficit in the balance of payments. Balance of payments is in equilibrium at the point where the demand for and supply of foreign exchange curves intersect.

Now let us examine an effect of interest rate change on the equilibrium of foreign exchange market. As mentioned before, at a higher interest rate there is an increase in the capital inflow as more and more financial capital would be allocated to domestic economy from abroad to gain from the higher interest rate. This increased inflow of foreign capital would create a surplus in the balance of payments of the economy. Therefore, an increase in the interest rate creates a surplus in balance of payments. On the other

Figure 16.1
Demand for and Supply of Foreign Exchange

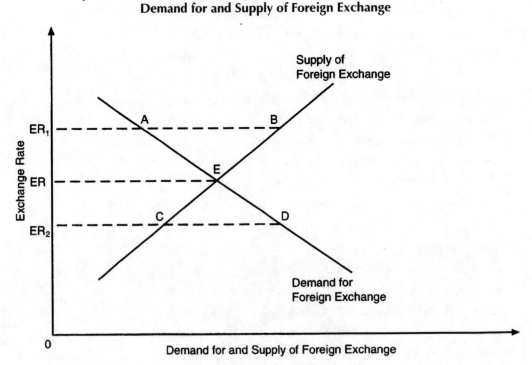

Demand for and Supply of Foreign Exchange

hand, as mentioned in import function, an increase in GNP of an economy would influence the amount of imports of that economy. Higher GNP would create higher quantity of imports, therefore, a deficit in the balance of payments of an economy. If we try to find out combinations of interest rates and income levels that keep the balance of payments in equilibrium, then they would be shown by an upward sloping curve from left to right. These combinations are shown in Figure 16.2 and are joined by a curve called *BB curve*. Thus, BB curve by definition is the locus of combinations of interest rates and income at which the balance of payments of an economy is in equilibrium. The slope of BB curve depends upon international mobility of financial capital. If capital is very mobile internationally then a small change in interest rates creates a large inflow and outflow of capital. This makes a large disequilibrium in the balance of payment. To have another point of equilibrium we need a large change in GDP to be associated with small change in interest rate. Hence, BB curve is flatter when the international capital mobility is higher. In fact, in an extreme case of perfectly mobile capital BB curve is horizontal. When capital is perfectly immobile, the slope of BB curve is vertical.

Shift of the BB curve is created by changes in exchange rate. If exchange rate increases (and domestic currency depreciates) then at the same interest rate we need a higher GNP level to have equilibrium in balance of payment. This is because increases in exchange rate creates a higher exports and lower imports hence to have BOP=O, we need to have higher Y with any given interest rate. Hence BB curve shifts to right.

Figure 16.2
The BB Curve

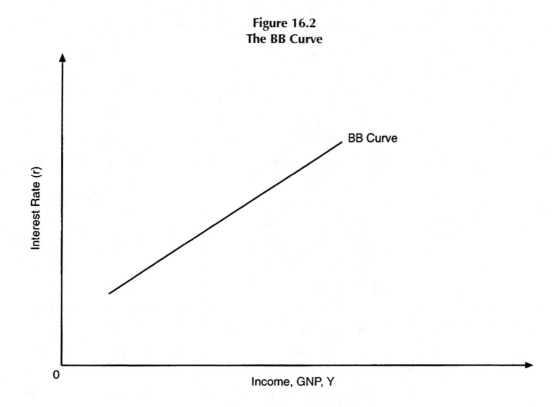

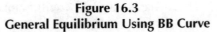

Figure 16.3
General Equilibrium Using BB Curve

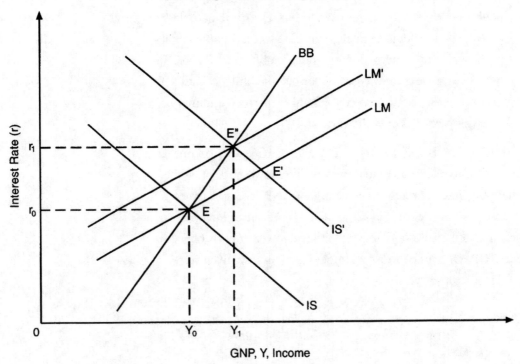

Recall from the discussion in Chapter 9 where we had derived the IS and LM curves. Together with the IS and LM curves, now we have the BB curve that can be used to redefine the general equilibrium in an economy. In terms of Figure 16.3 the money market, the commodity market, and the balance of payments of the economy are in equilibrium at point E, hence, the general equilibrium is said to be established at that point. There is a special reason why the BB curve will have to pass from the intersection point of the IS and LM curves. That special reason is given by Walras' law that states that if there are 'n' markets in the economy and if n-I markets are in equilibrium, then the nth market is also in equilibrium. When we consider only three markets in the economy, namely money, commodity and international trade, then by using Walras' law, it is obvious that the BB curve has to pass from the point at which the commodity and money markets are simultaneously in equilibrium, i.e., from the intersection point of the IS and LM curves.

Now let us analyze the changes in equilibrium combination of interest rates and income due to fiscal and monetary policy activities in an open economy setting. Let us suppose initially that the fiscal policy action happens to be expansionary, i.e., there is either an increase in government expenditure and/or reduction in taxes and/or both. Due to this, the IS curve would shift to the right. As the government expenditure is financed by selling bonds to the public, the supply of bonds would go up and the price of bonds would go down leading to a higher interest rate. But the higher interest rate leads to two types of effects in the money and international markets. In the money market, there is a decrease in the demand for money, and therefore, a movement on the demand for money curve to the left. In terms of the IS-LM-BB analysis, there is a shift of the LM curve to the left. Also, the higher interest rate is responsible for an inflow of foreign capital in the country. This leads to the surplus in the balance of payments of the economy. In terms of Figure 16.3, due to expansionary fiscal policy there is a movement of general equilibrium point from point E to E′ to E′ Thus, an expansionary fiscal policy is accompanied by a surplus of balance of payments, assuming that the higher GNP has no effect on the imports of goods and services. If the higher government expenditure is responsible for higher GNP, which in turn causes a higher amount of imports, then there could be a nullifying effect on the balance of payments.

Similar to the fiscal policy change, we can also use the IS-LM-BB curves to examine the effectiveness of monetary policy in the open economy setting. Let us suppose that monetary authority decides to increase the money supply. In terms of Figure 16.4, as the money supply is increased, there would be an initial change in the money market, leading to a right-ward shift of the LM curve to LM_1.

Figure 16.4
Expansionary Monetary Policy in Open Economy Setting

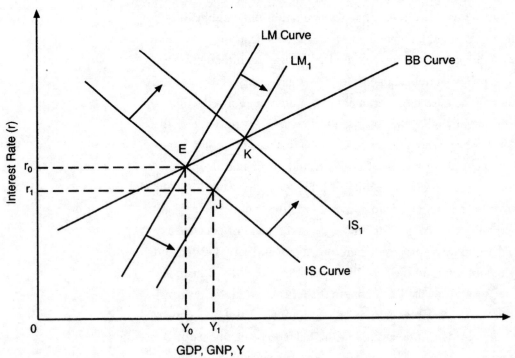

A rightward shift of the LM curve would lead to a decrease in the interest rate of economy and increase in the GNP level. A lower interest rate is also responsible for the increase in private domestic investment leading to higher GNP level. Hence, the IS curve would shift to the right to IS_1. The final equilibrium is reached in Figure 16.4 at point K.

Therefore, in terms of having an open economy equilibrium, it is better that an expansionary monetary policy is carried out. An expansionary monetary policy via lower interest rate created by it, leads to an inflow of capital. An expansionary fiscal policy, on the other hand leads to higher interest rate therefore, outflow of financial capital. Nonetheless, both policies lead to higher GNP levels which could create a deficit on the current account of an economy's balance of payments.

A more complicated analysis can find the effects of capital mobility on the effectiveness of monetary and fiscal policy. It can also derive a international autonomous expenditure multiplier. We shall leave these issues for an advanced international textbook and refrain from going into them here. In the following section however we will focus on different approaches to analyze the behavior of balance of payment of an economy.

16.3   Behavior of Balance of Payment: Survey of Approaches

One of the most famous approaches to explain balance of payment behavior is the Keynesian approach. It concentrates on values of elasticities of demand for export and import of an economy. With the help of a famous mathematical condition derived by two popular economists, Alfred Marshall and Abba Lerner and called *Marshall-Lerner condition*, Keynesian approach dictates that balance of payments behaves in a very special way. More specifically, a decline in value of country's currency may not lead to surplus in balance of payment if the sum of elasticities of demand for export and demand for imports is less than unity or one. Thus Keynesian approach takes the help of elasticities; many times is also referred to as the *elasticity approach*.

The second approach to balance of payment behavior was developed by Sidney Alexander in 1951 and is called the *absorption approach* to balance of payments behavior. To elaborate the absorption approach's arguments, a simple identity of total expenditure = total income is used. Consider therefore total expenditure of an economy as $C + I + G + X - M$ and total income as equal to the one level of GNP or Y as we have done in chapter 7. Moreover ignore the capital flows by assuming a perfect capital immobility. In this case then balance of payments is defined by export and import alone and therefore $BOP = X - Ml$. If we denote $C + I + G$ by one letter say A and call it the domestic part of total expenditure or *absorption* then $BOP = X - M = Y - A$.

Now, it is clear from the above that for any change to have a surplus in balance of payments, one needs to have either decline in A or increase in Y. Therefore change in exchange rate such as a depreciation of the domestic currency can lead to surplus in balance of payments only if it is accompanied by a policy of decline in A or increase in Y. Considering that increase in Y is outside the control of the policy members (another word for that is *endogenous*) then policy makers must have a decline in absorption to have balance of payments surplus. Hence as a consequence of the above discussion, absorption approach tells us that a devaluation of a currency must be associated with an action that leads to lower absorption—such as a decline in government expenditure (G) or restrictive fiscal policy to have surplus in balance of payment.

The third famous approach to balance of payments was developed by a few famous monetarists but it relies heavily on the works of late Professor Harry Johnson of the University of Chicago. Since this approach concentrates on capital (or monetary) flows and treats them as the main source of changes in balance of payments it is also referred to as the *monetary approach* to balance of payments.

The monetary approach claims that the excess demand for (and supply of) money can be responsible for the deficit or surplus of balance of payments. More specifically they argue that a surplus of money supply over the demand for money in the money market leads to the outflow of financial capital. If the domestic residents do not intend to hold it, it is natural that the capital outflow of the economy would increase, leading to the deficit in the balance of payments of that economy. On the other hand, if people demand money in a greater amount than the country's monetary authorities are willing to supply, then there would be inflow of capital from abroad, leading to the surplus of balance of payments of that economy. Monetarists, therefore, believe that the balance of payments changes of an economy can easily be analyzed by looking at the money market changes in the economy. Moreover, recall that monetarists claim the stability of the demand for money function as mentioned in earlier chapters. In terms of the balance of payments and the open economy, this may have some interesting repercussions.

For example, suppose that the demand for money is in fact stable and the domestic monetary policy is to increase the money supply in the economy. If people do not desire to hold more money than the stable demand for money function dictates then there would be an excess supply of money in that economy. Obviously this would lead to an outflow of capital from the economy and a deficit in its balance of payments. The effect of an expansionary monetary policy will be, in this way of thinking, only to create a deficit in the balance of payments. Obviously, the effectiveness of the policy change, as measured by the increase in the GNP level it causes, would be zero.

A change in the balance of payments can occur, according to the monetarists, only when there is either a change in demand for money or an exogenous change in money supply. The changes in demand for money would not occur unless there are changes in the GNP, real interest rate and/or the inflation rate—the variables that effect the volume of demand for money. But none of these variables are exogenously determined, therefore, the demand for money cannot change drastically. You may think that the interest rate can be changed by monetary policy, but do not forget that according to the monetarists, the interest rate elasticity of demand for money is marginal, and there is no big change in the latter variable because of a change in the former.

In conclusion of the above discussion, we can say that according to the monetary approach to the balance of payments, expansionary monetary policy leads to an outflow of capital and in the open economy setting, the effectiveness of the monetary policy is questionable. To continue the argument further, some monetarists claim that the effect of the deficit in the balance of payments created by an expansionary policy, due to the outflow of capital, is called the *offset effect*. Several monetarists were busy estimating the value of this offset effect in empirical terms. The empirical value of this offset is called the offset coefficient.

Suppose for a moment that the offset coefficient in reality is, in fact, significant and there is a great outflow of capital anytime a monetary policy undertakes an expansion of money supply. Also consider the world of a few small and many large economies. Let us assume further that the large economies undertake the expansionary monetary policies so that they incur a big out-flow of capital. This would naturally create an inflow of capital in the small economies who would find an involuntary increase in the foreign reserves component of their money supply. If the small economies are worried about the value of their domestic currency in terms of the currencies of the large economies, they have only two options to tackle the problem. They can either revalue their currencies or allow their domestic money supplies to grow with the world money supply. If they are forced to elect the second option, then the involuntary increase in their domestic money supply can create a round of inflation in the small economies. Thus, without intent, the small economies would import the inflation of the rest of the world. This is called the monetarist explanation of the importation of inflation. A number of economists have recently conducted studies in modern times to evaluate the validity of the monetarist model of the importation of inflation. Even if there are mixed results, the argument is valid in theory. The application of this model would depend upon several factors. First, the openness of an economy is very important. The higher the openness of the economy, the greater will be the applicability of this model. Also, the ability of domestic monetary authorities to revalue the domestic currency can determine the effect of international outflow of capital. Third, the effect of the increase in foreign reserves on the domestic money supply will not be high if the domestic monetary policy is to sterilize the increased foreign reserves. Sterilization process means reducing the domestic component of money to accommodate the increase in the foreign component. An increased sterilization activity puts additional pressure on the value of domestic currency. Hence, there is a practical limit to the ability of any monetary authority to carry out the sterilization of foreign reserves inflow. The fact remains that an excessive increase in the world money supply would be responsible for inflations in the small economies.

There is another theory on which the monetary approach relies. It is called purchasing power parity theory, and with the help of this theory, monetary economists can draw a law of one price. Both concepts mean that when there is an increase in the price level of one economy by assuming a two economy world, free trade and fixed exchange rates, we can show that there is one price that prevails in both economies. As one economy faces an increase in money supply, the excess money flows to the other economy via capital outflow, and the other economy suffers the problem of inflation. Moreover, the increase in price level of one economy creates higher imports of that economy and higher exports of the other. This again leads to an importation of inflation in the other economy if both allow free trade. In recent times, world trade has consistently been on the rise. The monetary theory of the balance of payments has, therefore, become even more applicable to the real world today than ever before. This completes our overview of monetary theory in an open economy setting. Obviously, in international finance classes and textbooks, more attention is paid to the detailed analysis of these concepts. Another important topic to be considered is the international monetary system. In the next chapter we present some of the new ideas put forward by economists to revitalize the international monetary system.

Suggested Additional Reading for Chapter 16

1.   Aghevli, Bijan and Moshin Khan. "The Monetary Approach to Balance of Payments Determination, An Empirical Test." Staff Papers. IMF, 1977: 275-290. Akhtar, M.A., Putman, Bluford and Wilford.

2.   Akhtar, M.A., Putman, Bluford and Wilford Sykes. Fiscal Constraints, Domestic Credit and International Reserve Flows. Unpublished manuscript, 1977.

3.   Bhatia, S. L. "The Monetary Theory of Balance of Payments Under Fixed Exchange Rates: an Example of India 1951-1973." *The Indian Economic Journal*, Jan-Mar 1982, No. 3: 30-40.

4.   Chen, Hang and Nicholas Sargen. "Central Bank Policy Towards Inflation." *Federal Reserve Bank of San Francisco Business Review*, Spring 1975.

5.   Courchene, Thomas and Karnail Singh. "The Monetary Approach to the Balance of Payment, An Empirical Analysis for Fourteen Industrial Countries." *Inflation in the World Economy*, Eds. Parkin and Zis. Manchester: Manchester University Press, 1976.

6.   Genberg, Hans. "Aspects of the Monetary Approach to the Balance of Payments Theory: An Empirical Study of Sweden." *Inflation in the World Economy*, Eds. Frenkel and Johnson. Manchester: Manchester University Press, 1976.

7.   Hean, Donna L. "International Reserve Flows and Money Market Equilibrium: The Japanese Case." *The Monetary Approach to the Balance of Payments*, Eds. Frenkel and Johnson. Manchester: Manchester University Press, 1976.

8.   Johnson, Harry G. "The Monetary Approach to Balance of Payments Theory." *Journal of Financial and Quantitative Analysis*, Vol. 7, March 1972:1555-1572.

9.   Kemp, Donald S. "Balance of Payments Concepts—What Do They Really Mean?" *Federal Reserve Bank of St. Louis Review*, Vol. 57, July 1975: 14-23.

10.   Kreinin, Mordechai and Lawrence Officer. "The Monetary Approach to the Balance of Payments: A Survey." *Princeton Studies in International Finance*, No. 43. University of Princeton, 1978.

11.   Kulkarni, Kishore and Sunil Dhekane. "The Monetarist Model of Imported Inflation in a Small Open Economy." *Economic Affairs*, Vol. 26, No. 3. July–September 1981: 288-505.

12.   Kulkarni, Kishore. "Stagflation as Caused by Worldwide Inflation in Small Open Economy with Special Reference to the Netherlands." Unpublished Ph.D. dissertation of University of Pittsburgh, 1982.

13.   Mussa, Michael. "Tariffs and the Balance of Payments: A Monetary Approach." *The Monetary Approach to the Balance of Payments*, Eds. Frenkel and Johnson. Toronto: University of Toronto Press, 1976.

14.   Salvatore, Dominick. *International Economics*. New York: Macmillan, 1983.

15.   Swartz, Antonie and Jan Kooyman. "Competition and the International Transmission of Inflation." *De Economist*, Vol. 123, 1975: 723-48. 194

16.   Tsiang, S. C. "The Monetary Theoretical Foundation of the Monetary Approach to the Balance of Payments." *Oxford Economic Papers*, Vol. 29, November 1966: 329-338.

17.   Tyson, L. D. and E. Neuberger. "The Impact of External Economic Disturbances on Yugoslavia: Theoretical and Empirical Explorations." *Journal of Comparative Economics*, Vol. 3, 1979: 346-74.

18.   Whitman, Marina V. N. "Global Monetarism and the Monetary Approach to the Balance of Payments." *Oxford Economic Papers*, Vol. 29, November 1977: 319-338.

19.   Zecher, Richard J. "Monetary Equilibrium and International Reserve Flows in Australia." *Inflation in the World Economy*, Eds. Frenkel and Johnson. Manchester: Manchester University Press, 1976: 189-215. 195

The Future of International Monetary System: An Analysis of New Ideas

17

17.1 Introduction

While forecasting the interest rates and other macroeconomic variables is a dangerous adventure, the predictions for the future of the international monetary system are much harder. Several prevalent theories try to make the predictions but they can be incorrect because there are several real-world economic events in which prevalent theories have gone astray. This chapter intends to analyze the ideas of the working of the international monetary and exchange rate system that proposes a practical solution for it.

17.2 International Monetary System: Past and Present

By 1880, the majority of the countries in the world were on some form of gold standard. Connolly [1] helps us in reviewing lessons learned from the past. The classical gold standard prevailed from around 1880 to 1914 with some aspects remaining until the Bretton Woods breakdown in 1971. The gold standard was a commitment by participating countries to maintain fixed prices of their domestic currencies in terms of a specified amount of gold, and to maintain fixed prices by being willing to buy and sell gold to anyone at that price. As we saw in Chapter 4, the gold standard broke down during World War I but was briefly reinstated from 1925 to 1931 as the Gold Exchange Standard. Other countries besides the United States and Great Britain would hold gold reserves under the Gold Exchange Standard. But this system again broke down following Britain's departure from gold in 1931 and was succeeded by "managed money."

The next attempt at a modified gold standard came about under the Bretton Woods system. Hawtrey [2] gives us some background of what was involved in Bretton Woods. He mentions how two projects arose from Bretton Woods in July 1944: an International Monetary Fund to promote International cooperation in monetary and foreign exchange policy, and an international bank to facilitate international loans in aid of post-war reconstruction. With the creation of the International Monetary Fund, every country contributed, along with gold, a quota of its own currency. Therefore, there appeared a stock of foreign exchange containing all the currencies in due proportion. Any participating country could draw, with limits, upon this reserve by buying whatever foreign exchange it might need with its own money.

The Bretton Woods system functioned smoothly in earlier years. But the inflation of the late 1960s resulted in large dollar outflows that strained Bretton Woods to the breaking point. But the initial breakdown was only partial. It was the gold convertibility of the dollar that fully ended in 1973 that was mainly responsible for the official breakdown of Bretton Woods. The International Monetary Fund is an important survivor from the breakdown, and the convertibility of currencies among each other and the importance of autonomy of national economic policies are the other two beneficiaries of the Bretton Woods system. Williamson [3] adds that another significant reason for the failure of Bretton Woods was the vagueness with which two important aspects of balance-of-payments were addressed. The first was the question of which country had the responsibility to initiate adjustment action and when, and secondly, the question of techniques that should be used to effect adjustment when desired.

There was, however, implicit incorporation in Bretton Woods that both surplus and deficit countries have a responsibility to seek payments adjustment. The system was equally ambiguous about techniques that were supposed to be employed to effect adjustment. The current account restrictions were frowned on but the capital account restrictions were permitted, and they could not contribute to current account adjustments.

Holding yet another view, Oppenheimer [4] had gone as far as stating that the breakdown of the Bretton Woods System had nothing to do with any inadequacies of the system itself. He believes it was entirely attributable to the refusal to revalue gold. Had the United States been prepared to reverse her previous stand and had she urged a decisive increase in the price of gold, it should have been possible to re-establish a smoothly functioning gold exchange standard, at least for a short time. Most economists did not doubt the feasibility of such a strategy, but they questioned its desirability, as opposed to the alternative of developing a fiduciary reserve asset.

Other reasons for the collapse of Bretton Woods were increased productivity of German, Japanese, and Swiss economies. There was also a greater awareness of the unjust benefits of the United States as perceived by the rest of the world. After the United States closed the gold window in 1973 and announced that she believed the currencies of other industrial countries should be revalued relative to the dollar, the participating countries had little choice but to float their currencies vis-a-vis each others' currencies. The immediate effect of this widespread floating was the breakdown of the gold standard. Along with the U.S. decision to press for the revaluation of other currencies, there was a mass incentive created to shift funds out of the dollar into the revaluation candidates that only the most dedicated countries could contemplate facing.

Cooper [5] believes Bretton Woods would have broken down sooner or later even without the inflation of the late 1960s. The convertibility of gold and the dollar was bound to become increasingly doubtful as dollar liabilities rose over time relative to the U.S. gold stock.

All of the above incidences set the stage for a new monetary system on the international level. In the aftermath, a few things were very clear. The formation of the European Monetary System (EMS hereafter) was an indication that countries favored stable over unstable rates. The recent catastrophes of Argentina, Brazil, Mexico, and Israel are the strong reasons for an order and discipline in the international monetary transactions. As late as in 1985, the increase in the value of the dollar created the fears of a trade war between the United States and Japan, necessitating a coordination in the whole system in general and among industrialized countries in particular. In the next section, we concentrate on some of the suggestions made by economists in dealing with the modern problems of international monetary disorder. A complex problem does not have an easy solution. Even if there are several views about the future of the international monetary system, the chance of any one being implemented in full is very small. All views stand a chance, which makes this topic so interesting to be pursued.

17.3   International Monetary System: What's Ahead?

How can the standards and benefits of the International Monetary System be improved? Meier [6] says, "The design of an international monetary system is a very difficult task. It involves policy choices that take international monetary affairs into the political limelight, affecting the benefits and costs among nations and often requiring the resolution of conflicting interests."

Southward [7] gives the list of what he thinks are the main objectives of an International Monetary System. The system must be capable of achieving monetary stability, restoring acceptable levels of employment and sustainable growth, and checking the present strong inflationary and stagflationary policies. It must be supportive of a process of global development, especially for the

Third World Countries. The interests of the majority of the world must be reflected. All countries should participate in the institutional arrangements for international monetary management. There should be establishment of an international currency unit as an international means of exchange and primary reserve asset. A certain degree of an automatic procedure is needed in transfer of resources through reserve asset creation, by the international community.

Some lessons from the European Monetary System can be easily learned. Connolly explains some of the pointers that may be taken from the EMS. All of the main currencies of the EEC participate in the EMS except the British pound sterling. The system aims at enforcing a fixed exchange rate among participating countries, at least within a band, whereas exchange rates are floating in relation with outside currencies (although there is dirty floating). The internal fixity of exchange rates implies central bank interventions, and a complex system of indicators has been designed to help in the determination of respective responsibilities of central banks.

Two systems have been given particular consideration by the EMS:

1) Snake-type system, like the early 1970s in which there is a need for intervention when the bilateral exchange rate between two currencies reaches its upper or lower limits, and

2) Basket-type system in which the need for intervention is determined by the fact that one currency reaches its upper or lower limits in relation to the basket of currencies (European Currency Unit for instance).

In actuality, a mixed system was adopted. The intervention of central banks is not obligatory until a currency fluctuates at least 2.25 percent above or below its parity in terms of another currency in the system. This is the same as the old snake system, but a new concept has been added: the divergence indicator. The divergence indicator is not the same for each of the currencies that make up the European Currency Unit (ECU). This is because the probability of reaching a given limit of fluctuation is not as great for a currency weighted lightly in the ECU as for one that is weighted heavily. The indicator acts as a signal; it does not trigger automatic action. The country concerned can then intervene in exchange markets, alter its monetary or fiscal policies, or make an adjustment in the currency's parity.

The advantage of central banks over the market in stabilizing the exchange rate is smaller, the shorter the period under consideration, even when central banks kept information on their monetary policies to themselves. EMS arrangements are in no way optimal since the central banks claim that they defend fixed rates within banks in the short-run, but not make any firm commitment for the long-run. Putting aside the solution of a truly competitive system in the production of money, a second-best solution would imply perfect flexibility of the exchange rate without intervention in the short-run, whereby some information would be given to the market for the long-run value of the exchange rate, either because all central banks would use a policy of monetary targets or because they would be committed to the attainment of predetermined values of the exchange rate for the long-run and would be able to hold to their commitment. Unfortunately, the EMS arrangement is just the opposite.

Predetermined exchange rates in the long-run are not necessarily "fixed rates." Fixity of exchange rates is an irrelevant problem, because if information on the future course of exchange rates was perfect, there would not be any reason to prefer fixed rates. Fixity would mean only that there is a link between national inflation rates, which has no justification especially if the "common" inflation rate is high. In fact, social welfare can be increased by central banks via two different ways: by giving good information of the future of exchange rates, and/or monetary policies and by following monetary policies to minimize the inflation rate. Exchange rate fixity does not imply that any of these functions correctly maintain the fixity of exchange rates.

There is much discomfort about the present international monetary system. One of the important reasons for this distress is the large external debt that has been accumulated around the world, more specifically, with developing economies. Due to the uncertainty inherent in the system, the international monetary arrangements are not stable. Dissatisfaction with very short-run and year-to-year movements in real exchange rates, combined with technological developments, will sooner or later force a desirable change in existing arrangements. Cooper has some additional suggestions: the creation of a common currency for all the industrial democracies, and a common monetary policy. In this arrangement, the individual countries could determine their fiscal policy actions, but those policies would be constrained by the need to borrow in the international market.

Presently, we have exchange rate flexibility that has helped retain an open trading and financial system. These flexible exchange rates have generally corrected for differences in national inflation rates. However, two features of the present exchange rate system will not be satisfactory over the long-run.

1. Movements in real exchange rates have a major unwelcome effect on national economies. But movements in real exchange rates cannot be easily controlled by the usual instruments of national economic policy. This is because determinants of exchange rates are diverse and complex. Nonetheless, sometimes policies have worked sufficiently because it is the other country's responsibility to recognize the effects of disequilibrium adjustment in the balance of payments of its partners.

2. The present arrangements of creation of reserves are not sustainable over the long-run. The dollar as the principal reserve medium has been accepted, but not without some uneasiness. In recent years the productivity in   U.S.

manufacturing has not kept up with the other developed economies. This has already created problems. Several other weaknesses of reliance on the U.S. dollar will become more apparent as the rest of the world starts taking doubts about the U.S. dominance.

With greater sensitivity of production to changes in real exchange rates, governments must reduce arbitrary movements in real exchange rates in order to maintain an open trading system. An adjustable peg system of exchange rates that requires occasional discretionary movements in market exchange rates is not likely tenable. Cooper believes these variables lead to the conclusion that we will need a system of credibly fixed exchange rates if we are to preserve an open trading and financial system. Exchange rates can be fixed if international transactions take place with a single currency. He maintains that this is possible only if there is a single monetary policy and a single authority issuing the currency and directing the policy.

Korteweg [8] argues that exchange rates should be government-determined, not market-determined, and should be used as an instrument of economic policy. For a macroeconomic view, a country's competitive position may be thought of as being determined by the value of its currency in terms of a trade-weighted basket of its competitor's currencies as well as by the country's tradable-goods price level relative to prices. In this system there would be less uncertainty compared to the present flexible exchange rates, if carried out over ambitiously.

In another view, Southward proposes an idea as he thinks the solution for the world monetary problem and makes a case for a world central bank. The purpose of a world central bank would be to provide a uniform and universally acceptable currency with stable purchasing power, and to exercise systematic control over the total supply of currency reserves. If the central bank was organized as a better version of the IMF, no changes in voting arrangements would be necessary. The system would separate the reserve currency function from the function performed by national currencies on the international exchange market. This could be accomplished by creating a new unit of international currency. This would avoid the complex dilemma faced by the U.S., authorities in the Bretton Woods system.

The uniform currency would be defined as equal to a basket of currencies, similar to SDRs, with each currency valued at its exchange rate and weighted in proportion to the country's share of world trade or according to some other appropriate economic measure. The central banks could deposit national currency holdings in a substitution account, receiving the new currency in return. The world central bank would issue any additional reserves needed for adequate growth of the world economy. The national currencies would constitute a steadily declining portion of the world's currency reserves. The idea of a world central bank is doubtful for implementation because many nations, especially developing nations, fear loss of sovereignty over their monetary affairs. And yet, national monetary authorities are far from being free to act independently. Southward's proposed system certainly does not completely shelter nations from the international consequences of ill-considered domestic economic policies.

There is one strong argument for supporting a world central bank because no alternative has satisfactorily worked. Each system without a central bank has generated instabilities in the world economy. Unless some link of international unity can be created in money matters, the probability of instability remains high. Hence, we support the concept of having a sole governing body so that irresponsible domestic policies would not be tolerated.

Bernstein [9] explains to us some steps that could be taken to give foreign monetary authorities greater confidence in the dollar. One solution proposed is the establishment of a *substitution account* in the IMF in which countries could place some or all of their dollar reserves. A participating country transfers to the account any dollar assets it does not wish to hold and receives a credit balance denominated in SDRs.

This substitution account would provide participation members with an automatic diversification of their foreign exchange reserves in the 16 currencies that comprise a unit of SDR in proportion to their importance in that unit. The purpose of the substitution account is to avoid large changes in the currency composition or reserves. Participating countries must be able to use their SDR- denominated reserve assets in BOP settlements in the same way they now use their dollar reserves. Most countries would likely want dollars when converting their assets. If the U.S. Treasury were to buy assets held in the substitution account, it could either become a holder of such assets itself or retire them in exchange for an equivalent amount of U.S. securities held by the account. The establishment of a substitution account could contribute to greater stability of the international monetary system, but only if the United States were to take responsibility for the SDR value of the assets in the account. Also, one has doubts about the overall cooperation from European economies and developing countries for this establishment as well, as they are disturbed even by the recent phenomenon of overvalued dollar.

Morse [10] describes an alternate way in which the international monetary system might be organized. A tiered system in which governments of the industrialized world would institutionalize their relations with each other by coordinating their action so as to reduce the ability of each to harm the others and to buffer as far as possible their own network of interactions from outside pressure (i.e., LDC). Governments in less developed countries would want to attach themselves to international institutional arrangements that would preserve a structure of economic stability and order and also guarantee them some participation in the formulation of rules, but not on an equal basis as the government of the industrialized economies would have to abandon the traditional liberal norm of universality. The system would be global in scope, so different rules would have to be applied to different types of activities and relationships. Any international codes that emerge should embody what government does with respect to the exchange rate regime, adjustment mechanism, and mode of handling convertibility.

Five or six governments would assume major responsibility for "managing" international financial relationships. There would be formal arrangements governing the determination of exchange rates and supporting mechanisms. There would be informal agreements concerning targets for domestic economic goals, and national sovereignty.

Morse further believes that his system could serve to enhance the major objectives associated with the liberal international monetary system: price stability, full employment, free trade, economic growth, and defused adjustment process. This system is geared more toward pluralistic international order in which no single society plays such a predominant role that it can abuse the autonomy and freedom of others. This system would depend partly on the willingness of the members of the club to work out an economic truce with one another. This in itself is doubtful.

17.4   Summary and Conclusion

This chapter surveys the existing views in economic literature about the future of the international monetary system and to find out if the future can be correctly predicted. The most striking view is an establishment of the Bank of Issue or some such agency that would oversee the smooth functioning of the monetary system. How should the decision making authority be shared by the member countries is a political issue, nonetheless, one can point out the size of the GNP of an economy as a criterion for beholding the authority. All of this needs an international cooperation and coordination. A system, whatever is its soundness in theory, would just not be successful in reality if the members do not agree to the basic rules of it. It is, therefore, suggested that conference or a summit to discuss the expectations, needs, and requirements of the member countries should be arranged. There is a little doubt that given a choice and given the willingness of cooperation, countries favor fixed exchange rates over completely flexible. A fixed exchanged rate system gives the policy makers one less policy instrument but at the cost of losing the instrument, they seem ready to accept the certainty about the future exchange rate. Uncertainty of future exchange rates embodied in the flexible exchange rate system, has proven to be undesirable by the rapidly growing international business community. What lies in the future of international monetary system would be decided significantly by the steps undertaken by countries' governments in the above areas. By including the present chapter, this book tries to expose students to the modern thinking about monetary theory in an open economy perspective. While this chapter was the only material on the open economy analysis, it is by no means suggested that international monetary theory has less importance now. In fact, international finance is one of the fastest growing branches of monetary theory.

Suggested Additional Reading for Chapter 17

1. Bernstein, E. M. "Outlook for the Dollar and Other International Assets." *The International Monetary System: A Time of Turbulence.* 1982: 410-429.

2. Connelly, M. B. "The European Monetary System." The International Monetary System: Choices for the Future 1982: 180-197.

3. Cooper, R. N. "A Monetary System for the Future." *Journal of Economic Issues,* Vol. XVII, 1982: 168-184.

4. Hawtrey, R. C. *Bretton Woods for Better or Worse.* 1946: 1-55.

5. Korteweg, P. "Exchange-Rate Policy, Monetary Policy, and Exchange Rate Variability." *Essays in International Finance*, No. 140, 1980: 1-28.

6. Meier, G. M. *Problems of a World Monetary Order,* No. XIV 1982: 242.

7. Morse, E. L. *Alternatives of Monetary Disorder,* No. XIV 1976: 28-29.

8. Oppenheimer, P. M. "World Monetary Developments and the Committee of Twenty." *Aussenwirtschaft,* 1974: 46.

9. Rivera-Batiz, L. Francisco and Louis A. Rivera-Batiz. *International Finance and Open Economy Macroeconomics,* 2nd ed. Macmillan Publishers, 1994.

10. Southward, F. A. "The Evolution of the IMF." *Essays in International Finance*, No. 135, 1979: 1- 65.

11. Williamson, J. "Why Bretton Woods Collapsed." *The Failure of World Monetary*, 1977: 8-29.

Index